How To Fix Modern Football

To the memory of my dad Mike, my inspiration –
the man who taught me everything, especially the
value of pushing myself and trying as hard as I can at
everything I do.
5 October 1944 – 26 December 2020

How To Fix Modern Football

CHRIS SUTTON

monoray

First published in Great Britain in 2020 by Monoray, an imprint of
Octopus Publishing Group Ltd
Carmelite House
50 Victoria Embankment
London EC4Y 0DZ
www.octopusbooks.co.uk

An Hachette UK Company
www.hachette.co.uk

First published in paperback in 2021

ISBN 978-1-91318-326-4

A CIP catalogue record for this book is available from the British Library.

Printed and bound in Great Britain

10 9 8 7 6 5 4 3 2 1

This FSC® label means that materials used for the product have been
responsibly sourced

Picture acknowledgements
Getty Images Alex Livesey 191; Catherine Ivill - AMA 1;
FP Contributor 79; John Peters 139; Oli Scarff 237.

CONTENTS

Introduction

Sport has been my life. It's been a constant for me in the near half-century of my time on this planet, both man and boy. And, of course, among all sports, football is the greatest of them all. I never get bored of it. I am its biggest fan. I am its biggest champion.

But, at this moment in time, something is rotten in the state of football. Actually, let's be honest – quite a few things are. Too many aspects of the game don't currently function as they should. They're undermining the sport and they need changing. When added together, they show that football is in need of quite a serious overhaul. And that's where I come in.

I've been in and around the game every day of my life. I'm the son of a former pro and I'm a former pro myself. I've experienced all levels, from a floor-scrubbing YTS lad to a Premier League winner. I've also played in the UEFA Cup final and represented my country at full international level. I even had a short spell as a manager in the lower leagues. From rejection to rejuvenation, from the lows up to the highs, I've seen it, smelled it, felt it. Football flows through my blood. It's the essence of my DNA. I know when it feels great and when it doesn't. I'm all too familiar with the good, the bad and the ugly. And as wonderful as the good times are, plenty of the bad and the ugly are still very conspicuous within football. Our wonderful game can be so much better.

It's not just my playing days that inform my opinions. My post-retirement life as both a newspaper columnist and a TV and radio pundit allows me the privilege of continuing to work within the sport that I've made my life. And I'm very lucky to have the opportunity to air my views, as vociferously as I like, right across the media. Very few people are this entitled. I get to observe, praise and criticise how the game is currently being played, managed and administered. It's not a bad day job by any stretch of the imagination.

My observations and opinions are formed as a result of the quantity of football I watch every week, whether in the BT Sport studio on a Saturday afternoon alongside a squad of other former professionals or up in the gods of a stadium, with the match summariser's mic in my hand, alongside the cream of the BBC's commentary team. Or, indeed, right here at home, keenly watching on TV while trading opinions with one or more of my kids.

And then, of course, there are the two hours every Saturday night in which, as half of the two-man team with Ali Bruce-Ball, I co-present BBC Radio 5 Live's evergreen football phone-in *606*. Here I get to further air the grievances I have with the modern game, as well as being able to spar – and occasionally agree – with those passionate fans who care enough about their teams to call up looking for sympathy, debate or, most often, the chance to have a good old moan. These are my people.

How To Fix Modern Football is a chance for me to drill deeper into the footballing issues that really matter, that really concern me, that really need fixing. And there's no shortage of those. I've handpicked 25 aspects of the modern game – set out across five themed sections –

which I believe aren't working how they should. As my 'You're Better Than That!' catchphrase suggests, there's room for improvement. Football can be better. It just needs to work harder and to reassess its priorities.

There's a wide variety of subjects that I've got in my crosshairs. From diving players to abusive fans, from the managerial merry-go-round to ticket prices, from agents to VAR, I aim to leave no stone unturned. And I won't pussyfoot around the issues. I'll tell it like it is and like I see it. I've never been mealy-mouthed and I've no intention to start now. But this is more than a grumpy man climbing on to his soapbox just to have a moan. There's a purpose to my preaching. While I've never been a legislator, and I don't sit on any fancy boards or governing bodies, I do have plenty of solutions to offer. Having diagnosed the ills currently infecting the modern game, I'm not going to shy away from also prescribing the treatment needed to cure them.

On occasion, my tongue might slip into my cheek. Elsewhere I'll be deadly, deadly sober in my pronouncements. But whether I'm light-hearted or serious, honesty and passion will be found in every word and in every sentence you read. As a player I was deeply committed every time I stepped on to a pitch; I wore my heart on the sleeve of every first-team shirt I put on. I'm the same today. I may have hung my boots up some time ago, but my faith in, and my fervour for, the game remains undiminished. I rant and I rave because I care. And I never want to stop caring about football. I owe it my life.

I guess this 25-point plan represents a call to action – one to be heeded by us all, whether it's those working within the modern game or those studying it closely from the terraces or via the TV. Football is failing both itself and those who love it dearly. But it's far from a lost cause. There are lessons to be learned from the past and examples of good practice from other sports to be followed. Some of the cures

I prescribe could be implemented very swiftly – as long as the want and the will are there. And it's crucial that they are, for the game must recognise that it needs to improve before it can move forward.

And improve it must. Because as we all know, football – that glorious, life-affirming sport that makes hearts sing and grown men weep – is better than that.

Chris Sutton

PART ONE
ON THE PITCH

Let's start with the fundamentals. Twenty-two players, a ball and a patch of grass.

Those are the basics. But the story of football has always been a story of flux and evolution. The game has never been trapped in amber, nor set in stone. It's been altered, modified, modernised and reshaped over the years and decades to the point where it's largely unrecognisable from the sport that was formalised during the second half of the 19th century – when the best teams revelled in names like Wanderers, Royal Engineers and Old Carthusians. Indeed, were a moustachioed player from the Victorian age able to jump into a time machine and fly forward 140-odd years to Anfield or the Etihad, he would have very little idea of what was going on. The existence of a penalty area would appear to him to be a revolutionary advance, never mind other head-scrambling concepts like substitutes, television cameras, goal-line technology, the offside law and those three dreaded letters V, A and R.

Of course, football – like every aspect of society and culture – moves with the times. It shape-shifts as everything else around it shape-shifts too. It becomes a reflection of the particular point in history that it occupies.

But not every evolutionary step, every innovation, has improved football. Sometimes the game has fallen victim to retrograde alterations that have worsened, rather than enhanced, the game as it's played out on the pitch. All too often, the fundamentals have got lost in a fog of misguided 'improvements' and petty rule changes. Football has become too complicated – and unnecessarily so. It needs simplifying and this can be achieved largely through the application of common sense. There are plenty of wrinkles that can be easily ironed out.

Players are very different beasts now too. The gentleman amateur of the Victorian era became an extinct species many generations ago, while the professional age produced players whose motivation and outlook were markedly different from those who went before them. By the time the cash-rich days of the early 21st century came along, the football pitch had become a crucible for both cynical attitudes and cynical methods. A sense of fair play got lost somewhere along the way.

What occurs on that patch of grass requires overdue attention. The game is better than that. Attitudes need adjusting and rules need straightening out. And here's how it all could be done...

1

Properly Punish the Divers

At approximately 7.45pm on any given Saturday evening during the football season, the voice of Tom Petty can be heard on BBC Radio 5 Live, straining to reach the high notes of his best-loved song 'Free Fallin''.

There's a reason why Petty can be heard every week. This is the song that announces the Simulation Game, one of the regular features on *606*, the station's long-running football phone-in show I co-host with Ali Bruce-Ball. If you're not aware of the feature, the clue is in the name (and also in Petty's lyrics). The Simulation Game sees myself and Ali naming and shaming players who, over the previous seven days, have – to our eyes at least – brought the game into disrepute with their theatrical tumbles. We get to hold football's disgraceful divers to account, putting them in the metaphorical stocks from where public scorn can rain down on them. It's a privilege to be able to humiliate these players in this way – to shame them for their dishonesty and deception. But I wish we didn't have to.

Plenty of the Premier League's top stars have been nominated for their antics since we began the feature back in January 2019, players at the very highest level who really are better than that. Sadio Mané has come under our scrutiny, as have Josh King, Ben Chilwell, Nicolas Pépé, Yerry Mina and a whole host of others. Newcastle's Miguel Almirón is a multiple winner of this most dubious of awards. So too is the England captain – one Harry Edward Kane. No one escapes our forensic attention. No one is exempt.

There are plenty of others who, to use that well-worn euphemism, go down too easily. There are several repeat offenders, those who've been booked on more than one occasion for simulation. These include Daniel James, Dele Alli, Raheem Sterling, Pedro, Leroy Sané, James McArthur and Wilfried Zaha. Zaha definitely had a reputation for it, but I think he's improved in this respect.

One particular week, we asked listeners to roll back the years and nominate their Diver of the Decade. We weren't short of suggestions, with the switchboard lighting up like a Christmas tree. Michael Owen, Wayne Rooney, Ashley Young, Arjen Robben and Gareth Bale were all nominated. Didier Drogba's name cropped up repeatedly.

> There are certain players in the Premier League who we've collared on the radio for being divers. And there's an easy way for those divers to put that right. Just stop doing it

There are too many cheats in the game who are getting away with incidents because they're 'not that type of player'. I think Harry Kane goes down easily, but you're not allowed to call him a diver. You can't say that about England's hero. But if someone burgles a house just once, he's still a burglar. You only need to rob a bank one time to be called a bankrobber. 'He's not that kind of character. He's a good guy.'

Well, he did it.

In some ways, the Simulation Game is tongue in cheek, but in other ways it's not. I think it's a very good service we're offering, calling out these cheats. It's there for everyone to see. And the bottom line is that nobody likes to be called a diver. Nobody wants to be tarred with that brush. It's not a badge of honour. But there are certain players in the Premier League who we've collared for being divers. And there's an easy way for those players to put that right. Just stop doing it.

Of course, many of the referees' calls on this issue will be subjective. The eyes of one official might judge a player tumbling to the turf to be as guilty as sin, but another may see that player as a paragon of virtue who's been unfairly dealt with by an opponent. A conman to one, a victim to another. But there are so many cases of diving where we can all see it with our own eyes, where there isn't the merest shade of grey that's colouring what's just happened. Why can't we just say what we see?

I thought VAR worked superbly at the 2018 World Cup in Russia. On a couple of occasions, Neymar went down easily in the box, the ref went over to the monitor and called him out for cheating. But now we've got VAR in the Premier League, players seem to be diving more. I'm still trying to get my head around that one. You'd think that it would have the opposite effect. I was sure it would clear diving up. But it hasn't. Far from it. It's more rife than ever.

I played in an era when English and Scottish clubs would go and play in Europe and come off worse. With Celtic, I lost the 2003 UEFA Cup final against Porto – José Mourinho's first big trophy. It's fair to say that while they deserved to win that particular match, they would have also won a Laurence Olivier Award for their antics. You ask any Celtic fan who was there. Even the soberest among them would tell you so. The Porto striker, Derlei Silva, was the biggest culprit that night. He scored twice and was named man-of-the-match, but spent plenty of time lying horizontal on the turf without seeming to have been touched.

I honestly couldn't name any British player who was a diver back in the day when I was playing. I don't want to sound xenophobic – foreign players weren't all at it, by any stretch of the imagination – but you would encounter plenty of divers in the European competitions.

I think it reached the stage at some point in the last couple of decades where British players thought *We actually need to start joining in here. We're losing out.* As a result, the old triple somersault is something that's only come into the British game in the last 20 years or so.

> Divers need to get what they deserve. The only way to cure their behaviour is to give them a three-match ban. No ifs, no buts

(That said, before I was born Francis Lee had notoriety for being a legend of the fall. The former referee Keith Hackett described the striker as having 'a reputation for falling down easily', while Lee gained himself a nickname during his playing days: Lee Won Pen.)

But, of course, when a British player dives they'll often be described as 'clever'. Pure hypocrisy. Just call it as it is. Don't dress it up for fear of causing offence. Don't pussyfoot. A diver is a diver.

However, simply condemning these players for their sins over the airwaves on the Simulation Game isn't sufficient punishment. They need more than public humiliation. Diving is cheating. Simple. It's no different to any other way that a player flouts the rules to get an unfair advantage, such as Maradona's 'Hand of God' at the 1986 World Cup or Thierry Henry's clear and obvious handball against the Republic of Ireland, setting up the goal that denied the Irish a spot at the 2010

World Cup. Those were clear examples of cheating and both players – both of whom were their side's captain, it's worth noting – should have been banned as a result. To me, diving is in the same category as a shamelessly deliberate handball. In both cases, players are trying to deceive the officials on the pitch. On that basis, you have to have a strong enough deterrent to encourage a player to just play honestly.

Divers need to get what they deserve. And the only way to really cure their behaviour is to give players caught diving, or seeming to dive, a three-game ban. No ifs, no buts. If that was applied straight across the board, football fans all over the country would absolutely understand. After all, it's one of the issues that really infuriates the average football fan. It's not a divisive subject. It actually unites fans of every stripe.

If I were a player and I got a three-match ban for diving, the next time I played I'd be thinking about the consequences of me taking that option. Because it's a choice. It really is. Diving is a choice. And it's not a difficult choice, either. You either want to dive or you don't dive. So if you're tripped, fall as you would fall. If you're not tripped and you're trying to dive, you'll know what's coming to you. The punishment doesn't fit the crime at the moment and that is a huge issue. Is a three-game ban over the top? No, it's not. Missing one game isn't enough. Missing three tells you the severity of the crime and sets out the parameters.

And let's not stop there. If a player chooses, after his first ban, to reoffend by committing the same crime again, why not stick one more game on top? So a four-game ban for a second offence, a five-game ban for a third and so on. That'll teach them.

It's really important that there's a far tougher stance adopted than there currently is. That's why players continue to do it, to chance their arm. They know they can. They're not going to get a ban. They might get a yellow if they're caught, but they might get a penalty if they're not.

I bet there are players out there who practise diving. And screaming. A good scream gives a dive real credibility, especially if it sounds like the diver has been shot in the nether regions.

I can't prove this, but I wouldn't be surprised if there were managers out there who actually congratulate their players on diving. 'Well done. You bought that for us. Earned us a good three points.' But as soon as there's a sufficiently strong punishment, managers who are currently patting their players on the back will find their star man is out with a three-game ban and will be telling their players that they need to stop that kind of behaviour. Managers aren't stood in dressing rooms philosophically discussing issues of morality – should players dive or shouldn't they dive? Instead, thanks to the short-termism of the managerial world, they'll be thinking *I need to win. I need to find a way of winning a game by whatever means necessary.* Getting rid of that mindset would certainly be a change for the better.

> A good scream gives real credibility to a dive, especially if it sounds as though the diver has been shot in the nether regions

Diving signifies a lack of discipline from a player. If I punched someone in the face, I'd get a three-game ban – and I might end up getting more. When you strip it all away, it comes down to personal choice. Players don't have to dive. You hear ex-professionals like Michael Owen and Robbie Savage say that if there's contact, you're entitled to go down. You're not. There has to be *enough* contact to cause you to go down. That's pretty basic.

By the same token, though, if there is enough contact, players should not be awarded penalties or free kicks if they're over the top with their antics – if they make a meal of things, doing the extra tumble and ending up spreadeagled on the turf. A rule should be brought in whereby that kind of behaviour actually supersedes the foul. In trying to con the referee, the player has committed a more serious act than the original infringement and so the decision gets rightfully reversed. That's another measure that would help to eradicate it from our game.

We've all got massive double standards, of course. There wasn't ever a moment in my playing days when I collapsed like a pile of bricks without any contact from an opponent. But as a centre-forward backing into a defender, did I go down even when the force was such that I didn't need to fall to the floor? Yeah, I did. So am I admitting to diving? Yes, I think I am.

But I did think I was pretty bloody good at it…

2
Stop the Pointless Rule Changes

Every year, new rules appear in our sport. They are rarely revolutionary. More commonly, they are minor tweaks and amendments. And that's understandable. Welcome at times, even. But while football continues to evolve, the basic framework has been in place for generations. The wheel was invented long ago.

Quite often, however, these tweaks and amendments produce no improvement to what is already in place. Sometimes they make things worse. On occasion, the pointlessness of a new rule has beggared belief.

Every rule has to be there to enhance the fan experience, to make the game more exciting, to make it more competitive. But all too frequently these principles appear to have been neglected or forgotten. For whatever reason (although executives justifying their own jobs isn't a bad first guess), there has been too much change for change's sake, producing rules that should never have been proposed, let alone passed.

Here, I'm going to run through some of the more stupefying rule changes of recent times. And, believe me, there have been some howlers. But before the steam begins to emerge from my ears, let's kick off with a rule change that has been highly positive – transformative, even – since it was brought in in the early Nineties.

'An indirect free kick is awarded if a goalkeeper touches the ball with the hand/arm after it has been deliberately kicked to the goalkeeper by a team-mate'

Ah, the back-pass rule. This is an excellent example of one of those rare occasions when the lawmakers got it right, when their metaphorical dart hit the cherry red of the bull's-eye. This intelligent change, which came into force in 1992, makes perfect sense and had an immediate, and extremely positive, impact. Previous to this rule, sides were taking the lead in a match and then killing the game: knock the ball back to the penalty box, keeper takes the ball in his hands, falls on it, slowly gets up, wastes more and more seconds. The teams who mastered the art of killing the game became the successful ones. It became harder to get the ball back off the top teams, because they knew how to neutralise the game right up to the final whistle. I perfectly understand why teams did it. They wanted to wind down the clock and guarantee themselves the league points or cup win.

The ultimate back pass has to be the one that Graeme Souness made while playing for Rangers against Dynamo Kyiv in the European Cup in 1987. With Rangers 2-1 ahead on aggregate, Souness took possession of the ball halfway inside the Kyiv half. Nowadays, players would head for the corner flag to run the clock down. Not back then, though – not in the days before the back pass was outlawed. Souness turned towards the Rangers goal and launched what had to be the longest back pass in history into the Glasgow night, the ball travelling a full 70 yards into the safe hands of his keeper Chris Woods. That was the mindset of the top players then. First and foremost, it was about winning and the smart players knew how to achieve that.

But this rule change really did transform the game. It put goalkeepers under pressure from strikers who knew their opponent couldn't pick the ball up. Keepers had to adjust (or be replaced) as a result and now, aside from shot-stopping, they're judged on their ability with the ball at their feet, which they hardly ever were before. Some have become phenomenal at this. Back in the day, a keeper just used his feet to punt a long ball down the pitch. The standard of the game has improved since this law was introduced and thanks to it football is now more of a spectacle. And the goal count has definitely risen as a consequence.

'The ball can be kicked in any direction at kick-off'

In sharp contrast to the back-pass change, this is a rule that doesn't outlaw anything significant. What on earth is the benefit of allowing the ball to go either forwards or backwards, when previously it could only go forwards, thus requiring two players in order to keep possession as opposed to only now needing one? How has it made the game one inch, one ounce better? Please, please someone enlighten me. I've thought long and hard about this, but there's absolutely zero material gain that I can find. There seems to be no reasoning behind it whatsoever.

But the bigger question is why anyone would think it up? You'd have to query exactly what that person actually knows about football if they think that this utterly pointless initiative would change anything at all. Actually, 'initiative' suggests someone's put their grey matter to a positive use. Not here they haven't. The meeting at which this idea was put forward must have been the dullest, most meaningless one ever. Wasn't the person who proposed it deeply embarrassed by even saying it out loud? And surely there must have been at least one person sat around the table with enough common sense to say 'Whoa, hold on! Why are we wasting our time with this?' and shoot it down in flames. But apparently there wasn't.

This may well be the most pointless rule change in football history. Well, let's see...

At a goal kick, 'the ball is in play once the kick is taken; it can be played before leaving the penalty area'

I could understand it if this rule, brought in ahead of the 2019–20 season, only applied to the under-10s level and below. Sometimes those little legs just can't kick a ball that far. But, no. It was applied right across the board, all the way up to the most senior adult level.

Perhaps its purpose is to encourage teams to play out from the back more, but I can't see why they wouldn't be doing that anyway. A few more yards aren't going to make any difference to a team's modus operandi. I suppose it creates a little more space on the pitch and so teams might have to tweak the way they press, but it seems pretty pointless to me. It hasn't made it better. It hasn't made it worse. It's changed nothing. So what was the point?

'Even if accidental, it will be a free kick if a player gains control/possession of the ball after it has touched their hand/arm and then scores, or creates a goalscoring opportunity'

Another new rule for 2019–20 was this further amendment to the handball law, the various tweaks to which over the years have already taken up plenty of space in the rulebook. It declares that any handball committed by the attacking team – whether deliberate or accidental – which leads to them scoring means that the goal will be disallowed. This removes the element of subjectivity from a referee's decision. If the ball touches either hand or arm, irrespective of distance or speed or the position of the arm, the goal will be disallowed and a free kick awarded to the opposition. It is absolute and immovable. No debate, no interpretation. It is black and white.

However, any handball committed by the defending side in their own penalty area remains a matter of subjectivity, of the referee interpreting the intentions of the player involved. If there was consistency between the two scenarios – whether both showed zero tolerance or both were subjective calls – that would be absolutely fair, but this tweak of the handball law puts the attacking side at a disadvantage. And there was me thinking we were trying to create a game that gave us more goals…

Surely there must have been at least one person sat around the table with enough common sense to say 'Whoa, hold on! Why are we wasting our time with this?' and shoot it down in flames. But apparently there wasn't

In January 2020, the iniquity of this new regulation made itself conspicuous in a match between Sheffield United and West Ham. The visitors to Bramall Lane thought they'd snatched a last-gasp equaliser when Declan Rice powered his way upfield before setting up Robert Snodgrass to score. But VAR ruled the goal out because of a handball by Rice in the build-up. He and Blades defender John Egan were running alongside each other chasing a bouncing ball when Egan headed it on to Rice's arm, which was a matter of inches away and not in an unnatural position. It was absolutely unavoidable.

However, had the pair's run continued into the penalty area and it was actually Rice who had headed it on to Egan's arm, it wouldn't have automatically been given as a penalty and would most likely have been deemed accidental. In this scenario, the attacking side gets punished both ways round. Any goal they score gets chalked off, while there's no guarantee of a penalty if the opposition commits the same 'crime'.

Just why has the good old-fashioned drop-ball been outlawed? It wasn't as if they were leading to a spate of fisticuffs and brawls

And this particular incident throws up a further talking point. What if Rice's handball had taken place on the edge of his own area and not a few metres outside the Sheffield United box? Would his position at that precise point be seen as a defensive one? Or, having subsequently dribbled the length of the pitch to set up Snodgrass, would the point at which he took possession of the ball qualify as part of the phase that created the goal? If the latter, it would be a farcical state of affairs to disallow it and bring play back to the other end of the pitch where the handball had occurred.

This particular law is an ass. It needs changing. Instantly.

'If a player who requires the referee's permission to re-enter the field of play re-enters without the referee's permission, the referee must caution the player'

It is already a frustrating, rather petty rule that declares that, after an injured player has been treated by the team physio, he has to leave the field of play before he can continue. And, of course, he can only do that with the referee's permission once the game has restarted.

In addition, though, if a player returns before having been waved on by the referee, he can be cautioned, even though his 'crime' is wanting to re-enter the fray and get his team up to its full complement of players. And if he's already been booked, he won't be coming on again now. So he gets clobbered by the opposition and an early bath is his reward. Double whammy.

'The referee drops the ball for one player of the team that last touched the ball'

This one really irks me. It now means that a drop-ball can no longer be competitive. A drop-ball used to be a great spectacle, with both teams putting up their hard men to compete it. It was pure theatre, a fabulous sideshow. They'd roll up their sleeves and get stuck in. Who's going to be quickest? Will they both miss the ball and end up decapitating each other? And it was brilliant to be involved in them. You'd get a huge adrenaline rush, all for something so inconsequential. They never had a massive impact on the game and it wasn't that important a contest to win, but everyone still wanted to be first to the ball.

Now, if there is an enforced stoppage in play, a player from the team that last touched the ball will be the recipient of the drop-ball. Any remote semblance of competition and conflict has been removed: 'all players of both teams, except the player receiving the ball, must be at least four metres away'. Are we going to take everything out of the game that made it a spectacle? It's an aggressive sport, but eventually we're going to ban every sort of physical act. Will we get to the point where, if a defender gives an attacker an angry glance at a corner, a penalty will be awarded?

Just why has the good old-fashioned drop-ball been outlawed? It wasn't as if they were leading to a spate of fisticuffs and brawls. I can't recall a single one that ever did. A non-competitive drop-ball is pointless. It's like going to watch a non-competitive sports day, applauding them when they've done a few star-jumps. I've been to a few of those. I'd rather see my kid finish last in a traditional sports day.

Don't call it a drop-ball when it's not what we know as a drop-ball. In fact, let's eliminate it entirely. We need more of a spectacle instead. Perhaps, to keep us entertained, the referee should do some tricks before volleying the ball back to the goalkeeper. But, of course, even that still wouldn't give us half the thrill that a meaty drop-ball contest would have done.

'A player is cautioned if guilty of excessively using the "review" (TV screen) signal'

In a lot of games, you see high-profile players getting away with far too much. They call the referee every imaginable expletive but he turns a blind eye – or ear. You can say virtually anything and not get cautioned, but make the old TV sign, as Lionel Blair used to do on *Give Us a Clue*, and the yellow card will be out of his pocket before you can say 'Three syllables. First syllable. Sounds like "knee"…'

A player could genuinely, and politely, ask 'I'm sure that I was onside. Could you check?' and draw an imaginary TV screen in the air, but into the book he'd go. What a crime. What an outcry. Many worse things go unpunished. Players can harass a referee en masse and receive little censure – as half of Manchester United once did with Andy D'Urso, chasing him around the Old Trafford pitch as he furiously back-pedalled. Only one of them – Roy Keane, naturally – got booked.

I can think of a few hand gestures that would land a player in hot water if they were directed at any of the officials, but the VAR sign is surely one of the tamest examples of non-verbal communication there could possibly be. Two fingers up to this rule.

Teams in the Champions League final can put 12 substitutes on the bench

Throughout the Champions League competition, three substitutes can come on during a match, with a fourth permitted should the tie go into extra-time. So why on earth for – and only for – the final did UEFA increase the number of potential substitutes on the bench from (a still-excessive) seven to a round dozen? No team needs that many. Even if you subscribe to the fanciful notion that a specialist player in every position needs to be there should the first choice get injured, that's still only eleven that's required. Twelve gives you more subs than there are positions on the pitch!

There is absolutely no point in cramming the bench with so many players, three-quarters of whom are unlikely to get on the pitch. It's a waste of everyone's time. But, if whether these players are going to play is immaterial, as it appears, why stop there? Why not invite the youth team to come and warm the bench as well? Let's make it a party.

There was nothing wrong with the era when clubs were limited to naming three subs – usually a defender, a midfielder and a striker. (OK, I'm feeling generous. You can have a goalkeeping sub too.) If injury befell their players, it was up to the team to improvise with what and who they had. It made for an intriguing, tactical challenge. Simply swapping like for like is no test at all.

'The occupants of the technical area must remain within its confines'

It must have been a rather unworldly person who drew up the plans for this one. While including substitutes and the coaching staff, this rule has one particular person in mind: restricting a manager's movements while naively assuming that a box painted on the turf will be respected and never breached. Fat chance. It's not strictly enforced and so everyone ignores it. It's a loose guide at best. And the worst response if a manager literally oversteps the mark is the fourth official politely asking them to take two steps back.

It's a token gesture to get the two sides to respect each other's boundaries. If something did kick off between the benches, it wouldn't stop a thing. So if you must have a technical area, at least keep the manager inside it somehow. Perhaps build a nice white picket fence around it, with a little gate, so he at least has to find his way out before confronting the opposition staff. What's wrong with that?

'The player being substituted must leave by the nearest point on the boundary line'

This is bonkers, isn't it? They're trying to quicken the game up by demanding that a player being subbed take the shortest possible route off the pitch, but there's no need. The ref should just stop his watch while the uncooperative player ambles towards the bench at the speed of a tortoise. If it's an attempt to waste time, not a single second will be lost. (That said, whenever I knew I was just about to be subbed, I'd wander to the furthest part of the pitch in order to have the longest, time-eating walk possible. It never made any difference.)

If a player leaves the pitch via the far touchline, there's going to be a walk of shame involved, almost certainly past the opposition fans. The protection of stewards, and possibly the police, will be necessary – a situation repeated with every substitution. This will put those looking after the safety of the stadium and its occupants under unnecessary pressure, as well as each substituted player being vulnerable to volleys of abuse from the stands. What's so wrong with avoiding this scenario and referees simply adding 30 seconds for each substitution? At a maximum of six substitutions in a Premier League game, the combined three minutes would be shorter than many VAR checks.

'A goalkeeper is not permitted to keep control of the ball in his hands for more than six seconds'

The six-second rule was introduced in 1998, a measure clearly devised to cut down on time-wasting and speed the game up. That was an admirable intention, but how often has it actually been enforced? If anyone can think of an example at all, most people would probably only have one in mind: the case of Simon Mignolet was the exception that proved the rule.

In 2015, in a Europa League match against Bordeaux, the then Liverpool goalkeeper mysteriously decided to hold on to the ball for a full 22 seconds. He was a rare victim to be punished under this rule. And Bordeaux did punish him. The next time he handled the ball, it was to pick it out of the net after the resultant free kick inside the box.

> Perhaps build a nice white picket fence around the technical area, with a little gate, so the manager at least has to find his way out before confronting the opposition staff

I suspect every goalkeeper breaks this rule multiple times in a match. By the time he's caught the ball, waited for his defence to reassume its shape and bowled it out to the right-back, six seconds would have long expired. And the referee, by now on the halfway line to keep up with play, doesn't care a jot.

So a rule is made but rarely, if ever, applied. And because no one can be bothered to uphold it, goalkeepers may even have forgotten it exists. It never needed to.

When facing a penalty, a goalkeeper must refrain from 'touching the goalposts, crossbar or goal net'

Poor old goalkeepers. They seem to really get it in the neck from the lawmakers. The only justification for this curious regulation is that a keeper might be attempting to make the goal frame wobble, either to put off the penalty-taker or to somehow manipulate the size or shape of the goal itself. But these goals aren't known for their flexibility. They're not made of bamboo. I say good luck to any keeper who can make a post wobble. Next stop, Britain's Strongest Man…

> Who went into a suited-and-booted meeting and piped up from the back: 'We need to stop the bar wobbling when there's a penalty. It could ruin the game as we know it'?

Again, the lawmakers have embarrassed themselves here. Who went into a suited-and-booted meeting and, when it came to 'Any Other Business', piped up from the back: 'We need to stop the bar wobbling when there's a penalty. It could ruin the game as we know it'? They should be sacked for even thinking of it.

'A player must be cautioned, even if the goal is disallowed, for removing the shirt or covering the head with the shirt'

I appreciate that goal celebrations where the player has leaped into the crowd could be interpreted as inciting supporters and is therefore quite possibly worthy of a caution. But I've never really understood why showing your delight by ripping your shirt off deserves a yellow.

Although I never chose to unburden myself of my shirt whenever I scored, celebrations are what football is all about: passionate expressions of ecstasy that allow the goalscorer to get thoroughly caught up in the moment. They aren't worthy of punishment. Obviously we don't want to see some blubber monster taking his shirt off if and when he finds the back of the net – we go on holiday to see that sort of thing. But if a player has been to the gym and is lean, mean and muscular, what's the problem?

'Referees must caution players who delay the restart of play by appearing to take a throw-in but suddenly leaving it to a team-mate to take'
Let's finish with this extraordinarily over-the-top rule and dissect its lunacy with a theoretical scenario. Imagine you're a wafer-thin winger who is urgently trying to create an equaliser for your side in a cup quarter-final. You make a run down the wing and are tackled, but you win the throw, 10 or so yards from the corner flag. You shape to take it yourself, but then notice that your right-back – him with the biceps of a lumberjack – is making his way up the pitch. He can launch it twice as long and twice as hard as your Twiglet arms can. But the referee stops play. He calls you over. He brandishes a yellow card. You were apparently time-wasting. It's beyond belief.

Sometimes change isn't for the better. The ridiculously petty rules that I've reeled off here are testament to that. Why are we overthinking the game to such a degree? We don't need to alter football that much. It's an inherently simple game and these modifications only serve to complicate and confuse. Strip it back. Hold dear the fundamentals. Keep the tinkering to a minimum.

Are these lawmakers from the IFAB (International Football Association Board), these mandarins, drawing up these rule changes for the sake of the game or to look busy and protect their jobs? They really need to take a long, hard look at themselves. You can imagine them in their committees, having pointless meeting after pointless meeting. It must be like the People's Front of Judea from *Monty Python's Life of Brian*. 'Let's have a meeting about a technical area. How big should it be?' 'Let's have another meeting about how many subs are allowed on the bench, even though only three can play in a match.' 'How about ruling out touching the crossbar when it's a penalty? Yes, put that on the agenda for next time…'

While we might be laughing at these absurd modifications, there are big issues getting lip service at best, or being totally ignored at worst. The authorities need to get to grips with the issues that really matter. Sort out racism. Sort out sectarianism. Silence the verbal abuse. Tackle the dementia issue affecting former players.

Instead, these pen-pushers and committee men would rather focus on issuing a yellow card to someone who's decided to leave a throw-in for his team-mate to take. Come on lawmakers, you're better than that.

3
Remind People That
Football is a Contact Sport

Sit down with a pen and a piece of paper and it's easy to list them. Every club had at least one. Some had three or four. The hardmen, the enforcers, the players who didn't give an inch. Roy Keane, Patrick Vieira, Vinnie Jones, Julian Dicks, Paul Ince, Terry Butcher, Neil 'Razor' Ruddock...and their kind go back across the decades, Norman Hunter, Tommy Smith, Billy Bremner, Ron 'Chopper' Harris...

These were tough guys who carved out a reputation for themselves because they could effortlessly strike fear into opposing players. They were superheroes with a real aura around them. It's been 35-odd years since Harris hung up his boots and a high proportion of today's football fans wouldn't recognise him from Adam. But his legend lives on. They'd know his stock-in-trade, his modus operandi, just from his nickname. After all, you don't get called Chopper because of your delicate, fleet-of-foot, tiki-taka style of play.

Trying to list the hardmen of football today is a much harder pursuit. That piece of paper would remain relatively blank. They're a near-extinct species now. Someone should tell David Attenborough.

It's all down to changes in the rules over the years and to what referees are prepared to let go – or, rather, what they're allowed by the authorities to let go. It's a less ferocious game these days – and quite possibly an easier one. We talk about the beautiful game, but you can't tell me there's one person out there from the era I played in and before who doesn't enjoy a 50-50 challenge where both players are off their feet and there's an enormous noise because the ball nearly bursts. I think the game is worse off for it. It's less of a spectacle.

> All I remember is lying on the Carrow Road turf, looking up at the blue sky in a daze. Terry Hurlock had totally wiped me out

I certainly loved playing in those more physical times. I think the first hardman I came up against was a guy called John Gayle. I was playing centre-half for Norwich City reserves against Wimbledon reserves and he really bashed me around. He treated me like a rag doll. It was a steep, sharp learning curve and he taught me quite a lot just in that one game – about picking your moments, about not trying to win everything up against a big guy. As a youth-team player, it was brilliant playing in the reserves against players who had plenty of first-team football under their belts –wily old pros who'd been around the block. They were like old boxers who had probably been whacked many times themselves, but who had far too much nous for young, up-and-coming, exuberant players like myself.

Once, when Millwall came to Carrow Road, I remember Terry Hurlock coming in for a tackle. I knew his reputation – he looked more like a doorman than a footballer. Or maybe a long-haired Aberdeen Angus. But I was young and up for any challenge, and I was ready to prove myself in that moment. I was going to be the destroyer of the destroyer. I reckoned the ball was 60-40 in my favour, but big bad Terry was coming towards me and he was going to get it. Then the collision. I don't really remember it. All I remember is lying on the Carrow Road turf, looking up at the blue sky in a daze. He had totally wiped me out. The curly perm of Tim Sheppard, the Norwich physio, came into view. 'Where are you hurt?' 'Everywhere, Tim,' I mumbled. 'Everywhere…'

I was a young person coming into the game and I had to learn to accept these kinds of challenges. We used to play Arsenal with their famous back line. Whenever the ball was clipped in to me from one of our full-backs, I used to count to three in my head. By the time I'd got to two, I was normally lying on the floor with either Tony Adams or Steve Bould standing over me, having been absolutely walloped. But it was all part of the game. And it was a part that, I have to say, I really enjoyed. I loved it.

As a young player, it was a test of your mettle. You learned from the experience of playing up against the likes of Adams and Bould or Steve Bruce and Gary Pallister. They were really hard, tough men. I wouldn't say they were fair, but that was part of the game. And then you learned to not be fair yourself. You'd sharpen your elbows and be ready to look after yourself. For instance, when I first used to head a ball, I never used to put my arms up to protect myself. But after getting my face smashed numerous times, I soon became switched on in terms of what I had to do.

The physical aspect was also a test of your mental capacity. Were you prepared to go through that? The old adage 'Do you want it?' certainly did apply. And on the flip side of that, if you're dishing it out, it worked the other way. If you knew somebody wasn't quite mentally up for the physical scrap, that's where you could bully certain types of players, because you just knew that they couldn't stomach it.

If you were a tricky winger, you knew that if a ball was rolled in to you within the first two minutes, the likelihood was that the opposing full-back was going to come through and kick you up in the air. Then the defender would say to the referee, 'That's my first one. You can't book me for that.' It was all about laying down a marker.

I have to say that I was pretty all-in and eventually learned to handle myself. Or, at least, I realised when things were 60-40 in my favour and when they were 80-20 against me. I would pick my moments, I'd box clever. Well, eventually, that is. But when you're young, stupid thoughts go through your head. Call it the exuberance of youth.

I remember playing for Norwich in the UEFA Cup against Vitesse Arnhem in 1993. I wanted to get my revenge in first on this older, clearly experienced midfielder. *I'm going to do him. I'm going to do him.* I went in so high on him, but he went in higher. I had a cut on the inside of my leg, all the way up. He'd studded me and my balls were bleeding. That really, really hurt and was the closest I came to having the snip. Experience won the day. That was a lesson learned.

Or perhaps it wasn't. A full five years later, I was playing for Blackburn against Arsenal. We had a corner, but Patrick Vieira elbowed me and broke my nose before the kick was even taken. My eyes were watering and he just smiled at me. I thought, *I'm going to top you!* I went to top him with a two-footed challenge but missed – he was too smart for me. I got a straight red and Emmanuel Petit pushed me over and I face-planted on the turf. A broken nose and a straight red card. That was a bad evening.

Back then, the game was undoubtedly tougher – and not just because of the physicality. Going up against these hardmen was a mental test. If you weren't prepared to take the hard knocks, ultimately you might not end up playing and having a career. It was a test of character, with the physical challenge causing the mental disintegration. 'If I keep kicking you, are you going to keep getting up?'

A hardman is a master of psychology. Anybody can go out and throw a lazy punch or hit someone when they're not looking. A hardman is someone who can dish it out but who also, when someone launches into them or elbows them, can take it and come back. That's a hardman.

A hardman is also somebody who has the mental strength to take that drive and mentality on to the pitch every time come match day. In my view, Jeremy Goss was a hardman at Norwich. He'd run through a wall. He wasn't the most talented player, but he would give absolutely everything. He could be naughty too, and that's what a hardman is.

I knew plenty of players who weren't the most technically gifted but who were mentally impregnable. They struck fear into almost everyone. I played alongside Billy McKinlay at Blackburn who intimidated

I had a cut from the inside of my leg all the way up. He'd studded me and my balls were bleeding. That was the closest I came to having the snip

people throughout his career but who told me it was all a front. He played in the holding midfielder role, protecting and shielding the centre-halves. He was a good stopper, effective at breaking the play up in a robust manner. But he was naughty at times. He would leave a bit on the opposition, as they say. I admired him as a team-mate, aside from one time he squared up to David James at Ewood Park. The truth is David James could have picked him up and sat him on top of the crossbar. I wished he had've done; McKinlay definitely overegged it that particular day. After our careers finished, he told me he used to play in fear. He just fronted it out and made a good career thanks to his psychology. He had me fooled, along with the Blackburn fans!

Those two tests – the physical and the mental – are now lacking in football. Modern players have got it easy. I can understand people saying the game is now better because of the skill, speed and movement, but it's made it a totally different sport. Previously, that heightened psychological challenge measured your courage. Players don't have that test now. And that test sometimes began before we were even on the pitch. You'd be trying to concentrate on the game but would be getting psyched out in the tunnel. Wimbledon were famously masters of this.

These days, opponents are fist-bumping or hugging or high-fiving each other before they get on to the field of play. That would have been absolutely unheard of in my day and it's something I despise. You're supposed to be playing for your jersey. After the game, do what you like, but beforehand, you're all in it together as a team. I used to feel like it was going to war and that's how the teams I played for used to feel. You train all week for this match, getting your armour ready. You should be on the edge, 100 per cent committed, not 'How are you mate?' You wouldn't have seen that when the Roman gladiators were going into the Colosseum. There would have been none of this 'How are you getting on? How's the family?' nonsense.

We live in different footballing times. People talk about Lionel Messi being the greatest player of all time, but it's impossible to compare him to someone like his compatriot Diego Maradona. The times have completely changed, the context has radically altered. I don't think Maradona ever got a tackle below his ankles. Most of them were at knee height or even up around his hips, and this is a far greater test of courage. This is why the likes of Maradona and George Best have to go down as the real greats, because of the type of challenges these guys had to put up with, week in and week out, game in and game out. It's not the same in the 21st century. Players are an overprotected species now. We can all applaud Messi and Ronaldo and say their stats and their numbers are great, but there's a strong argument to say Maradona and Best were better as they had to put up with a far greater physical and mental challenge. If Messi and Ronaldo had played back in the Sixties, Seventies and Eighties against 'Chopper' Harris, Billy Bremner, Billy McNeill and guys like them, it would be fascinating to see how they would have coped with being tackled around their waist a couple of times, to see if they had the courage and temperament to deal with it.

> When the Roman gladiators were going into the Colosseum, there would have been no fist-bumping and none of this 'How's the family?' nonsense

Best was great, Maradona was great, Kenny Dalglish was great. And it wasn't just the physicality they had to contend with. They weren't playing on the carpet-like pitches of today. They were performing on cow fields with the ball bobbling everywhere. These guys were properly skilled. That's why I have total respect for the players from that era. They had to put up with much more. And some of them used to have to take their kit home and wash it too!

Young players are so over-pampered these days. The old apprenticeships made youngsters respect what they had. They understood the ladder, the hierarchy, the pecking order. They knew what it would take to become a top player. Nowadays they have everything done for them. They waltz into the dressing room, with their headphones on, where their 'kit coordinator' has laid everything out for them – possibly including gloves and a snood. A snood! It's hardly a breeding ground for rabid, frothing hardmen anymore, is it?

I admit that I wore gloves and a hat in training when it was freezing. But I never, ever wore gloves in a game. That was a matter of principle. I mean, how can a football fan watch their team and think a player is committed when he has gloves on? I just don't get it. And we're not exactly living in the frigging Arctic, are we? And then you have the football player who wears short-sleeved shirts and gloves. Explain that! You couldn't make it up. So you let your arms get cold, but not your hands? You buffoon!

> I'm calling for a loosening of the laws. Let's return the game to a more adversarial contest

Some of the older ex-players must look at today's game and think *God, they've never had it so easy. Not only do they get paid an extraordinary amount of money, but they are not allowed to tackle anymore.* And that's true. When I'm working as a pundit, if anyone comes into a tackle off their feet, you automatically say 'Yellow card'. The referee's left with no choice. Back in the day, if a player didn't come off his feet, he'd be coming off the pitch. The manager would be hooking him off – 'You're not giving it your all.'

I'd have loved to have played now. It would be so easy. But football's not supposed to be easy. So I'm calling for a loosening of the laws, such as the resurrection of the rule that allows tackling from behind as long as you get the ball. Let's return the game to a more adversarial, more gladiatorial contest.

I'm not talking about elbowing someone in the face, or whatever.

Far from it. I'm talking about the art of tackling, of being allowed to make full-blooded, all-in challenges. It simply makes the game a better spectacle. If you come off your feet and you win the ball, what's the big deal? There's all this talk about 'endangering', but where does that end? Running over a bump in the pitch and tweaking an ankle is seen as endangering. It's ridiculous. Every time someone jumps for a header, or every time someone goes into a challenge, that's endangering. Football shows real signs of becoming a non-contact sport. It kind of is already. This needs reversing.

I understand that the game is a different art form these days, one based more on passing and interceptions and athleticism and fitness. But most fans of a certain vintage would agree that it was much more of a spectator sport when it had physicality, when committed players would fly in with ferocious tackles. Come on, let's tell it like it is. Was the game better for robust, all-in challenges? Yes, it was.

Football is missing both the physical and psychological aspects. The edge is lacking. Today's robots need to show human qualities again.

And they need to leave those bloody gloves in the dressing room.

MY TOP TEN **HARDMEN**

To prove that football isn't a game of tiddlywinks, here I've selected who I believe to be the game's true hardmen – the most ruthless players who never gave a single inch.

10 ALAN SHEARER
Southampton, Blackburn Rovers, Newcastle United and England

People might not think Shearer was a quintessential hardman, but the reason I've picked him is because we played in the era of tackles from behind, when people could give you one. And he took a battering. But he loved it, relished it. He wasn't the biggest player, but he was like a bull, with formidable physicality and tremendous spring. When you talk about hardmen, you talk about the physical aspect, and he could certainly handle himself against the toughest opponents – the likes of Arsenal and Manchester United. But when you add on top of that his psychological strength and his mental capacity, he was on a different level, he absolutely was. A couple of serious injuries came his way, but he had the toughness to come through them and to keep up the quality of his play. And that's why he had the career that he did, scoring all those goals. Off the pitch, Shearer conducted himself well, but on the pitch, he was absolutely ruthless. He was also an intelligent player, very smart – such as the time he didn't get into a fight with Roy Keane but let him lose his head and pick up the red card. He used his brain well in the heat of battle.

Shearer says: 'Sometimes going in for a hard tackle generates a louder cheer than a great pass.'

9 BOBO BALDÉ
Marseille, Mulhouse, Cannes, Toulouse, Celtic, Valenciennes and Guinea

He was 100 kilos and six foot five. There wasn't an ounce of fat on him – he was just pure muscle. He couldn't pass the ball very well over 10 yards but, boy, could he tackle. He would take the ball *and* the man. Even once when we were playing a charity game, after we'd all retired, he absolutely took out Dimitar Berbatov. A charity game! I was glad I played alongside him not against him – you wouldn't want to cross him. Although I did once, in the dressing room at the training ground. During a bust-up with Stiliyan Petrov, who was complaining about his passing abilities, he had Petrov by the throat. I tried to rescue Petrov from being dismantled by giving Bobo a shove, but he just picked me up and threw me into my locker. He broke the door. And Alan Thompson was inside the locker, cowering! Still, I did save Stiliyan's life. Bobo was a lovely guy off the pitch. Other than that incident, of course…

The Celtic fans say: 'Bobo's going to get you!'

8 JOHAN MJÄLLBY
AIK, Celtic, Levante and Sweden

I played with Mjällby at Celtic. The captain of Sweden was an Adonis – the only guy I ever went on holiday with who wore Speedos and could carry it off. He first came to prominence in the UK when he scored the winner against England in a European Championship qualifier in 1998, popping up in open play where a striker should have been, despite the fact that he was a centre-back. He signed for Celtic two months later. He was a really combative character with a never-say-die attitude – as I once found out at the dining table. We had both ordered poached eggs on toast and the waitress brought one plate of them out. I took them and, suffice to say, he explained that they were his. After a couple of expletives and a threat to rip my head off, I just said 'Well, you have them, then.' And this was before a game. This was three hours before kick-off!

Mjällby says: 'I've calmed down [as a manager]. I don't get angry, but I still lose my temper – especially if the defence don't do their job properly.'

7 DAVID BATTY
Leeds United, Blackburn Rovers, Newcastle United and England

Alongside Gary Speed, Gary McAllister and Gordon Strachan, he was part of the Leeds midfield that helped to win the final First Division Championship before the Premier League arrived. So I knew of his reputation before I faced him. He had a fantastic engine and was the snap and the bite in their midfield. He wasn't the biggest, most intimidating figure, but was super-fit and super-hard, and carved out a tough-as-nails reputation across the footballing world that extended into winning 42 caps for England. When he came to Blackburn, I saw from close quarters what a little terrier he was. If someone kicked him, he'd just go back in, but would go harder. With Batty it was all about desire, about making that ball your own going into a 50-50. He didn't understand the concept of second best. Don't back down. Don't show weakness. He epitomised what I think we all thought about

Yorkshiremen – that they're stubborn and tough. He was a footballing version of Geoffrey Boycott, if you like. Only a bit more energetic…

Batty says: 'The one thing I have always given every game is 100 per cent. I would defy anybody to say different.'

6 PATRICK VIEIRA
Cannes, AC Milan, Arsenal, Juventus, Inter Milan, Manchester City and France

I've had my battles with him over the years and once came a cropper that ended with me receiving a red card (see page 28). But it was his head-to-heads with Roy Keane – either on the pitch or in the tunnel – that largely defined the bitter rivalry between Arsenal and Manchester United during that particular part of the Premier League's history. It was enthralling to observe, and people watched the matches for that head-to-head alone. And these were the captains! With most of these hardmen, the one consistent thing is that they could dish it out but they could also take it. They didn't cry and moan when somebody gave it back to them. It's normally the smaller, more tigerish players who are the aggressive midfielders, but he had both the height and the intimidation factor. He was a fearsome competitor who was very strong in the tackle, but he was a skilful player too. He was a real all-rounder who gave plenty of steel to that Arsenal midfield.

Vieira says: 'My commitment, and my desire to win the ball or make a tackle, will never change. But you grow up. I'm not 20 anymore.'

5 JOE JORDAN

Morton, Leeds United, Manchester United, AC Milan, Hellas Verona, Southampton, Bristol City and Scotland

One from an earlier era, but his legend went before him. Not only was he a monstrously effective centre-forward in domestic football in Scotland, England and Italy, he also carried his reputation on to the highest international stage, starring for Scotland in three World Cups. And losing his front teeth during his early days at Leeds only added to the sense of menace and threat. But, for me, the incident involving him that's most indicative of his character and his toughness was when, as Tottenham assistant manager, he squared up to Gennaro Gattuso on the touchline at a Champions League match against his old club Milan. Jordan was 59 at the time, and is 26 years the Italian's senior. Gattuso probably thought *I'll go for the old guy in the technical area.* He clearly didn't know of Jordan's reputation, despite the Scot's time in Serie A. Bad move. Maybe square up to Harry Redknapp instead. Don't square up to Joe Jordan because he won't back down. And he didn't. Everyone was thinking *Blimey, Gattuso's a brave man. However young and fit you are, you've picked the wrong man there.*

Jordan says: 'I've lost it a few times. Not that many. I rarely got sent off. I wasn't going to move [away from Gattuso]. Not a chance.'

4 STUART PEARCE

Coventry City, Nottingham Forest, Newcastle United, West Ham United, Manchester City and England

Anyone with the nickname 'Psycho' isn't going to be a shy and retiring wallflower. As a left-back, he played in an era when full-backs could give one to a winger early on and he never disappointed in that respect. He was a fearsome opponent – just the size of his thighs alone, with his shorts pulled up, was a sign of his physicality. One sight of those and you knew what you were going to get. I played against him many times, but I used to peel off on to the right-back instead. He was an all-in character who absolutely didn't shirk a challenge. He took the bull by the horns, head on. He's summed up by his response to that penalty miss against Germany at Italia 90. Six years later, at Euro 96, he fired his spot-kick home against Spain and then roared his defiance for all of Wembley to hear. Redemption!

Pearce says: 'If opponents were scared of me, so much the better. I would do it coldly and deliberately; emotion didn't come into it.'

3 DUNCAN FERGUSON
Dundee United, Rangers, Everton, Newcastle United and Scotland

He was an iconic figure. His stare, his presence, his reputation – they all went before him. I think it was genuine fear that centre-halves had of him. Best not to rile him, best not to fire him up. I never played centre-half against him, but I always stayed on the right side of him. I remember playing against him for Blackburn at Ewood Park and he got sent off for calling David Elleray a baldy so-and-so. That didn't make him hard, but I thought that made him accurate! He did, though, once get a three-month prison sentence for headbutting Jock McStay of Raith Rovers in 1994. The thing I enjoyed the most about him was actually after he retired, when those two lads were stupid enough to burgle his house. He detained one of them, who then apparently had to spend three days in hospital. I mean, they could have picked any other house on his street…

Ferguson says: 'I have spent an entire career trying to shake off a reputation I earned in one day.'

2 ROY KEANE
Nottingham Forest, Manchester United, Celtic and the Republic of Ireland

Another all-in, fearsome competitor, like his great foe (and fellow box-to-box midfielder) Patrick Vieira. Keane personified that whole United era. People give Alex Ferguson the credit for creating that mentality, but Keane was the driving force on the pitch. He was the one who took United to that different level. Everybody who played in the 1990s would have wanted Roy Keane on their team. Hardmen tend to be leaders – they want to be the centrepiece. They take responsibility, they bear the weight of the team, and nobody did it better than Keane. The evidence is there. They had talented players in the team, but he's the one who got the most out of them. He was the one out there in front. He used to stand in the tunnel looking so intense. You wouldn't want to make eye contact with him. He could have gone out and played on his own against teams; that was how motivated he looked. In retirement, I think he's become the hardman of punditry as well. He doesn't hold back.

Keane says: 'I played centre midfield. I wasn't a little right-back or left-back who can coast through his career without tackling anybody. Or a tricky winger who never gets injured. I played in the middle of the park.'

And my favourite hardman is…

1 TERRY BUTCHER
Ipswich Town, Rangers, Coventry City, Sunderland, Clydebank and England

One of England's greatest captains. Butcher was someone you definitely wanted on your side rather than facing him. I'm younger than him so I never played against him – and I don't think I would have liked to either. As hard as nails, that's what he was. A legend of both East Anglian and Glaswegian football (although for the wrong side in both cases!), he was a stalwart for both teams during respective great periods for them. He was the glue at the back, holding everything together. And he was a monster of a man, really physically imposing. Like with all hardmen, you just wouldn't mess with him. Stay on his right side, don't do anything to upset him. If you did, you'd know you'd be on the end of one. But he was a player with a massive heart. That famous picture of him, with blood pouring down his face and on to his England shirt after a World Cup qualifier against Sweden in 1989, completely sums him up.

Butcher says: 'The quiet hardmen were always the worst and didn't need to advertise their toughness.'

4

VAR Needs Sorting or Shelving

There are two words which every fan of a Premier League club dreads in the aftermath of their team scoring. Put together, these words weren't part of football's vocabulary even a couple of years ago, but everyone is familiar with their pairing now, thanks to their appearance in giant letters on big screens in stadiums up and down the country. They are two words to chill you to the bone.

Checking Goal.

These twelve letters invariably put stadiums into a strange lull of both anticipation and dread. One side's support is hopeful; the opposing fans fear the worst. Celebrations are put on hold and players left in limbo. The adjudication comes from elsewhere, many miles away on an industrial estate on west London's furthest fringes. This is the location of Stockley Park, the nerve centre of English football's VAR supremos. But here, despite all the high-tech equipment being deployed, and all the refereeing experience being called upon, there's no guarantee that justice will be served.

I was all in favour of VAR's arrival in the Premier League in August

2019. The previous summer, I had been working for 5 Live at the World Cup in Russia, where I first encountered the process up close and personal. I was impressed. The decision that converted me came in Brazil's group match against Costa Rica. Neymar, who has trouble staying upright at the best of times, took a tumble in the box and Brazil were awarded a penalty. The Dutch referee was then advised to pay a visit to the touchline VAR screen, from which he realised that the tumble was all the striker's own work. Decision reversed. 'Bloody good on you,' I muttered to myself. These were exactly the kind of wrong refereeing calls that the technology was there to right. The only aspect I disapproved of was that Neymar wasn't cautioned for his ridiculously theatrical dive.

It felt like VAR would promise certainty where once was doubt. It would turn grey areas into either black or white. A new era of indisputable absolutes was upon us

There were a few hiccups and teething problems, but VAR worked to pretty decent success at the World Cup. In my view, it was pretty nailed on certain that the game in this country would benefit from its presence. It felt like a new dawn for football, promising certainty where once was doubt. It would turn grey areas into either black or white, yes or no. A new era of indisputable absolutes was upon us.

That was the theory, anyway.

Before the start of the 2019–20 season, I was among the legions of commentators, pundits and journalists invited to Stockley Park to understand the principles behind VAR and how it would be applied to the English game. Although it quickly transpired that its adoption in the Premier League wouldn't mirror how it had worked in the World Cup, despite there being a clear, pretty successful blueprint to follow, I came out of the briefings feeling positive. Really positive. I thought it was all going to work well. I was confident.

From the start, though, they made such a pickle of it. It really didn't need to be this way and the failure to follow the precedents set at the World Cup is at the heart of things.

Firstly, the policy of dissuading referees from consulting the pitchside monitor – erected for this very purpose – is curious at best, deeply flawed at worst. I'm still scratching my head as to why Mike Riley, the head of the referees' body, the PGMOL (Professional Game Match Officials Limited), told his officials to use the monitors sparingly – especially as this is against the protocol of IFAB, the organisation responsible for the global introduction of new rules, and is the approach used widely across Europe. One of the reasons given was to prevent lengthy stoppages to the game, but that has proved misguided, with delays in play while the video team go back and forth over slow-motion footage having been shown to be even more time-consuming.

There was also apparently a concern that referees would become too reliant on looking at the pitchside monitors when they should be placing faith in the judgement of their Stockley Park colleagues. Well, Premier League referees certainly can't be accused of being over-reliant on these screens. It wasn't until January 2020 that a referee in England came across to the touchline to see for himself, when Michael Oliver did so in the FA Cup third-round tie between Crystal Palace and Derby.

Now, people may still argue that Oliver got the sending off of Palace's Luka Milivojević wrong and that it was harsh, myself included. Do you know what, though? I say 'Good on him'. I can accept it because he went and had a second look. He made the decision with his own eyes. It was his interpretation. I just don't understand why it took so long – half a season! – for the first referee to trot over to the side of the pitch to check things out for himself. You would have thought that the main hurdle in the whole VAR story was getting approval for its introduction into the English game. But that appears to have been comparatively straightforward. It now seems that the biggest issue is finding referees who have the balls to actually use the technology themselves.

If the on-field referee is not going to use the pitchside monitor, there has to be trust between him and the folks back at Stockley Park. If I were a referee and someone else had the apparatus and equipment to look at all sorts of different angles but gave me the wrong information, and this happened week after week after week, eventually I would take matters into my own hands. I would look at the monitor to untangle the situation myself. After all, I've got the ultimate responsibility. I'm carrying the can. It's baffling as to why other referees hadn't already chosen the course of action that Oliver did.

Here's an analogy. Imagine being a spaceman trying to land your spacecraft on the moon. Years and years of training and dedication and commitment have been put in for you to get to the required level where you know you can trust yourself. You've passed all the exams.

> Getting approval for VAR's introduction appears to have been comparatively straightforward. The biggest issue seems to be finding referees who have the balls to actually use the technology themselves

You know you can do it. But in being responsible for the landing, you are also part of a bigger team. As you approach the moon, the team back at base keep giving you the wrong information and you keep making mistakes, and then repeating these mistakes, thanks to the boffins at Mission Control. Ultimately, you have the final decision. As you trust your training and you trust your instincts, and you no longer trust the boffins who are continually letting you down, you say 'Enough is enough'. From now on, you're going to rely on yourself and your own judgement instead. And this is the situation that referees find themselves in in the VAR age. They need to trust their judgement more to make a decision, based on paying a visit to the monitor to see for themselves. It's not rocket science…

> VAR has been so universally intrusive in the Premier League that when a team scores, their fans now instinctively hold back from completely losing themselves in the moment

I don't always agree with him, but José Mourinho was absolutely spot on when he described VAR as a video referee rather than a video *assistant* referee. He hit the bull's eye. It's there to *assist* the referee, to advise him. It shouldn't have the last word. Its remit is to indicate when the referee has made a howler, when he's dropped a clanger. But in the first season of its operation, there were plenty – and I mean *plenty* – of questionable decisions that the video assistants made. And sometimes these decisions were definitely incorrect. VAR hasn't empowered the on-field ref. It's undermined him. He hasn't had the final say. He's left with egg on his face – and possibly a dent in his reputation.

The other way in which VAR was misguidedly implemented in the Premier League was the early adoption of a 'high threshold' – that is, a policy of limited intervention, only in cases where there has been a 'clear and obvious error'. It is an approach that muddies waters that should be pretty crystal clear. You don't want either a high threshold or a low threshold. You just want a decision. You don't want the video guys at Stockley Park to feel that they have to back the on-field referee. Their job is to uphold the laws of the game and to offer a correction when the referee has made an error or missed an incident. This is what players and managers and fans expect. There shouldn't be any slant, any pressure to back a colleague's decision. It's simply calling it right or wrong. That's their job. That's why they exist.

They should never have put themselves under pressure with this high threshold. Just do the job and say what's been seen. If something is wrong and the on-field referee has got it wrong, they shouldn't have to ask themselves, *Well, should I back him in this instance?* Instead it should be, 'You see it that way, but I see it this way. It's your call, though.'

There has been, of course, huge dissatisfaction about the effect of VAR on the rhythm and intensity of the match, thanks to long and protracted discussion and analysis of video evidence. When VAR first came into world football, Lukas Brud, the secretary of IFAB, offered reassurance that the game as we knew it would not be fundamentally altered. Brud promised 'minimum interference and maximum effect. We don't want to create something in football that's constantly interruptive and destroying the game.'

You'd have difficulty finding any football fan who believes that the English implementation of VAR has upheld this objective. It's been so universally intrusive in the Premier League that when a team scores, their fans now instinctively hold back from completely losing themselves in the moment, concerned that the Stockley Park detectives will spot a minor infringement from 30 seconds earlier. At its best, football gives us unfettered joy and sheer ecstasy. It's now tempered by a sense of mild concern and worry. A truer reflection would be 'maximum interference and maximum effect'.

Along with the muted celebrations, the delays while video evidence is checked, checked again and checked once more for luck can be interminable. The pace and immediacy of the match dissolves, as players linger and lurk, waiting for the verdict to come down the line. And with the delays comes the lack of communication. Players and fans alike are left in the dark. This is simply unacceptable, especially as fans have coughed up a significant wedge of cash to be there and yet aren't remotely kept in the loop. Knowing what the reason for the delay is and which aspect of play is being double-checked should be part and parcel of the price of admission, whether communicated up on the big screen – where the incident itself could be reshown – or via a mic'd-up referee, as it would be in rugby or American football. Ignorance isn't bliss. Clarity is all.

It used to be the case that somebody at home would call someone at the match to find out what was happening and what the score was. It's the other way around now. The person in the stadium is calling a friend or relative at home in front of the television to learn exactly what the delay is. That's a bonkers state of affairs.

I accept rugby union is a different game and that it has more natural stops, but I actually think it plays out these decisions beautifully, thanks to the referee being mic'd up. You don't always have to agree with what the referee says; we can all interpret decisions in a different way, after all. But at least the referee will say, 'Well, I've given this decision because this is the way I see it.' That's very, very difficult to argue against. He's been clear and communicative. You then don't have to agree with that, but at least you have had an explanation. He's shown you his workings. He's done his qualifications to get to that high level of refereeing and he trusts himself that he'll make the right calls.

Why not simply replicate that in football? There's often been a case made for referees to be interviewed after matches to explain certain decisions, so why not feed that appetite by getting him to explain big decisions as he goes along? 'This is the way I saw it. It's a red card for violent conduct' or 'I gave a penalty because of the distance the ball travelled before it hit him on the arm, which was also in an unnatural position'. Just let him say what he sees.

> Any part of the body that a goal can be scored by is subject to VAR in an offside referral. A little toe? A hint of shoulder? An oversized buttock?

Of all its failings, the VAR controversy that has aggravated fans of Premier League clubs the most is its interference in offside decisions. Out comes the software that can measure video images to the smallest margins – all those geometrical lines across the screen which indicate whether a striker was ahead of the defender by the thickness of a cigarette paper. And there are many who declare that offside is offside, no matter the miniscule advantage there might be for the attacking player. I was once a strong advocate of this way of thinking. But I've since come round to an alternative view.

Across Europe, VAR's brief is to step in when a player is in a 'clear and obvious' offside position and a goal has been scored. However, the English interpretation doesn't adhere to this principle, instead relying on ultra-precise software to detect whether a player has strayed offside, even – or especially – when the margin is invisible to the naked eye.

Not only that, but what's being measured is questionable. Any part of the body that a goal can be scored by (so everything bar hands and arms) is subject to VAR in an offside referral. A little toe? A hint of shoulder? An oversized buttock? Perhaps even a floppy fringe – in which case Todd Cantwell needs to be careful.

I mean, when a goal has been ruled out because the scorer's armpit was in an advanced position, we're in trouble, aren't we? Since when has anybody ever scored a goal with their armpit? Answers on a postcard please.

I did chuckle when, ahead of their FA Cup third-round tie against Watford at Vicarage Road, Tranmere Rovers sent a tweet concerning their imminent first experience of VAR: 'Any lads in the squad with particularly big noses or feet, time your runs a tad later please.' Brilliant.

I could fill half of this book detailing the various episodes that VAR threw up in its debut season in the Premier League

Dozens of goals were ruled out by those unforgiving VAR measurements during that first season, goals that would have stood when the naked eye was the determinant of an offside decision. It's the triumph of forensics. In the words of the *Independent*'s Lawrence Ostlere, the technology 'has unearthed sins we didn't know existed'.

We all want to see more goals being scored and there are a few alternative approaches that could assist with this. One school of thought suggests that it's the position of the attacker's foot – the main tool of his trade, after all – relative to that of the last defender that should be the determining factor. That would certainly be less ridiculous than the current anything-goes approach. Graeme Souness came up with another interesting solution: if any part of the body is onside, then the player can't be deemed offside. That is, every part of the attacker's body would need to be in advance of the last defender for the goal not to stand. I like this. It's a positive move. And it would certainly add to more goals being scored. The technology is already there. It would just be the simplest of rule changes.

But the approach I favour – and which would alleviate the need for all those lines on the screen, thus not causing the game to be delayed quite so much – is the one used in the MLS (Major League Soccer). If the decision goes to VAR, the video team make a judgement on how they see it on the screen. If they feel they would have to scrutinise the footage to the nth degree to decide, they allow the goal. This seems like common sense to me. Not everybody would like this, but I think most would accept it.

I could fill half of this book detailing the various episodes that VAR threw up in its debut season in the Premier League – goals wrongly allowed, goals wrongly disallowed, penalties denied, red cards wrongly awarded. Very few matches seemed to escape controversy. It lurked around every corner. Here, though, are my takes on some of the most memorable VAR incidents – and, when I say memorable, I don't necessarily mean that positively.

Trent Alexander-Arnold, Liverpool vs Manchester City

It was the biggest game of the season so far, the two overwhelming favourites for the Premier League title going head-to-head, punch for punch, at an electric Anfield. The atmosphere didn't need further spice, but it arrived just five minutes in when the ball struck Alexander-Arnold's arm, which was, it has to be said, not in the most natural of positions. The referee waved for play to continue and Liverpool launched a swift counter-attack that, 22 seconds later, ended with Fabinho firing them ahead. The VAR check didn't judge the handball to have been deliberate, which I have to say looked pretty plum to me. Rather than City getting an early penalty, they found themselves conceding the crucial first goal in a crucial match. Liverpool went on to take a screw-turning 3-1 win.

Youri Tielemans, Leicester City vs Bournemouth

Another illogical decision that left me bemused. One of the four criteria that VAR is empowered to investigate is whether a straight red card can be issued in the event of serious foul play. And when a Tielemans challenge on Callum Wilson was so dangerous that it could have broken the Bournemouth striker's ankle, the video team moved into action. Imagine the collective surprise – possibly even from Leicester fans as well – when the Belgian's foul was not deemed worthy of a sending-off. It was. It really was. As clean a cut, straight red as you're likely to see. But VAR's numerous angles were apparently blind to the truth.

Marcus Rashford, Manchester United vs Liverpool

This was one of the decisions of that first VAR season that really made me question the implementation of the technology – or, at least, the competency of those operating it. Rashford's goal simply shouldn't have stood. Divock Origi was clearly fouled in the build-up when Victor Lindelöf kicked him in the calf. You felt sure that the team at Stockley Park would swiftly confirm the impediment, but no. I'm still at a loss to understand how the goal wasn't chalked off, a goal that significantly contributed to Liverpool's first dropped points of the season. The referee, Martin Atkinson made a clear and obvious error and yet the VAR team exonerated him. How could they miss it?

John Lundstram, Spurs vs Sheffield United

This was one of the tightest offside decisions of the season, with the technology demonstrating that, as he crossed for David McGoldrick to score, the Blades midfielder was offside by no more than the length of a toe. And, going by the Premier League's principles of application, it was the correct decision. But what made this particular incident stand out was the length of time it took for the decision to be made. If an assistant referee is required to judge marginal offside decisions in a split second and raise their flag accordingly, I'm utterly baffled as to why it would take multiple officials, in front of multiple screens showing multiple angles nearly *four minutes* to adjudicate.

Teemu Pukki, Norwich City vs Spurs

For me, this was one of the landmark VAR decisions of that first season – and not because it involved a Norwich striker. Controlling a long ball from the left, it was a glorious first touch and finish by the bearded magician of Carrow Road that left every home fan, and anyone watching on television, purring with delight. 'Sumptuous' is a word that would describe it well. However, those watching at Stockley Park weren't purring. Despite Pukki's feet being well behind those of the last defender, the Finn was leaning forward, ready to pounce on the ball. This put a slight part of his shoulder ahead of the Spurs man, something which the naked eye would never have spotted. But no goal. That law is an ass.

There are innumerable further examples of controversial, game-changing interventions by VAR. Potentially season-changing interventions, in fact. A late penalty wrongly awarded could mean two points dropped and a fundamental effect on a club's final league position. So could a dubious red card or a phantom goal unfairly ruled out. In its initial form, VAR hasn't brought in that much-anticipated new era of certainty. And I'll hold my hand up here. As I admitted earlier, I was a major cheerleader at the outset, metaphorically shaking my pompoms and chanting 'V-A-R!' from the sidelines. My position, though, shifted throughout the first half of that initial season – and it moved in one direction only. My faith was weakening.

By Christmas of its first season, I got to the stage where I would have preferred to bin VAR for the time being and go back to the technology-free days of the previous season. Ali Bruce-Ball disagreed with me: 'You can't shelve it. It's here to stay.' But if something's not working, you either get it mended or you get rid of it, don't you? You don't carry on putting your dirty laundry into a broken-down washing machine. It'll just stay filthy. And you don't sit in front of a television set that won't switch on. So why would we persist with VAR in this fractured, misfiring state?

It was brought in to assist with the big mistakes and incorrect decisions that can frustrate and infuriate lovers of the game. We're talking the 'Hand of God', or Frank Lampard's phantom goal against Germany – those kind of wrong calls. But the pernickety and petty way it's sometimes applied in this country has simply got the collective hackles up. Every week on *606* the phone lines are dominated by VAR-related calls, with fans united by how their game is being reshaped and redrawn. VAR was supposed to neutralise those controversial flashpoints that cause such indignation. Instead, it's been the source of a depth of anger rarely heard from our listeners, whether that be Livid of Leicester, Angry of Arsenal or Pissed-off of Palace.

By the time you read this, you'll hopefully have a fine grasp on what – if anything – will be changing in respect of VAR in the Premier League for future seasons. And, by Lord, I sincerely hope that sense has been seen and that it falls closer in alignment to what happened in Russia in 2018.

Hopefully Mike Riley will at some point hold his hands up and admit that he got it wrong on several counts. I'm not holding my breath, though. But severe questions do need to be asked of him. What was the philosophy and purpose behind the principle of the high threshold? Why do our Premier League referees use monitors when they're officiating Champions League matches but don't do so at home? And can we sort out the utter, utter mess that these offside decisions are making?

Riley's not the only one with blinkers on who needs to wake up and smell the coffee. I'm still flabbergasted by the comments of Neil Swarbrick, the Premier League's VAR supremo, when he went on 5 Live to defend the process against the overwhelming chorus of criticism. Halfway through the season, he was asked how successful he thought the opening months had been for VAR in the Premier League. He suggested a score of seven out of ten was an accurate reflection. He's a nice man, but I did feel sorry for him and his miscued overview. Seven! Seven is what Len Goodman used to give good dancers in *Strictly*! Sadly, VAR hasn't shown such fancy footwork. Perhaps it should have been voted off early doors.

As well as 'Checking Goal', there are two other words that regularly appear on the big screen of Premier League grounds. But these words

> You don't carry on putting your dirty laundry into a broken-down washing machine. So why would we persist with VAR in this fractured, misfiring state?

don't bring a chill. Rather, they bathe one set of supporters in a wave of relief. No further action is needed. 'Check Complete'.

The check on VAR itself, though, is far from complete.

5
Stop Renaming On-field Positions

_____

'The game doesn't change. The goalposts don't move. It's still eleven versus eleven.' These are the wise words once passed down to me by John Robertson, the former Nottingham Forest winger and one of my coaches at Celtic. And they're bang on. They contain the fundamentals about the sport we love – the indivisible, unimpeachable truth. No amount of debate, discussion and disagreement can shift them.

These words can be confidently applied to the way teams line up on the field of play. You can dress up playing positions in any amount of new words or phrases, but they're not describing anything new. Those who create and use this new terminology – the tactical analysts – are simply trying to invent the wheel all over again. Why can't we just keep it as it was?

All manner of supposedly new positions have come into the game in the digital age. But many of these are actually nothing new. They're simply positions that have been renamed and rebadged to give the sense that they're describing something cutting edge and contemporary. We always used to – and many of us still do – call the deepest-lying midfielder, the one lending the most assistance to his defence, the holding midfielder. Over the last couple of seasons, though, it's been increasingly replaced by the word 'pivot'. It means the same thing. It's describing the same position. So why the name change?

Another type of midfielder rejoices in the glorious epithet of 'shuttler', which sounds more appropriate to use it to describe a commute using public transport. It's actually applied to the kind of player who covers a lot of ground up and down the pitch, supporting both his team's defensive line and its strike force. Steven Gerrard would be an example of one. Patrick Vieira is another. But why the need to give this role a new name? Box-to-box midfielders is what they are. Everyone understands the type of player you're describing when you use that phrase, so why swap it for something else? Why start confusing people by calling them shuttlers?

This is just the tip of the iceberg. 'Central-wingers' sounds like a contradiction in terms, but it describes those players who offer width to their team's central playmaker, but who are more likely to cut in than to try to get to the byline. Others might call them 'half-wingers' or 'inverted-wingers'. David Silva and Juan Mata are examples.

'Rest-defence' sounds like a new, innovative concept that's redefining how a team's back line sets itself up. It turns out it merely describes how a defensive line keeps its shape and structure when its forwards are busy on the attack. You know, just how defences have operated for decade upon decade. Does that really need a name?

Then there's the quarterback, the playmaker who actually operates much deeper than a conventional number 10 – an Andrea Pirlo figure. Let's not forget the *raumdeuter*, a German word that broadly translates as 'space investigator', describing a player who has the luxury of being allowed to roam wherever he wants. Thomas Müller calls himself one. The name might be new, but the concept is anything but. Paul

Gascoigne was granted such freedom 30 years ago, after all. And many more before him.

We've all heard of the false 9, the ghost striker who comes much deeper than a traditional centre-forward, bringing defenders with him and thus creating space for his team-mates to attack into. Messi has been a master of it at Barcelona. I don't have too much of a problem with that as a concept, but it doesn't stop there. Some bright spark then introduced the notion of a 9½, a player similar to the false 9 but who might drift a few yards deeper but not so deep as a number 10. These players existed before a new name was dreamed up for them. Roberto Baggio was one such player. We just called him an attacking midfielder. That seemed to be good enough.

If the difference between a 9 and 10 is 10 yards, then a 9½ must be 5 yards. I appreciate it's all about small gains these days, but where does it all end? A 9¾? A 9⅞?

The people who use this new and enlarging football lexicon are trying to describe something that in their view didn't previously

> Certain positions have been renamed and rebadged to give the sense that they're describing something cutting edge and contemporary, but they're actually nothing new

exist. For instance, the emphasis put on a 4-4-1-1 formation these days suggests that that pivotal playmaker, the number 10, is a relatively new creation. Well, tell that to Ferenc Puskás. Or Gianni Rivera. Or Liam Brady.

This thinking assumes that, going back a couple or more decades, 4-4-2 was a rigid, unyielding formation in which there was no fluidity.

The assumption is that two strikers just played up alongside each other and that neither of them ever dropped in to turn and slide a ball through to the other. When I played at Blackburn alongside Alan Shearer, Alan was the main man – and quite rightly so, because he scored the goals. I played a secondary role, so when the team lost the ball, I would be the one to drop on to the holding midfielder. When the opposition were on the attack, Alan and I weren't just hanging around the halfway line, waiting for the long hoof out of defence to charge on to.

So when we were out of possession, we'd be playing 4-4-1-1 and yet that formation is trumpeted as if it's something new and revolutionary. It's the thought that, in my era and before it, no one ever adapted the way they set themselves up, that no one was able to think for themselves. Surprisingly enough, we weren't robotic. We didn't stick to a particular position, unable to adapt and improvise. There weren't exclusion zones on the pitch into which we dared not move. And yet we're led to believe that an interchanging, fluid forward line has revolutionised football. I mean, really?

When Nottingham Forest travelled to Madrid in 1980 to defend the European Cup against Kevin Keegan's Hamburg side, an Achilles injury kept out Trevor Francis, the match-winner 12 months earlier. Rather than replace him with another striker, Brian Clough selected the 18-year-old midfielder Gary Mills instead, playing five across the middle of the pitch and leaving Garry Birtles on his own up front. This 4-5-1 formation was successful too, with Forest keeping hold of that famous trophy. This was a full 40 years ago, but some still regard the idea of flooding the midfield as a new one.

Pep Guardiola has been lauded for innovative, often revolutionary tactics. One of these has been the deployment of a W-M formation, which effectively means five outfield players on defensive duties and the other five in attacking mode, forming the shapes of a W and an

M across the field. Those without a deep knowledge of footballing history are unlikely to be aware that this was the favoured formation of Herbert Chapman, the celebrated manager of Arsenal who led them to two of their five league titles in the 1930s, a time when this was genuinely a revolutionary approach. What might appear to be a new idea ain't necessarily so. Adaptable formations aren't the sole preserve of the modern era.

People are getting jobs off the back of inventing new positional names, despite – as John Robertson said to me that time – the game essentially staying the same. The notion of a false 9 wasn't invented in the Messi era. Look at Kenny Dalglish. He was a prolific goalscorer, yes, but less of a 6-yard poacher type than someone like Gary Lineker. He would drop deeper to look for the ball, to affect play more than a fox-in-the-box would.

> Back in the day, we didn't stick to a particular position, unable to adapt and improvise. And yet we're led to believe that an interchanging, fluid forward line has revolutionised football. Really?

As well as 10s and false 9s, other numbers are also used. 'He's an 8. They're a 6.' But referring to positions in this way is utterly baffling in the era of squad numbers in domestic football. It can only confuse the layman. A player with a 6 on his back was always one half of a centre-back pairing. Similarly, a player wearing 4 would invariably be the holding midfielder, but look at the best players in that position in the Premier League today. Eric Dier wears 15 at Spurs, Man City's Fernandinho favours 25 and Declan Rice goes as high as 41. It's one thing to confuse us with new names for positions, so don't make it even more confusing by referring to numbers too. They were never the greatest guide, anyway. If you're talking about some of the best 'number 10s' in history, Johan Cruyff will be for ever associated with the number 14, while Zinedine Zidane wore the 5 shirt at Real Madrid.

If you were a Martian who had just landed on our planet and you had to process information about football positions and names of positions and numbers, you couldn't possibly make head or tail of anything, other than probably a goalkeeper. You would get back in your flying saucer and clear off as quickly as possible, thinking *Those football people from Earth are on another planet…*

This new language bolsters the reputations of analysts and tacticians, and helps them justify their jobs. That's the long and short of it. They'll be analysing analysts soon, won't they? And there's so much smoke and mirrors going on with all this data. I played with Alan Thompson at Celtic, who used to manipulate his Opta stats that calculated how much distance he covered in a game. Whenever the ball was out of play – for a throw-in, for instance, or if someone had got injured – he used to go on runs to get his stats stacked up! It's genius when you think about it – giving the manager the impression that you're working harder than anybody else.

Maybe there are elements of hypocrisy underlying this whole rant of mine. In my father's era, it was all wing-halves and inside-forwards – terminology that had become well out of date by the time I played. Am I just clinging to the terminology of my own era as the world shifts around me? After all, you become used to whatever's the norm of the particular times you live and play in. Who knows, in 20 years from now, the next generation might be raging about a new term that has superseded the use of 'pivot'.

So what's the cure? Perhaps there isn't clear action that can be taken. Perhaps grumpy, middle-aged men like myself simply need to move and adapt with the times, to use – and become at peace with – the world of shuttlers and *raumdeuters* and central-wingers (and I haven't even got started on overloads, underlapping, transition, high blocks, low blocks, counter pressing…). Maybe it's up to us to accept that times change and that we shouldn't become outdated. Acknowledge that time passes, that there's a handover between generations.

Still, the bottom line is that, while new words come and go, the positions on a football field remain the same, despite what the analysts might think. The fundamentals don't alter, the goalposts don't move.

And it's still eleven versus eleven.

MY TOP TEN **MOST ENTERTAINING TEAMS**

The clichés say that football is a result-based industry, but it's also a branch of the entertainment business. Here are the teams that have entertained me the most over the years…

10 NEWCASTLE UNITED, 1995–96

This was the last full season of Keegan's first reign at St James' Park, when his policy of all-out – and possibly gung-ho – attack gave them the nickname 'The Entertainers'. While their fast, full-blooded style failed to land them any serious silverware, it did earn them many admirers, thanks to the stirring performances of David Ginola, Peter Beardsley, Les Ferdinand, Faustino Asprilla and others. If only they'd kept their bottle and held off the challenge – and the mind games – of Alex Ferguson's Manchester United. For the neutral, it was sickening they were never champions.

Kevin Keegan said… 'We were naive in many ways. It was part of our charm, and one of the reasons why so many people liked watching Newcastle, but ultimately it counted against us.'

9 EVERTON, 1984–85

For a handful of years in the mid-Eighties, Everton threatened the domestic dominance of their neighbours across Stanley Park. Howard Kendall's blend of seasoned pros (Peter Reid, Andy Gray) and young bucks (Trevor Steven, Gary Stevens) was a winning combination, in particular during the 1984–85 season. They narrowly missed out on an historic treble that season: they won the league and the Cup Winners' Cup, but lost out in extra-time at the FA Cup final to Ron Atkinson's Manchester United. Despite being champions, though, they were denied a tilt at the European Cup by the ban on English teams in Europe following the Heysel tragedy. Who knows what heights they might have reached?

Howard Kendall said…'They were fighters. They got to a point where they thought they were the best and I think if you've got that mentality, you've got a hell of a chance.'

8 CHELSEA, 2004–05

Now this was an impact. He might be miserable these days, but when he first arrived in England, José Mourinho had no small amount of charm and swagger – and he backed up this cockiness by winning the Premier League in his first season at Stamford Bridge. While they went on to win the Champions League under Robert Di Matteo, I regard this side to be the greatest and most entertaining Chelsea side ever, thanks to that season's judiciously selected new signings – Petr Čech, Arjen Robben and Didier Drogba among them – hitting the ground running. Mourinho's own description of himself as the 'Special One' might have raised eyebrows and hackles, but he backed himself to deliver Chelsea's first title in 50 years. And deliver he did.

José Mourinho said…'We have top players and, sorry if I'm arrogant, we have a top manager.'

7 MANCHESTER CITY, 2017–18

Having finished the previous season without a trophy for the first time in his managerial career, Pep Guardiola more than made amends the following year, winning his first Premier League title with a City team that became the first ever to reach 100 points – half of which, extraordinarily, came away from home. They also scored more league goals (106) than anyone else in a season, thanks to the potency of both Sergio Agüero and Raheem Sterling. City's fluid, devastating play ripped their opponents apart and they neatly reached the 100-point mark on the last day of the season. A terrific team.

Pep Guardiola said… 'Everything was perfect this season. It finished the way it deserved to finish.'

6 ARSENAL, 1997–98

I believe Arsenal's thrilling 1997–98 side pips the 2003–04 Invincibles, based on the style with which they secured the double in Wenger's first full season at Highbury. Twelve points behind Manchester United at the end of February, ten straight wins saw them overhaul their bitter rivals. Despite it being the new manager's first Arsenal side, its balance was perfect, from the sturdy English defence (Adams, Bould, Winterburn and Dixon), through the French steel in midfield (Vieira, Petit) and the attacking flair of Dutchmen Overmars and Bergkamp, alongside free-scoring Ian Wright. They were the complete team and saw off United in their pomp, securing the title with two games to go. An FA Cup triumph a few weeks later completed the double.

Arsène Wenger said… 'They were ready to go to war with you. You could be in the trenches with them.'

5 LEICESTER CITY, 2015–16

The bookmakers didn't fancy Leicester to win the Premier League title, putting odds of 5,000-1 on them. Not many other people fancied them either, what with the Foxes having only narrowly avoided relegation the previous season and boss Nigel Pearson getting the boot. In short, this collection of waifs and strays, now under the control of Claudio Ranieri, were no-hopers. But with the pace of Jamie Vardy and Riyad Mahrez allowing them to counter-attack clinically and quite brilliantly, they made a good start as front-runners, a status they continued to sustain as the season progressed. *They're going to have a blip*, you'd tell yourself. *They're going to have a blip.* But they didn't. And they won. Probably the greatest story in Premier League history.

Claudio Ranieri said…'Why can't we continue to run, run, run? We are like Forrest Gump. Leicester is Forrest Gump.'

4 CELTIC, 1966–67

Winning the European Cup was a phenomenal achievement for this particular Celtic team, the first British team to do so. And the Lisbon Lions did it by taking the game to two-time winners Inter Milan in the Portuguese capital, brilliantly unlocking the ultra-defensive Italians with flair and guile. And they did this with a completely home-grown XI: the only 'outsider' was Bobby Lennox, who hailed from Saltcoats, a full 30 miles from Celtic Park! We'll never see the like of that again. Extraordinary. They were true trailblazers, led by the indomitable Billy McNeill.

Jock Stein said…'We are going to attack as we have never attacked before.'

3 MANCHESTER UNITED, 1998–99

Obviously plenty of silverware had already come Alex Ferguson's way (multiple titles, multiple FA Cups and a Cup Winners' Cup), but this was surely the season when they reached the summit proper, when there was nowhere left for them to go. With an unparalleled treble at stake, they left it late in the Champions League final in Barcelona, when two strikers came off the bench to both score in injury time. They were quite probably the greatest Premier League side ever – swashbuckling and easy on the eye, with goals coming from right across the team. If the opposition fancied getting anything out of a visit to Old Trafford, their goalkeeper would have to put in a world-class shift.

Alex Ferguson said…'I can't believe it. I can't believe it. Football. Bloody hell.'

2 NOTTINGHAM FOREST, 1978–80

Four months after his ignominious exit from Elland Road, Brian Clough pitched up at Second Division Nottingham Forest in January 1975, where he was joined a little while later by his lieutenant Peter Taylor. Having won promotion in 1977, in their first season back in the top flight they loosened Liverpool's grip on the championship by winning the title. They then followed that up by winning two successive European Cups, making it the greatest managerial spell of one of the greatest managers. And – aside from genuine superstars Trevor Francis and Peter Shilton – it was achieved by a raggle-taggle team of wily veterans and a former carpet-fitter plucked from non-league. A wonderful story.

Brian Clough said…'You win something once and people say it is all down to luck. You win it twice and it shuts the buggers up.'

And the team that entertained me the most is…

1 LIVERPOOL, 1976–77

Bill Shankly might have built the club up, but it was Bob Paisley who brought home the bacon. Having succeeded Shankly in 1974, under his guidance the Reds swept up six league titles, three European Cups, the UEFA Cup, three League Cups, the UEFA Super Cup and five Charity Shields (plus another one shared). Only the FA Cup eluded him. The season in which they won their first European Cup, 1976–77, was arguably the best, adding glory in Rome against Borussia Mönchengladbach to the retention of the First Division title. Fired to success by the dynamism of players like Keegan, Terry McDermott and Jimmy Case, in winning nearly everything under Paisley they invariably did so with great style and panache.

Bob Paisley said… 'I've been here during the bad times, too. One year we came second.'

6
Ban Coloured Boots

Picture the scene. It's Christmas morning at some point during the early 1980s and, in a quiet Norfolk village, the Sutton family have gathered around the tree, eager to open their presents. I'm rattling the parcel I've just been handed by one of my sisters. It's shoebox-sized and, from the clunking sound it's making, I reckon it contains a pair of football boots. In a flash, the wrapping is off, the lid of the box is lifted and I'm gazing at the treasure that lies within. The white 'P' on the boots' tongue indicates that they're not Adidas or Gola, the names favoured by the cooler kids at school. They're a pair of Patricks, a brand that – despite their top-end boot being endorsed by Kevin Keegan – were a Second-Division option when it came to what football-crazy kids put on their feet.

But am I disappointed? Not a bit of it. For unlike Billy Dane – the teenage hero of 'Billy's Boots', the strip in the *Roy of the Rovers* comic, who only played well when wearing the ancient footwear of goalscoring legend 'Dead Shot' Keen – even my pre-pubescent self knows that it's not the type of boots on my feet that will make me a better player. The brand doesn't matter. Having been born in Nottingham, I'm a Forest fan and I appreciate that in order to follow in the stud-prints of my hero Trevor Francis, I must apply myself. I must practise and practise and practise. I have to do the hard yards.

Spool forward several decades and there are legions of footballers who seem to genuinely believe that the colour of their boots – the colour! – will determine how well they play. Not for them the standard all-black pairs of yesteryear, of yesterday's men. Instead they opt for the gaudiest shades imaginable: oranges and yellows and pinks and blues and greens that emit a glow as if they're radioactive. Indeed, were a floodlight failure to occur during a match these days, play could simply continue, illuminated by the light source provided by 22 pairs of luminous boots.

> Were a floodlight failure to occur during a match, play could simply continue, illuminated by the light source provided by 22 pairs of luminous boots

Even my Patricks would have looked impossibly futuristic to the owner of the first recorded pair of football boots. Rather extraordinarily, that was one Henry VIII, who in 1526 commissioned the royal shoemaker Cornelius Johnson to make him a pair of ankle-high leather boots to wear when he played football with the young noblemen of his court. Of course, the game Henry played was unrecognisable from what would become association football. It was brutally violent and unforgiving; definitely not the place for the Day-Glo footwear of today. Indeed, you can imagine what the reaction of the famously intolerant Henry would have been on seeing such a pair – and what punishment he might have meted out for the wearer of such boots. After all, the king wasn't shy when it came to dishing out stiff retribution. Just ask a couple of his wives.

Of course, it's not just the very upper echelons of the game where these colourful monstrosities appear. Right down the pyramid, as far as under-10s leagues, they're a staple of every football pitch in the land. I think it's fair to say that, years ago, young players growing up just used to think and to dream purely about playing. Nowadays, and from a young age, people seem to think more about the trappings than the game itself – and this is a huge problem. The focus is not on the process of how to reach the top of the game, but it's on what they look like, their haircuts and what they wear. All the gear but no idea.

> When coloured boots came into the game, the feeling was that if you wanted to wear them, you had to make sure you were the best player on the park

Perhaps it's just sour grapes. I may be slightly bitter on this subject as my mum used to cut my hair until I was about 14. Out of the kitchen cupboard came the pudding bowl for the old basin haircut. She sometimes cut my fringe too high and it was often wonky. She was partially sighted in one eye and the left-hand side of my hair would be shorter than the right-hand side. It was all pretty desperate – being of high-school age and your mum still cutting your hair. I bet James Maddison never had a bowl cut.

It extended to clothes too. When everybody else wore Sta-Prest at school, I had big flares. And there are pictures of me in my younger days in horrific 1970s cardigans. I look like a bloody hippy in some of them. I was stitched right up by my parents. So this is why I may be slightly envious that kids nowadays get their hair cut by proper barbers and can buy trendy clothes. Because of my haircut, I was rejected romantically at school. But I suppose that being unlucky in love meant I kept my eye on football.

I perfectly understand that when you're young, you want to try to keep up with the trends. But when I was that age, that wasn't the most important thing. It was a principle drilled into me at a young age: it's not about the clothes you choose or the boots you wear. It's about what you *do*. Not that I had a choice. When I look back at the photos, my parents seem to have taken that option away from me!

I played in the era when coloured boots started to come into the game. The feeling back then was that, if you wanted to wear them, you had to make sure you were the best player on the park. You had to make sure you were a bloody good footballer with a bag of tricks up your sleeve – stepovers and the like. (I used to have a stepover in my younger days at Norwich, but by the time I hit my thirties, you could see it coming about half a minute before as I tried to set it up.)

I remember the young lads at Celtic who used to wear coloured boots when they came to train with the first team – talented lads like Aiden McGeady and Shaun Maloney. We just used to kick lumps out of them. There were levels of respect to observe as much as anything. Don't get above your station. When you're in the company of top players – and they were training with the likes of Henrik Larsson, who was the ultimate player – what gives you the right to come to a training session with those boots on your feet when you're not at that level? You have to have a mentality problem, as much as anything. The older players certainly questioned it. Or at least they did back then. Coloured boots are the norm now.

It was a natural reaction. People will think, *Who do you think you are? You fancy yourself.* And it extends beyond the colour of a player's boots. Just look at Robbie Savage. People just wanted to boot him for bleaching his hair. And then they got to know him and they wanted to boot him even more! I'm joking, of course…

It's a curious equation: the notion that the more expensive or the louder the boot, the better the performance. We can't deny that a lot of youngsters think that way, but anybody who does really believe it shouldn't be allowed to play football. Young kids see Ronaldo or Messi wearing these high-end boots and think that, at least partially, this is the secret of their success. So they pester their parents to buy them an 80-quid pair, despite the fact that they won't make them play any better than if they were wearing an old pair fished out of the PE department's lost-property box.

I may be misremembering, but I've never knowingly bought my kids coloured boots. I've been in sports shops with them when they've held up pairs for me to admire. 'Dad, what do you think of these?' Then they see the look on my face and the steam coming out of my ears and swiftly put them back on the shelf. They probably think I'm from the dark ages.

Everyone wears them now though. You'd probably be looked upon as some sort of caveman if you ran on the pitch in black boots these days, so I accept that I'm sounding like some old fogey here. But I still stand by the principle. It's not about what particular colour of the rainbow your boots are or what your hair looks like or how many tattoos you have. It's actually about what you do on the pitch. Get your head down and play football. It's as simple as that.

Players have got to prove themselves. They've got to earn the right to act a bit flash. But they're trying to become a brand too early. Years ago, when we'd been a pain in the backside, the youth-team manager used to make us scrub the changing-room floor with a toothbrush as a punishment. We cleaned boots, put kit back on pegs, picked dirty slips up off the floor – which is far from a nice thing when one of the first-team players has had a curry the evening before. It was character-building. That probably sounds really old-fashioned and people might look at that and think *What on earth are you talking about?* But this kind of discipline is good. It makes you appreciate what you have.

When you're good enough to be a brand, by all means go and enjoy all the trappings. I take my hat off to players at the top level, those playing Premier League football. They deserve everything they get because they've made sacrifices. Who I'm talking about are the players the rung under that. I suppose once they're 18, they can do what they like and if they want to buy a flash car, that's their prerogative. I don't have a problem with that, as long as they're keeping their eye on the ball and training hard. Everybody has natural talent to some extent. Some people are golden and can just rock up and be a success. Most have had to undertake years and years of training, repetition and possibly rejection to get where they are.

Look at James Maddison now. He's not shy, but he's been around, he's done those hard yards. He was at Norwich, went up to Aberdeen on loan, came back, worked hard in the Championship and carved himself a really good career. There's Jack Grealish, too. In his younger days, he seemed to be a bit of a Jack-the-lad, but the penny has since dropped. These players deserve everything they get and fair play to them.

Ultimately, you have to be known not for your boots or for your hair, but for your brilliance on a field. Football is a working-class game and I can understand that people are attracted all the trappings that come with it. I don't have a problem with people who've earned those. But the trappings come *after* success. They don't – and never have – arrived before. It's not a good mentality to worry more about your boots than your training and the effort that you're putting in – the running and the drills and the repetition and such like.

And it's not just the boots (which, incidentally, might well be personalised to have their initials on them, or the initials of their kids, or the names of their pets…). Young players obsess over their hair more than they should. It needs to be spot on. The tattoos need to be conspicuous, the shirt tucked in perfectly. It doesn't end there – gloves, snoods, leggings, socks pulled up immaculately just under the knee and so on. By the time they've sorted out their appearance, there's a good chance they've forgotten who the manager told them to pick up at corners. Concentrate on the game, not your appearance.

So how do we stop players getting above their station, of them suggesting – through their choice of footwear – that they've reached a level they're actually nowhere close to? My tongue is firmly in my cheek here, but it's got to be a ban, for these young upstarts, on football boots that are anything other than black in colour. Just like I applied to my kids.

> By the time they've sorted out their appearance, there's a good chance they've forgotten who the manager told them to pick up at corners

And then, why not institute a system where coloured boots are treated like medals and therefore actually mean something? They would remain the preserve and the privilege of first-team players, those who've earned the right to wear them. Even then, they would be colour-coordinated to match their club's kit – so yellow and green for Norwich, claret and blue for Burnley or Aston Villa and so on. If you reached the level of being an international player, this would be the plateau on which you were free to choose whatever shade or colour you wanted to stick on your feet. You'd have earned the right. To the winners, the spoils. But this would only be in matches when you were representing your country. You'd be back to your club colours for the next domestic game.

If you reached the very pinnacle of personal footballing endeavour and won the Ballon d'Or, you'd be afforded a unique privilege. For the next 12 months, you would be the only person in the world allowed to play football in gold boots. With the winner's feet 'crowned' at a lavish coronation, this would be the ultimate accolade for a footballer, one of more worth and prestige than a garage full of Lamborghinis or a home on every continent.

Those gold boots would be the carrot dangling in front of every wannabe superstar. To get remotely close, these players would have to apply themselves wholeheartedly. To escape the world of boring black boots would take knuckling down and focus. Creating a brand would have to take a back seat. Eyes on the prize. No distractions.

And that's the serious message at the heart of things here: football is not about being materialistic, in any way, shape or form. It's about being switched on and it's about being single-minded. I'm proof of that. I was someone who only managed to carve out a professional career through graft and sacrifice.

For that lanky, knock-kneed 13-year-old with spots on his chin and a bowl haircut up top, it certainly wasn't about the look…

PART TWO
OFF THE PITCH

A football pitch is not an island. What happens on that field of dreams isn't contained by the white paint of the touchline. It's affected by everything around it. Football isn't simply a 90-minute match and its protagonists aren't merely those chasing after a polyurethane ball.

Off-field activities define and determine football and its culture as much as a crunching tackle or a thunderbolt of a free kick into the top corner. They're part of the fabric of the game, whether it's occurring in clear view elsewhere in the stadium or out of sight behind the scenes.

And there's plenty on the sidelines and beyond that needs adapting and improving, whether that's a case of just tinkering around the edges or making sweeping and wholesale changes. For instance, up in the stands, the behaviour of certain elements in the crowd needs special – and immediate – attention. The toxicity of particular football grounds has reached a level way beyond what is tolerable. This dissent and abuse affects the experience of both the fans and the players going about their jobs. And it poisons and pollutes the sport that we love.

The off-field side of football definitely needs to raise its game. It's gone too far in the wrong direction and needs to retrace its steps. Am I calling for the clock to be turned back, for the game to return to more tolerant times? Call me a dinosaur, perhaps I am, but the past isn't necessarily a bad place to be.

Like Joni Mitchell once sang, you don't know what you've got 'til it's gone.

7

Verbal Abuse Needs to Stop – Whether Racist, Homophobic, Sectarian or Just Personal

When the number 34 appeared on the electronic substitutions board, the home fans made their delight more than audible. But the cheers quickly turned into jeers as the substituted player, their own captain, made his way towards the touchline with the slowest of saunters, despite the current scoreline suggesting he show a little more urgency. The boos only got louder as the player raised two arms sarcastically in the air, before cupping his ear with his hand, prompting the jeers to become even fiercer. After greeting his manager in a decidedly lukewarm manner, he then committed the cardinal sin in the eyes of his club's fans: just before he disappeared down the tunnel, he ripped the team shirt from his back.

This was the tale of Granit Xhaka in what turned out, after Unai Emery later stripped him of the honour, to be his final match as Arsenal captain. It's always unwise for any player to make sarcastic gestures to the faithful, let alone show apparent disrespect for the shirt. It's doubly unwise if you're the skipper, the person who's supposed to have the most level head in the entire dressing room.

But I had some sympathy for Xhaka that day against Crystal Palace. His was a natural reaction to what he was hearing. Did he cover himself in glory? No. Should he have reacted as he did? No. But with the Arsenal fans already frustrated and angry at their team for letting a two-goal lead slip, they made Xhaka the scapegoat. The boos of tens of thousands of fans was laced with some of the choicest cuts of Anglo-Saxon that would have made even a docker blush.

But the Arsenal fans didn't think twice about their actions. They felt perfectly within their rights to vent their anger in such a potty-mouthed way, but ignored the double standard at play: football fans can hurl verbal abuse at a player, but when that player reacts, he's deemed a disgrace. 'He can't do that. Fine him, ban him, kick him out of the club. He's not fit to wear the shirt.' Well, there's a strong argument that those dishing out the abuse aren't fit to wear the scarf…

When it comes to fan abuse of one of their own players, the Xhaka incident was as extraordinary and extreme as it gets. On a scale of 1–10, it took maximum points for the level of vitriol and disdain shown by those in the stands. But it was merely the latest example of the increasing toxicity of football. It was also further evidence of a growing sense of entitlement among certain sections of fans that, having coughed up the price of admission, they can behave in whatever manner they fancy. It's definitely getting worse.

'We pay our money,' they'll argue in their defence. 'We can say what we like. We can boo. We can jeer.' And, yes, I understand that going to see top-flight games regularly can be a real financial undertaking, but does that justify that kind of behaviour? Absolutely not. It doesn't give anyone the right to shout obscenities at someone else. People pay good money to go to the theatre and the cinema, but you don't hear them screaming abuse if they don't think the acting's very good. I buy tickets for the panto every year, but does that mean I have free rein to rant and rave at whoever's playing Dick Whittington or Cinderella? Oh no it doesn't!

Ranting and raving is one thing, but the mark is so often overstepped. However much you might feel he's mismanaged the football side of affairs at Old Trafford, a chant calling for Manchester United chief executive Ed Woodward to die is disgusting and well beyond the pale (as was, of course, the flare attack launched at his home). Similarly, the aeroplane gestures made by Manchester City fans during derby matches, referencing the Munich air crash of 1958 where United players and personnel were killed, has absolutely no place in society, let alone in our sport. As human beings, as a species, aren't we better than that?

> I buy tickets for the panto every year, but does that mean I have free rein to rant and rave at whoever's playing Dick Whittington or Cinderella? Oh no it doesn't!

These are extremes, but there's a definite fickleness and impatience among particular sections of football fans these days. That makes itself clear on *606* quite regularly. One week a player is a god, the next they need to be sold. A manager can be a saint on a particular Saturday, but lose the next game or two and there are calls for his head. It seems to be a very turncoat culture.

Certain fans – although I'd question the depth and legitimacy of their fandom – seem to think they have licence to behave any which way.

In my dad's playing days, fans went to watch the game and to *support* their team, despite any frustration they might have felt. And, yes, back when I was a young pro, people would certainly let you know if you had a bad game. But it's at another level now. Heavy abuse has become the norm, thanks to the baying mob who feel that they are quite within their rights to unleash their invective, whether through social media or at the game itself. Fans think they've earned the privilege of expressing their views in whatever manner they please. They feel legitimised. Everyone enjoys a strong opinion, of course, but it's now reached the point at which the level of abuse is well over the top.

> On the pitch, a player has to ignore the verbal abuse. He has to stay focused and shut out the outside noise

If a player is sufficiently self-disciplined, he can bypass the online abuse by simply avoiding social media. Turning a blind eye is probably the best way to rise above it – 'I don't actually need to be part of this. It won't improve my life.' Some players, though, do choose to interact with their club's supporters in this way, as they realise that there are plenty of sensible football fans out there who are thrilled to have direct access to their heroes via social media. There are a lot of decent human beings around who are good to interact with.

However, the results aren't always as positive and life-affirming as they might be. Just ask the Celtic midfielder Ryan Christie. In October 2019, he was rightfully sent off against Livingston for a horror tackle which contributed to a 2-0 defeat that day. Christie knew what he'd done. He held up his hand, agreeing that it was a stupid challenge and that the straight red was deserved. Despite his conciliatory words, the keyboard warriors among Celtic's own support had already got their retaliation in on Twitter, blaming the player for a scoreline that, bearing in mind the tightness of the title race with Rangers, could be a highly significant result. They did not do this using calm, qualified language. They did so using the very worst vocabulary imaginable. You could almost see the steam rising from their tweets. Christie, showing infinitely more wisdom than when he went into that tackle, took swift action. He deactivated his Twitter account. 'I've realised it's maybe just a platform for people to come at you,' he admitted. 'The quicker you get rid of it, the better.' He wasn't wrong.

There's no grey on social media. It's black or it's white. It's love or it's hate. And that's what people seem to enjoy. But these morons are just going to push the top players away from Twitter, Instagram and the like, thus depriving the fans who do know how to behave online. Why would any modern-day footballer ever look at what somebody writes about them on social media? You wouldn't. You just wouldn't. Certainly, if I were still playing, I'd be steering well clear, concentrating instead on my game rather than letting criticism from some knuckleheads affect me.

On the pitch, a player has to ignore the verbal abuse. That's his job. He has to stay focused and shut out the outside noise. I had a difficult time at Chelsea – I was getting booed in the warm-up, before I'd actually done anything wrong in the match. It's one thing being jeered for missing an open goal. It's quite another when you're just going through your pre-match stretches. It seemed pretty brainless to me.

And let's be honest, being booed is not nice. You do lose confidence as a result. I know I did, especially as I didn't think my performances warranted people to jeer me in that way. Surely it's counter-productive. Why would you want to dent the confidence of your own player ahead of a match? Every action has a consequence, after all, so what is the desired outcome of all this screaming and shouting? Perhaps the intention of such supporters – and perhaps the Xhaka-baiting Arsenal fans are an example of this – is to get that player out of the club. But if they're successful, they'll just repeat their behaviour every time another player has a moment in a match where it doesn't go quite right. They could end up hounding out most of the squad. Team selection by mob rule.

The Xhaka episode was a rare example of fans really turning on one of their own players. Mostly the venom is reserved for the pantomime villains in the opposing team. If you sat behind the dugout and listened to the abuse that away managers get at games, you'd have to agree that it is nothing short of abhorrent. And their management team. And, of course, their players.

I remember one time when I was playing for Celtic away from home and I went to take a throw-in. Some guy near the front of the home crowd called me a merchant banker and did the hand gesture. His son, who must have been no more than six or seven, did exactly the same. Then they turned to each other and laughed. I was gobsmacked. I mean, properly gobsmacked. It was as if it were a rite of passage, a coming-of-age moment. 'Well done, son. I'll buy you a bag of crisps on the way home for that.' These days, even as a pundit I still get a hard time – a hangover from my playing days. The fact that I have to have security at certain grounds tells you everything.

You're made acutely aware of the toxic nature of football when you take your kids to matches. It's eye-opening, it really is. You sit in the stand and the language is appalling. It's not a great example of the adult world to expose your son or daughter to. I ended up not feeling the need to take them unless I got good seats – by which I mean up and away in the directors' box where they wouldn't hear the language and abuse. That's not great, is it?

It seems to be a case of anything goes within the crucible of a football ground. You don't get this level of tribalism in other sports. You certainly don't get it in rugby. Rugby fans sit next to each other and have a drink together. The only time I've been to a rugby match was when I went to see England versus Ireland at Twickenham. I found it so strange. Walking to the game, I didn't feel like I was going to get my head kicked in.

You don't want fans to simply be sycophantic. You want them to hold sturdy opinions. But there's always a line over which they shouldn't cross. I think we're in an age where, if you went to any ground around the country, certain fans would be regularly crossing that line. They're still in a minority, but there are plenty who go way over the top. And they do so because the repercussions are minimal. They know they can push the boundaries, that it's a free-for-all, a bile-fest. Why do they do it? Because they can.

> You don't want fans to simply be sycophantic. You want them to hold sturdy opinions. But there's always a line over which they shouldn't cross

Should the stewards step in and do more? Yes, because that's what they're there for. But I don't blame them if they don't. It's not easy to go and deal with an excessively angry and abusive fan. In their right mind, why would any steward, being paid £7 or something an hour, voluntarily tackle one aggressive individual when his behaviour is being replicated around the stadium? It's not worth it.

At grounds across the country, people scream the most horrible things, while the police, despite being well within earshot, stand there and choose to do nothing. But if you walked through any city centre and someone began hurling abuse at you and calling you every name under the sun, there'd be the very real prospect of them being arrested. And yet this behaviour is tolerated in football grounds full of 40, 50 or 60,000 people.

In an ideal world, I would love it if someone filmed these so-called fans at the game and then made them watch their antics back later on. Perhaps then each one would start to realise what an absolute buffoon they'd been. I wonder, though, whether they would even recognise themselves, because these people are like sheep. They soak up the behaviour they see and hear around them in the stand and repeat and replicate it. Who knows if they're in their right mind when they're dishing it out? The fact that hundreds, if not thousands, around them are doing likewise appears to give them permission to act in a way they'd never consider outside a football ground. But, of course, it's very difficult to single out individuals when this misconduct is being replicated by a large volume of people.

> A fine of just £10,000 isn't showing racism the red card. It's giving it the mildest talking-to

We see it in the Scottish Premiership where, at Old Firm games, tens of thousands of fans will be singing sectarian songs to goad the opposition's fans. Now, obviously you can't eject anywhere close to that number of people from a stadium in one fell swoop, so the punishment being meted out needs to affect the clubs instead – whether that's properly hefty fines or playing a certain number of games behind closed doors or being disqualified from certain competitions. Simply picking out a few individuals and giving them life bans will cure nothing. It won't create the necessary cultural shift that's needed to confine these songs to history, to make them an outdated expression from the past.

But the verbal abuse that needs the most pressing attention, the most immediate action to eradicate it, is the disgusting and overt racism that's on the rise again at football stadiums. According to the Kick It Out campaign, reports of racism at football matches in England rose by 43 per cent during the 2018–19 season. It is so depressing that it's even an issue that still needs tackling in the 21st century. We've been talking about this for decades and decades. It feels like Groundhog Day. And it's not an issue confined to football crowds in Eastern Europe or in Italy or Spain. Recent events have shown that it's still very much a live problem in English football. It's right on our own doorstep. And we need to clean it up right away.

Football needs to tackle the issue with sharper teeth that it's used thus far. In August 2019, Millwall were fined £10,000 due to a section of their supporters singing racist songs during an FA Cup tie against Everton the previous January. In isolation, this seems like a meagre amount, a tame punishment. Set it against other fines dished out by the authorities and it's insultingly low.

The month after Millwall received their fine, Huddersfield were fined £50,000 for wearing fake Paddy Power-sponsored shirts in a pre-season friendly. Judged on the fine alone, the crime was apparently five times worse than racist singing. Earlier in the year, Leeds were fined £200,000 for the incident known as 'Spygate', when a member of staff was discovered in the vicinity of Derby County's training ground. So apparently that was an incident deemed 20 times more heinous than what the Millwall fans were guilty of. And let's not forget the time that Besiktas were fined £30,000 for 'insufficient organisation' – namely, allowing a cat to wander on to the pitch during a Champions League qualifier. A fine of just £10,000 isn't showing racism the red card. It's giving it the mildest talking-to.

Much tougher sanctions need to be put in place. For their fans' racist abuse of England stars Raheem Sterling, Danny Rose and Callum Hudson-Odoi in March 2019, Montenegro were hit with a £17,396 fine and a one-match stadium ban. 'Hit' is the wrong word here. They would have barely felt the punishment. In these circumstances, make them feel pain where it hurts. Throw them out of the competition. Perhaps even ban them from the next one, too.

Back home, it was disappointing that the Crown Prosecution Service decided against criminal proceedings in the case of the Chelsea fan accused of racially abusing Raheem Sterling at Stamford Bridge in December 2018 – but respect to Chelsea themselves for issuing him with a lifetime ban. Clubs shouldn't shy away from showing they are tough on racism. Make an example of them. Shame the abusers by printing their names and photos in the programme for the next home game. And tell their employers this is the kind of person who works for them.

What happens in the stands is an echo of what's happening across the country at large. Gary Neville has apportioned blame for the rise in racist abuse at football matches in this country to a toxic general election where the two main political parties were directly accused of in-house Islamophobia and anti-Semitism respectively. And the adversarial nature of British politics of late appears to have given certain elements of society both licence and legitimacy to air their disgusting views. When these views are heard in and around football, criminal action has to be pursued as fiercely and stringently as possible. These abusers need to be hit where it hurts. Custodial sentences are very much appropriate in these circumstances. This is where the government need to show their muscle and join forces with the football authorities.

Accountability is the main issue. Nobody appears to be taking sufficient ownership of the problem. There needs to be more BAME representation in the corridors of power. At the moment, positions on high-level boards and committees are almost exclusively filled by white, middle-class appointments. Take the FA Board, for instance. Just one of the ten people who sit on it – Rupinder Bains – is of BAME heritage. This compares to a third of Premier League players being BAME. Equal representation is surely a fundamental that needs correcting. It's only then that racism can be put at the top of football's agenda and people can start to believe it can be truly kicked out.

After three supporters – two from the home stands and one from the away section – were ejected during a Chelsea visit to the Amex Stadium in 2020, having unleashed a combination of racist and homophobic abuse, Brighton's chief executive Paul Barber expressed his deep frustration. His call for tougher sanctions has to not just be heard and agreed with – it needs to be actioned. 'If the prospect of a life ban from watching their clubs play football isn't a strong enough deterrent, we have to ask the question as to whether the courts should be given the power to hand out more severe punishments … We are sick and tired of the game's reputation being tarnished by these people.'

Talk is cheap and words are no longer enough. It's time for action.

8
Slow Down the Managerial Merry-Go-Round

Imagine starting a new job and you only get four chances, four tilts, four shots at being successful. If you were a straight-out-of-college teacher, you'd have just four lessons to prove your worth or be given your cards. Or if you were a newly qualified doctor, you'd have to make spot-on diagnoses of your first four patients or face being struck off. Or, if you were a freshly appointed football manager, you'd have to avoid humiliation in the first four matches of the season to sidestep the sack.

Frank de Boer only got this many chances. The Dutchman was just four league games into his new job as Crystal Palace manager when he was shown where the Selhurst Park exit door was. Each of those games had been a defeat, sure, but this was no way to treat any new appointee, let alone one with such an impressive and glittering CV, having led Ajax to four consecutive Eredivisie titles. The decision was one of lunacy. It didn't make any sense whatsoever.

De Boer's experience in September 2017 is probably the most extreme example of a Premier League manager getting the bullet from a trigger-happy club. But he was far from alone. De Boer was simply the first of 15 Premier League bosses to clear their desks that season. It didn't end there. Across the 92 clubs in the Premier League and Football League, no fewer than 65 managers left their jobs in 2017–18, 54 of which were sackings. The average length of service of those 54 managers was little over a year. This wasn't an atypical season. The following campaign, 2018–19, saw 59 bosses leave their roles, whether of their own volition or, more likely, having been given the boot.

The managerial merry-go-round is spinning faster than ever, with managers holding on for grim life. Back in the day, when I started as a player, there certainly weren't the impulsive, knee-jerk sackings there are today. A manager was given time to mould his squad. But football's clearly a short-term game now. Owners want instant success and they're not frightened to make changes the minute they feel their club is on the slide. And this short-termism goes against everything that football clubs stand for.

> Managers used to know that they'd get time and opportunity. Now, if a side doesn't win for six or so games, the boss knows he's on the brink

Managers used to know that they'd get time and opportunity. Now, if a side doesn't win for six or so games, the boss knows he's on the brink. That never used to be the case. When Martin O'Neill first went into Leicester City in 1995, it took him eight games to register his first win, but look at the job he eventually did there, getting them promoted in that first season and then winning the League Cup twice.

This growing impatience is borne out by the numbers in the history books. Take Sunderland, for instance. Between 1980 and 2000, the club appointed eight permanent managers. In the first two decades of the 21st century, they appointed 16 – exactly double the number of appointments over the same time frame. They're not alone. Southampton also employed 16 managers between 2000 and 2020, but just six over the previous 20 years. Leeds are in the same ballpark: 17 appointments this century compared to half a dozen across the final two decades of the last.

In the ten seasons between 1999 and 2009, 78 Premier League managers moved on, whether pushed or jumped. This figure rose by almost 30 per cent by the end of the following decade to a straight one hundred. It's a clear measure of the merry-go-round's continuing acceleration.

Within these increasing numbers, sackings have risen out of all proportion. The 1995–96 season, the first to feature a 20-team Premier League, saw just three managerial departures. Over the next two seasons, only four of the sixteen managers to leave their jobs were sacked. Just a quarter. The remainder left of their own volition, in the main heading onwards and upwards to better roles. Ten years later, in the 2007–08 season, seven of that Premier League campaign's eleven departures were firings. By 2013–14, almost all managerial departures in the top flight – eleven out of thirteen – were at the behest of an impatient board or a chief executive with an itchy trigger finger. What's hard to understand is that these days – in most cases – the manager goes through a rigorous interview process for the highly competitive job that it is. He'll sit in front of the owner or the board and will tell them he's got a long-term plan. Every candidate will say the same thing – that the job is about developing youth, about nurturing from within. But they're not being straight. The owners will say, 'Fantastic interview. You've really impressed us. You've got the job.' The truth, however, is that they want success in the shortest amount of time possible.

Nurturing from within is not a swift process. But swiftness is what the game's about now. Quick fixes and instant success. Unfortunately, though, there's only one team who can win the Premier League each season, or the FA Cup or the League Cup or the Champions League. If a big club doesn't win one of those, it's a season of failure in the eyes of many of its supporters.

In de Boer's case, the Palace owners' excuse was simply that they'd made a bad decision. But think about the process, the outlay, the contracts. Think about how competitive the process is. Think about how much detail would be involved. And then to hand somebody a job before sacking them after just four games. It doesn't go hand in hand with what they say. 'We have every faith in you. Here's your three-year deal. We want to you to be here long term.' And yet you lose four games and you're out of a job.

These days, there's no room for manoeuvre. Managers have to win games right from the off, so logic would tell most of them to go for tried and trusted – perhaps signing a player in his mid-twenties who's played two or three hundred games and has international experience, rather than taking a punt on a seventeen-year-old who's showing promise in the youth team. This obviously goes against the grain of what managers say in the interview process, when they've pretended to be all about the youth team. The reality is that it's win at all costs. And not just that – it's win *early* at all costs.

While they would have an interest in young players, that's not really a new manager's job these days. At the top level, it's about trophies, it's about honours, it's about money. The youth team will always be further down the list of priorities. The primary objective is to win fast. If you don't do that, you're out of a job. That's what it is now.

Take Chelsea, for instance. In 2008–09, Luiz Felipe Scolari felt the guillotine's blade in February. The first World Cup-winning coach to manage a Premier League club wasn't even given a full season to prove himself in English football. And even when a manager has brought success to Stamford Bridge, there's no guarantee that they'll be there for anything like the long haul. Roberto Di Matteo was, after all, given the boot just six months after delivering both the FA Cup and Champions League.

Chelsea's ruthless, unsentimental nature has undoubtedly worked, though. Whatever people say, Roman Abramovich's time there has been absolutely phenomenal. He's had great success. There's not a lot of common sense in this approach though – unless a manager has the backing of the owner to spend money. Then you have a chance. At the top end at least, you can see how this short-termism can produce success if you have the spending capacity. Abramovich has certainly been the benchmark and the model for other overseas owners.

> Sentimentality is in short supply. Mauricio Pochettino left north London less than six months after he guided Tottenham to their first-ever Champions League final

Di Matteo isn't the only manager who might have thought the success he brought to a club may have granted him a little more job security. In November 2019, Mauricio Pochettino left north London, despite in the previous five years having taken Spurs to their most consistent run of high-placed top-flight finishes since the early 1960s. And, of course, the Argentine's departure came less than six months after he guided the club to its first-ever Champions League final. Sentimentality was clearly in short supply. Claudio Ranieri knows all about that.

Precisely 297 days after leading Leicester City to their first-ever title – and undoubtedly the most romantic fairy tale in the history of the Premier League – the Italian drove out of the King Power Stadium's car park for the last time, having been informed his services were no longer required. *Grazie e arrivederci.*

In running their clubs, ruthless owners and chief executives do still have to pay attention to fans. They are the lifeblood of any football club and will have strong feelings about who should be recruited as the next manager. Doing so successfully comes down to ambition and expectation. A massive problem now is what's being said on social media. Do clubs pay attention to it? I think they do. And that's not necessarily wise. Football clubs are big businesses. Listening to outside influences may not make commercial sense.

But clubs do listen to fans. And certain fans have it in for certain managers. There are managers out there who are met by negativity when their names are mentioned whenever there's a vacancy. When jobs come up nowadays, everybody wants the new, young, up-and-coming forward-thinkers, but I still think there's a place for the likes of Sam Allardyce and David Moyes. I thought Moyes actually did a good job in his first spell at West Ham. They cut back on players, but he kept them in the Premier League. And he was rewarded with being replaced.

While a lot of football fans view these kind of managers as dinosaurs, I think they deserve more respect for their work at the clubs they've managed. They must have something about them. Everybody nowadays wants a manager who's animated in the technical area, jumping up and down. But what purpose does all that leaping about actually serve? Fans want to see passion, but I feel that sometimes those managers are behaving like that for effect – that they feel obliged to do that because that's what fans want. It certainly feels more natural for some managers, like Jürgen Klopp banging his fists on his chest.

But to others it doesn't feel right. And it doesn't necessarily make you a better manager. Isn't the job more about the information that players are given throughout the week and at half-time?

If fans see a manager standing still, they interpret his body language as him not caring. But that's just balls. There's not a manager stood in his technical area who isn't desperate to win. People just show it in different ways. But a lack of passion is the first thing cited whenever a team goes on a bad run. And that's one thing that some fans get really badly wrong. I've never played alongside a player, nor been in a dressing room with a manager, who didn't want to go out and win the game, who didn't have the fire in the belly.

Managerial changes can, of course, destabilise a club and bring about player insecurity – especially if they happen frequently. An incoming manager might prefer a certain player over another. Kenny Dalglish signed me for Blackburn Rovers and we won the league, but then he went upstairs into a director of football role. Ray Harford inherited the job and left me out, leaving me to scratch my head wondering why. These things happen. Football is a game of opinions.

It was similar at Celtic when Martin O'Neill, a manager I really liked and respected, left and Gordon Strachan took over. I had respect for Gordon when he first came in, but then we fell out pretty quickly. And managers are quite within their rights to change things. They have their own ideas on players – as they should have. I've never known a manager to go into a new job and not want to give himself the best opportunity. In the current climate, managers are absolutely entitled to think selfishly. It's a matter of survival. They'll adopt whatever means to stay in the job as long as possible. We'd all do the same if we were in that position.

A player shouldn't fear a managerial change, though. His security comes from his ability and from knowing where he is in the pecking order, whether he should be playing or not. I played with the likes of Henrik Larsson, Alan Shearer, George Weah and Gianfranco Zola, and understood where I was in the food chain. But when you're left out in favour of a player who you deem to be inferior to yourself, that's when the problems start. That's when the disagreements come in.

Players will always be susceptible to the vagaries and opinions of managers, but they are especially so in the current climate when managerial turnaround is so high. At the start of the 2019–20 season, the managers of eleven of the twenty clubs in the Premier League had each been in their jobs for less than 18 months. In most cases, clubs do not prosper under short-term appointments. Watford are an exception to the general rule. What's happened there is absolutely remarkable. Nigel Pearson marked their tenth managerial appointment in a six-year period (and rather a left-field one when considering those

There's not a manager stood in his technical area who isn't desperate to win. People just show it in different ways

who'd gone before him), but where you might think the resulting instability would surely bring the club crashing down, they've enjoyed a decent level of success over that time – promotion to the Premier League, reaching the FA Cup semi-final in 2016 and the FA Cup final in 2019. The turnover of players has been pretty extraordinary too. It's been like a cattle market there. A change of manager usually sees a big overhaul of players, so if you're a young player at Watford coming through the ranks, you must be thinking *Where's my pathway?* From afar, it doesn't seem the right way to do things. Long-term success from short-term gain? It's illogical, but it works for them. There must be method in their madness. But how long can it continue?

The further you go down the scale, though, the harder it gets. Rapid-fire hiring and firing doesn't make sense down there. Look at what happened to Fulham. They sacked two managers – Slaviša Jokanović and that man Ranieri – during the 2018–19 season, and the guy running the recruitment there is the owner's son. He spent in excess of £104 million bringing in new players, but they sacked the managers? Surely the head of recruitment is the one to be sacked. Certainly that's how it looks from the outside.

> When it comes to selecting and appointing a manager, there is a strong argument that we need more football people in club boardrooms

At certain clubs, there are non-football people, from more of a business background, who are making purely football appointments, such as selecting a manager. There is a strong argument that we need more football people in club boardrooms making these decisions. But, of course, just because a person had a good football career on the pitch doesn't necessarily mean they become the best managers. Far from it, in certain cases. A great number of the most successful managers didn't have stellar careers as players.

I had five managers in my five years at Blackburn, but this was different to the hiring and firing that's happening now. That was the result of circumstances. No one could have foreseen Kenny going upstairs. The thought process at the time from the owner, Jack Walker, was of continuity, hence promoting Kenny's assistant Ray Harford. I felt that was a logical progression, even if the appointment didn't particularly help me in my second season at Ewood Park. But then things didn't go well under Ray and, from that moment, the club was always scrambling.

Tony Parkes was caretaker boss for the best part of a season before the club announced Sven-Göran Eriksson was going to be the manager. But Sven changed his mind and went to Lazio instead. Then Roy Hodgson was brought in. He was sacked less than 18 months later with the club bottom of the league. Brian Kidd replaced him, a coach with a fantastic reputation at Manchester United as Fergie's sidekick. But that didn't work out either and the club were relegated. The decline all stemmed from fact that we had lost Kenny, the manager who'd won the club's first title in 81 years. As players, we felt we had lost our figurehead.

It was the same when I was at Norwich City when Mike Walker, the most successful manager in the club's history, left. There had been a long-term plan around Carrow Road – everyone was talking about keeping the squad together and about the chairman Robert Chase loosening the purse strings. We had finished third in the Premier League the season before and had famously defeated Bayern Munich in a UEFA Cup tie. On our day, we could beat absolutely anybody. I signed a new deal just before Christmas, which paid out £500 a goal if we won or drew. I scored twice against Spurs the day after Boxing Day and was absolutely flying. The club was in a really good place.

But, at Norwich, long-term planning on the pitch and off the pitch amounted to two totally different things. Less than two weeks later, Mike Walker cleared off to Everton and they then sold Ruel Fox to Newcastle. That was the end of the long-term plan. In such a short space of time, the positivity and the aura that that team had around them disintegrated. The wheels hadn't gradually fallen off. They had snapped off overnight.

That was a quarter of a century ago. Long-term plans have long since disappeared from the agendas of football managers altogether. They're too busy trying to find the magic formula that delivers instant success. But something needs to change. There has to be a solution to this churn of managers and to the insecurity it brings upon clubs and the game in general. The logic has gone and we need to rediscover it.

I can certainly see the sense in introducing a managerial transfer window, one that operates in the same way as the transfer window for players. This is how it could work: owners, chairmen and chief executives would be restricted to two periods in a calendar year when they could remove their existing manager and recruit his replacement.

With such a system, the interview process would need to be more stringent. Clubs would have to get the appointment absolutely spot on. And, when it comes to nurturing players and allowing managers to do what they say in the job interview, I think it's a strong idea. It would be good for the game. We might actually see some youth development from the big clubs. We're certainly not seeing enough at the moment.

Clubs would argue that they need to retain the right to fire or hire managers when they want to fire or hire them, that they need to have the decision on timings in their hands. An owner would feel that, having put money into a club, they couldn't have this power taken away. I get that.

But, conversely, a managerial transfer window would breed more stability for clubs across the season, with managers unable to have their heads turned by other teams at inopportune times. The owners would have to show patience and faith. Further down the line, they'd have more of an idea of their manager's ability because he would have had longer to prove himself – to prove the appointment right or to prove the appointment wrong.

Patience is a much-missed virtue in football. It used to exist. Alex Ferguson famously went 42 months before he won his first trophy at Old Trafford. He's the greatest example of a long-term approach paying dividends, of being able to give young players the opportunity on merit. He was the benchmark. There have been echoes of this patience on display in recent years at Anfield, where Jürgen Klopp took almost the exact same amount of time before his first piece of silverware as Liverpool boss. And then he went and won the biggest one of all, the Champions League, in what was effectively the last game of the four-year period in which he promised to win a major trophy.

> Long-term plans have long since disappeared from the agendas of football managers. They're too busy trying to find the magic formula that delivers instant success

Largely, though, gone are the days when, if you were the manager of a big club, you were treated with patience. Look at Ole Gunnar Solskjær. He went into Manchester United in the December, passed his audition with flying colours, had a dodgy end to the season when things started to unravel and all of a sudden people were questioning him. At Old Trafford, they don't seem to remember the slack given to Fergie back in the day.

Fergie's short-lived successors – David Moyes and Louis van Gaal – would certainly have welcomed the breathing space that a managerial transfer window may have provided.

And it goes without saying that Frank de Boer would have been in favour too.

9

Stop Fans Leaving Games Early

We've all seen them. They're hard to miss. And quite often the TV cameras are keen to pick them out anyway. The quieter types might show their dissatisfaction with a shaking of the head as they disappear, but others among them are more apoplectic – ranting, raving and gesticulating, before one last look back in anger at the action on the pitch.

Fans who leave matches early. They are a species I have great difficulty understanding and identifying with.

I'm not necessarily talking about those who leave in stoppage time in order to beat the rush out of the car park or to catch the last train home. Here, my sights are fixed on those who leave ten minutes, or often more, before the end because they don't like what they've seen from their team over the previous hour or so. But a true supporter sees it through, don't they? It's a bit of a cliché, but supporting a football team is rather like a marriage. You'll have your good times, you'll have your bad times. The rollercoaster climbs high and dips low, and you have to ride it out.

It's all very well saluting your team at the final whistle when they're top of the table or winning a cup. It's the easiest thing in the world to be a fan of a successful team that's charging through a golden period. Everyone stays until the end when things are hunky-dory. It's when the team encounters the first sign of trouble that the turncoats show their true colours. They want a pain-free existence, but sadly for them, that's not the football fan's lot.

At half-time in their home match against Arsenal in December 2019, West Ham fans were purring with contentment. They were 1-0 up against Unai Emery's misfiring Gunners. Nine second-half minutes reversed the mood, when the visitors scored three times. Cue a mass exodus from the London Stadium. We're not talking fifty fans or one hundred fans, here. Hammers supporters were departing in their *thousands*. Not only did they not believe their team could find a couple of goals in the last 20 minutes against an Arsenal side who hadn't kept a clean sheet for something like eleven games, but they couldn't find it within themselves to urge their team to try to find those goals. They'd just totally given up. They were no longer supporting their club.

Those West Ham fans showed no shame in leaving so prematurely – and the following Saturday evening on *606*, they again showed no shame in calling up to justify their early exit. The main line of argument was that they'd paid for the privilege, for the right, to leave whenever they felt like leaving. I understand that fans

> When the team encounters the first sign of trouble, the turncoats show their true colours. They want a pain-free existence, but sadly for them, that's not the football fan's lot

are forking out a pretty penny to watch their team week in, week out and that ultimately it's their money they're throwing up the wall.

But if you're buying tickets – that are, of course, very expensive – you're investing in that club, aren't you? Surely that gives you some sort of stake in what happens on the pitch, even if it's just an emotional one. You pay your money and you see it through to the end. You wouldn't leave a theatre ten minutes before the end, would you? If you did that when you went to see *The Mousetrap*, you'd have to find out later that – spoiler alert! – it was the policeman who did it. But if you leave well before the final whistle, it's my belief that you lose the right to call yourself a proper football fan. You're simply not a true supporter, someone who's all in, through thick and thin. The clue's in the name. You *support* your team. That is, you help them when they most need it. Anyone who doesn't is simply a phoney.

> If you are a diehard fan, supporting your team isn't a take-it-or-leave-it situation. It really isn't. You have to see it through

What's even sadder is that nothing beats the rush of seeing your team come back in the last ten minutes of a game. Unless one team is genuinely out of sight of the other, there's always plenty of time for the score to be affected. And being behind by just two goals is never a reason to head for home well before time.

Less than a week after that West Ham game, Cardiff visited Leeds in the Championship. Now, imagine if Cardiff fans had vacated Elland Road after an hour with their team 3-0 down. They would have missed an outrageous last half hour where they scored twice, had a man sent off and then still equalised in the final couple of minutes. Had those

Bluebirds fans thrown their toys out of the pram and demanded to be let out of the ground, they'd have surrendered the chance of seeing what was probably their side's most extraordinary game of the season.

There have been some unbelievable comebacks over the years. I particularly remember one from my younger days at Norwich when we were 3-0 down at Sheffield Wednesday but got it back to 3-3. The most famous comeback in Premier League history is probably the time in 2011 when Newcastle, 4-0 down at half-time to Arsenal, scored four times in the last 22 minutes to earn a draw. St James' Park has probably never heard a roar like it when Cheick Tioté's screamer of an equaliser went in.

Of course, Manchester United fans know not to leave early. During Sir Alex's reign, there couldn't have been an empty seat as each match approached 'Fergie Time'. That's when you expected them to score. You could almost guarantee turning up to watch as late as the 80th minute and seeing a goal or two. Imagine any United fan leaving Camp Nou early in the Champions League final of 1999...

Even if their team doesn't manage a memorable comeback, the true diehard fans will remain in situ until the game is over. It might be appreciation they're showing, or it might be frustration. But the important thing is that they are there to show it and not already halfway back to the train station. The tough times are when a club needs its fans to stand alongside the players and the manager and say: 'We're here. We support you wholeheartedly. We're not clearing off.' Leave that kind of behaviour to the fickle, fair-weather brigade.

If you are a diehard fan, supporting your team isn't a take-it-or-leave-it situation. It really isn't. You have to see it through. It's a grind and that's what really makes football and football clubs. The devotion of supporters is what defines the game. What did Jock Stein say? 'Football is nothing without fans.' There have been loads of managers who have echoed those sentiments over the years. They know the truth.

The good times taste sweeter when you've experienced the bad old days, when you've gone through the pain barrier and emerged on the other side. Take Sheffield United. Three years before they arrived back in the Premier League in 2019, they were down in League One where the likes of Walsall were doing the double over them. Now they were turning up at Stamford Bridge and Goodison Park and the Tottenham Hotspur Stadium and getting results. The fans had shown their faith against Chesterfield and Rochdale and Scunthorpe, and now they were reaping the rewards, basking in the glow of better days. They'd been there for the whole journey. It's like that Dolly Parton quote: 'If you want the rainbow, you got to put up with the rain.'

These fair-weather fans don't like it when the metaphorical dark clouds gather. So how can these chumps – those who don't think twice about leaving ten, fifteen, twenty minutes early if things aren't going well – be rooted out? Or, at least, how can we change their behaviour? My tongue is firmly back in my cheek here, but if they are season-ticket holders, there's an easy punishment that can be meted out. You simply revoke their season ticket if they prematurely head for the door. A steward would confiscate it and then allocate it to a more deserving diehard fan who was patiently biding their time on the season-ticket waiting list. It's the latter who should feel this sense of entitlement. They appreciate the undertaking

> Put their faces on the big screen at the next home game, or on wanted posters outside the ground. 'Have you seen this man? He left early last week'

that being a supporter dictates. And they'd be more than willing to comply. To them it's the natural thing to see out the full 90 minutes.

If the revocation of season tickets sounds a little draconian, fans leaving early should at least be named and shamed. Put their faces on the big screen at the next home game, or on wanted posters outside the ground. 'Have you seen this man? He left early last week. Do you know this guy?'

Perhaps we should stop them leaving the stadium in the first place. Offer a disincentive so they stay in their seat for the duration. On arrival at the ground, everyone has to hand over a £20 deposit which will be returned to them only if they last the whole match. It would certainly make the early leavers think twice before hurling their final volley of abuse at their team's players and turning on their heels. If you want to leave early, you've got to pay for the right. 'I'm desperate to go, but I'm not paying 20 quid to leave. There's no way I'm paying that. I've got to stay for the last ten minutes of this rubbish.'

There are a couple of exceptions for which I'd show some leniency. It would be perfectly permissible for you to leave your seat and head for the nearest exit before the final whistle if your car's registration number has just been read out on the public-address system and is in imminent danger of being towed away. Or if the PA announcer has just informed someone – and 40,000 other folk – that their wife has gone into labour and they need to get to the maternity ward as quickly as their little legs can carry them there. But those are the only Get Out of Jail Free cards. No other excuses will be indulged. Call yourself a football fan? You've got to stay put and do the time.

Perhaps a little peer pressure is also in order. If the person in the seat next to you ever rises up with quarter of an hour left and with your side a couple of goals down, put them in an awkward position. 'Where are you off to, mate? You've got to see out the full 90. They need your encouragement. Remember Sunderland away? That was a comeback, wasn't it? Lightning could strike again. And you wouldn't want to miss it, would you?'

And you'd be right. Who would want to hear those cheers of celebration reverberating around the stadium while they angrily strode across the car park towards home?

Come on, early-exiting fans. You're better than that.

10
Make Post-Match Interviews More Honest and More Exciting

'Oh my days! It was the best feeling ever. I just can't stop smiling. Oh my days! Best game ever, best game ever!'

After 63 minutes of the 2019 Scottish League Cup final, you wouldn't have expected Jeremie Frimpong's post-match reaction, less than an hour later, to have sounded anything like this. The teenage Celtic defender had conceded a penalty and received his marching orders on his Old Firm debut, but Fraser Forster saved the spot-kick and Celtic scrapped hard to hold on to their single-goal advantage and win the trophy. And the nation was soon hearing the relief in Frimpong's voice.

I've not seen or heard many post-match interviews as gleeful as his. In fact, for me, that was the greatest one of all time. He expressed exactly what it means to play professional football. It was so authentic. It was from the heart.

Wearing an ear-to-ear grin and with his eyes dancing with joy,

Frimpong broke with convention and allowed the true emotion to spill out. He reacted as you would hope a cup winner would, all boyish enthusiasm rather than seasoned detachment. These weren't dour, poker-faced answers that make you wonder if the interviewee was on the winning side or not. The medal round his neck aside, you'd have had no doubt about the result. This was the unfettered delight of a winner.

But it wasn't just his exuberance that caught the eye and ear. It was his raw, unvarnished honesty. When asked about conceding a potentially match-changing penalty, most players would avoid an admission of guilt, hiding behind the kind of blame-swerving clichés we've come to expect. 'There was a coming-together.' 'I might have made contact.' 'I was committed to the challenge.' Not so our man Frimpong. 'He was through on goal and my first instinct was to give him a nudge,' he admitted, 'I had to.' These were two minutes of utterly refreshing television and I'd advise anyone who's not seen the interview to seek it out. May we always get such entertaining and honest post-match reaction from this sparky individual.

That Frimpong was so genuine and funny and charming emphasises the fact that at least one of these qualities, and sometimes more, is often lacking from most post-match interviews. We've become too accustomed to and too accepting of players' words that are defensive and non-committal – words that fail to enlighten us and that show very little of the player within.

I know this. I've been there myself. Everybody wants players to be authentic and honest and upfront and frank, but you don't want to give anything away. It's all about protecting yourself and your team. Unless I was caught in a bad moment – and there were plenty of those – I would always play a straight bat, a comfortable forward-defensive stroke. We all did. It would even be discussed in the dressing room: who could give the least interesting answers in pre- and post-match interviews.

This wasn't a game, though. It was to avoid putting each other under unnecessary pressure. Why would I want to say, 'I'm going to dominate their centre-half' in front of a television camera? How will that benefit me in the match itself? Similarly, if your team is in a title race, don't say, 'We're really confident. We've got the momentum. We're going to win it.' Don't say anything daft that will give a motivating leg up to the opposition.

There's a reason why so many players roll out the 'Each game as it comes' cliché. I've almost certainly been guilty of it on occasion. The best policy is to stay tight-lipped and instead go out on the pitch and prove yourself. And if you do hold your nerve in the

> We've become too accustomed to and too accepting of players' post-match words that are defensive and non-committal, that fail to enlighten us

title race, the end of the season is your chance to crow about it.

Everyone bar the player wants a headline, of course, so it's his duty to sidestep being the one who provides it by not speaking in an ill-advised manner. Reporters are smart, clever people who, if you don't have your wits about you, can lead you down some paths you really should be avoiding. It's their job to ask the questions, after all. That's what they're paid to do. So, in your public pronouncements, you've got to be watertight, giving nothing away. If you do unintentionally leave a morsel, it will get pounced upon. We know how headlines are formed.

These days, players have the advantage of being media-trained, but I was a complete plum when I first went in front of the cameras. I just clammed up. I didn't have anything of importance to say. I'd gone from having a job at Norfolk County Council to playing Premier

League football in two years, and came from a little village outside Norwich where we barely knew what television was! Then suddenly, after scoring the winner in one of my early matches for the first team, I was chucked in front of the cameras.

It was really embarrassing. I was wet behind the ears and I didn't know anything. I think I got in so many clichés – 'to be fair', 'at the end of the day', all of that nonsense. I'd love to see it back. I was a total sheep when I first did interviews because all I'd do was listen to what the other sheep said. No one should have expected a teenager to be a wise sage, a great philosopher.

We're in an entertainment business and that's what people crave. Truth and honesty and emotion. They don't want to hear yet another bland and asinine interview

I did graduate to becoming a more forthright interviewee, but this wasn't always to my benefit. On the last day of the 2002–03 season, Celtic beat Kilmarnock 4-0 away, but were denied the title on goal difference – by a single goal – because Rangers had put six past Dunfermline at Ibrox. And I was apoplectic. I was standing in the tunnel waiting to do the post-match interview when the referee Kenny Clark went past me to do his warm-down on the pitch. I called him every name under the sun and he red-carded me.

I was still waiting to do the interview when he came back, so gave him both barrels again and he gave me a second red card. Then I went on air on BBC Scotland and accused Dunfermline of lying down in their match. For these comments, I was charged with bringing the game into disrepute and handed a further one-match ban on top of the four-match one I'd received for the sendings-off. But I was speaking from the heart. I certainly didn't go into that interview with a straight bat.

As soon as a player says something that the rest of the dressing room feels or that fans feel, they get a lengthy ban and fined for speaking out of turn. I spoke out of turn. I was out of line and I knew that. The aftermath was bedlam. I was threatened with legal action from the Dunfermline chairman and was subjected to all sorts of threats and criticism from other quarters. Most quarters, to be honest. It's funny because I was merely saying out loud what my team-mates were feeling and I expected everyone to come out in support of me. But not a jot. It was a case of 'You said it. You're on your own now.'

I'm still reminded of this incident the best part of 20 years later. If the interview had been the day after, there's no way I would have said those things. I wouldn't even have ranted and raved had it been just a couple of hours after the final whistle. Looking back, do I regret saying those things? Not necessarily, because that's what I felt at the time. But should I have spoken to the referee like that? Probably not. Should I have said those things to the television cameras? Probably not. But that's how I felt and that's why I said it. We're in an entertainment business and people crave truth and honesty and emotion. They don't want to hear yet another bland and asinine interview that they'll have forgotten about within five minutes, if not quicker.

'What did you think of the match, John?'
'Yeah, it was a good game. We scored and they equalised.'
'And Terry elbowed you and broke your jaw, John. How did you feel about that?'
'Well, it's all part of the game. Terry's a good guy.'

That's not good enough. Those are answers which satisfy no one and simply waste a minute or two of television airtime. What we really want John to say is, 'I wanted to rip Terry's throat out. I still do. I'd love to go into their dressing room right now and smash his face in.'

I'm not saying we've got a thirst for casual violence, but we do have a hunger for authenticity. We fondly recall the memorable post-match interviews because they come along so infrequently. They're as rare as hen's teeth. Many people will remember the brilliantly to-the-point nature of my old team-mate Tim Flowers' interview after the penultimate game of Blackburn's title-winning season. He showed he was more than a match for Alex Ferguson's psychology, for those suggestions that we didn't have the mentality to see the season out as champions. 'Don't talk to me about bottle,' Tim forcefully told the interviewer. 'Don't talk to me about bottling it. Cos that was bottle out there.' A year later, of course, Kevin Keegan succumbed to Fergie's mind games in a very public way with his still-painful 'I will love it…' rant.

We want to hear more of these candid, emotional, in-the-moment interviews. Everyone likes to see someone lose it, don't they? The best interviews are usually on the final whistle, when players are still pumped up with the adrenaline coursing through their body. Win, lose or draw, there's always something riding on the game and there are always key moments that require further discussion and analysis – red cards, offside decisions and such like. These are the talking points, the issues which no football fan wants a manager or player to skirt around. They want to hear the reporter asking straight questions – 'What happened? Why did it happen? How do you feel about it?' – and they want the response to be equally upfront and candid.

Charlie Austin certainly let the *Match of the Day* interviewer know how he felt in a post-match rant after Southampton's draw with Watford in late 2018. Wearing a face of thunder, he let off both barrels, angrily bemoaning a disallowed second Saints goal that would have given them all three points. 'Help the officials out! Clearly they need help!' he raged, this being in the days before VAR. 'They cost us two points today. It's a joke!' That's more like it. Raw, honest and emotional. That's exactly what we want.

Interviews like Austin's come once in a blue moon. In their current form and tone, post-match interviews are tedious, repetitive and lacking in any real insight. You can rely on a handful of players to offer up answers that are always entertaining or enlightening – Troy Deeney is one, at ease with shrugging his shoulders and saying whatever he thinks – but most others don't have that confidence.

We need to empower them to do so, to abandon those dispassionate answers and to give heartfelt reaction to events that have just happened. We want their raw, emotional take on a match that's finished just a few minutes earlier.

Footballers aren't robots. They are human beings. But so many players – and I'd include myself among them – play, or played, with a mask on. People think they know you, but they don't know you at all. There are players whose public personas show them to be lovely blokes, but who are the most ruthless and outspoken individuals – in a good way, that is, for the benefit of their team. Take my former strike partners – Alan Shearer and Henrik Larsson. Very few players I've ever encountered are more ruthless than those two. And that's why they were who they were, that's why they were the best. (Speaking of Shearer, that was another legendary interview. Blackburn had just won their first title in 81 years and he was asked how he was going to celebrate. 'I'm going to creosote my fence…')

It's time for the mask to fall and for us to get genuine insight into who players really are and what makes them tick. The safe party line and the straight-bat clichés don't need to be heard anymore. We want players to forget their media training, to be let off the leash and to reveal their true selves. No more careful, judicious answers in interviews. No more biting of the tongue. And they must be free to do so without any repercussions.

So here's my plan. For the first 20 minutes after the final whistle, players are allowed to say whatever they think about what has happened over the previous 90 minutes. It would be the footballing equivalent of diplomatic immunity. They would be free of any repercussions. No action would be taken against them. No fines, no bans, no lawsuits. Just an open platform to reveal their naked emotion, what they felt there and then – the joy, the anger, the sense of injustice. It's time to loosen players' straitjackets and let us hear the truth. We can handle it!

But let's not suggest that players are the only ones guilty of not giving us what we want in post-match interviews. Their managers are also culpable of hiding their true emotions behind a facade of platitudes and clichés. So the offer of immunity I've just made to players would also be extended to them too. They could definitely prosper from this. All too often, managers bite their tongue for fear of facing an FA charge, giving lily-livered responses that please neither interviewer or viewer. Like their players, they too are emotional people, especially in the aftermath of a fiery match. For the previous 90 minutes, their emotions have also traced a parabola, the time-honoured rollercoaster. They've been put through the ringer too. It's just that managers play out the game in the technical area rather than out on the pitch.

Those FA charges often come with a price. Neil Warnock was hit with a £20,000 fine following a Cardiff City defeat to Chelsea, after declaring that the Premier League officials were 'the worst in the world'. Joey Barton has also had to put his hand in his pocket as punishment for a heat-of-the-moment summation of events out on the pitch. 'We needed a good referee to control what was a very good game of football,' the Fleetwood Town manager observed after his side's match against Bristol Rovers. 'Unfortunately we didn't get it.' There are others: Rafa Benítez and Jürgen Klopp have both attracted hefty fines (£60,000 and £45,000 respectively) for speaking out of turn, while José Mourinho is certainly no stranger to the FA's disciplinary committee.

Small wonder that the more shy and retiring bosses choose to keep schtum, but giving managers this same 20 minutes of repercussion-free verbal freedom would make their responses much less predictable. The master of the predictable pronouncement was undoubtedly Arsène Wenger who – whenever quizzed about an incident or a controversial moment that ultimately benefited his Arsenal side, perhaps an iffy penalty or a dubious handball – would often claim that he hadn't seen what had happened and was therefore insufficiently qualified to tender his opinion. This became his natural default.

No more careful, judicious answers in interviews. No more biting of the tongue. And they must be free to do so without any repercussions

Just how many times did he claim not to have seen an incident? What on earth was he looking at from the touchline instead? I'm unsure quite how he can analyse games, or deliver inspirational half-time team talks, or make a match-changing tactical switch, if he's not watching his players go about their business. And it's interesting to note that he began this defence very soon after arriving at Highbury. That soon-to-be-familiar statement made its debut in the aftermath of only his second match in charge: 'Frankly, I did not see what happened.' You would have thought he might have made that trip to the opticians right there and then.

There was a point at which Wenger's trademark get-out statement tipped over into cliché. We would expect to hear it every time a microphone was thrust into the Frenchman's face after the final whistle. You'd watch the post-match interview on *Match of the Day* and would be waiting for the question that would tee it up. A typical interrogation might go something like this:

'So to your mind was it a penalty?'
'I didn't see it.'
'Was the red card a little harsh?'
'I didn't see it.'
'OK, thanks Arsène.'

Wenger did later admit he had been economical with the truth over the years. 'Sometimes I see it, but I say that I didn't see it to protect the players,' he confessed, 'and because I could not find any rational explanation for what they did.' The truth will out. And the truth is refreshing.

Sometimes, in protecting his players and defending his club's reputation, a manager can end up saying something tortured and ultimately illogical. My mind goes back to 2013 when the then Southampton manager Nigel Adkins was asked about the penalty awarded to Jay Rodriguez against Aston Villa. Hearing his answer once wouldn't have been enough. It needed repeated attention to untangle it. 'It's not a dive. The lad would have kicked him. The challenge has come in and our player has evaded the challenge...If the player hadn't taken his leg out of the way, there would have been clear contact.'

Defending the indefensible through the use of hypothetical

scenarios doesn't sound the wisest approach. Everyone can instantly tell that you're grasping at straws in the absence of proof. Perhaps the Arsène Wenger approach would have been a more judicious course of action for Adkins. Or, just coming clean and admitting that his side had got away with one there. A sheepish grin and a hand raised in acknowledgement at a lucky break would have served him better. Instead, he seemed to be suggesting that there was no foul, but if there had been, it would have been a penalty. When he finished the interview, Adkins must have walked away and thought *Did I really say that?* That wasn't doublespeak. It was triplespeak. He should have fined himself after that.

> In interviews, managers behave as though they've been put under a spell or into a trance where they only speak garble, waffle and gobbledegook

The best piece of manager doublespeak I ever heard came from Mark Warburton while he was in charge of Rangers. It was absolutely priceless. 'I'm reading in the paper Celtic are on a record-breaking run. If they won four games less, they would be thirteen ahead. If we won one of our games, it would be ten.' Extraordinary.

What is going on with managers? It's as if they are normal, rational people when they're appointed but once in office they seem to morph into an entirely different species. They behave as though they've been transformed by a spell or a magic hat, and put into a trance where they only speak garble, waffle and gobbledegook.

Try this, from Claudio Ranieri. 'Footballers are like a parachute,' the Tinkerman once reasoned during his time at Chelsea. 'At times it doesn't open. Here, it is an umbrella. Mary Poppins.' Perhaps something got lost in translation. More homespun philosophy came courtesy of another Rangers manager, Mark Warburton's successor Pedro Caixinha. 'There is a Portuguese saying – "The dogs bark but the caravan keeps going". That means we are focused in our work and together in the same direction.' Caixinha lasted seven months at Ibrox.

Blinkers are a popular fashion item for reality-dodging managers. Freddie Ljungberg was clearly wearing a pair when he was interviewed during his short stint as Arsenal's caretaker manager following Unai Emery being relieved of his duties. After the Gunners' 3-1 victory at West Ham, when three quick-fire goals in the second half turned the score around after an abject Arsenal performance in the first hour, Ljungberg tried to paint a picture several shades rosier than how the rest of the stadium had seen it. His side had been truly awful for 60 minutes, but he was insistent on talking positively about his players' level of fitness and their hunger and desire. It felt like he'd been watching a different match to me.

> Life is precarious for a football manager and his instinct for survival seems to include the slight bending of what's really happened

I don't get that urge to paper over the cracks, to suggest there was a level of endeavour and passion that simply wasn't present. Most people can see right through these words. Just come out and tell it like it was. You'll gain more respect for doing so. 'We were crap for an hour and we weren't in it at all. We somehow managed to finally turn it around though, so fair play to the players – good on them. They dug in and grabbed us a good three points. I'm very relieved.'

At times, of course, their motivation in explaining things away is good old-fashioned self-preservation under what is enormous pressure. Life is precarious for a football manager and his instinct for survival seems to include the slight bending of what's really happened. Say something enough times and people will start believing you. And if they believe you, you've managed to buy yourself a little more time in the job, even if it's only a week or two's grace until you have to spin a story around your team's next underwhelming performance.

It's perfectly expected that managers will come out in support of their players, even when their observations are not supported by the evidence of the previous 90 minutes. Fans want to know that their manager is defending the honour of the club, that he's one of them. And they want him to be vociferous in this defence. Ideally he should be a chest-thumper, someone who shows emotion in the technical area. And if he doesn't behave that way, he's perceived as not caring for the cause.

I have an element of sympathy with managers. They do so many interviews throughout the week, whether for local media, national media or the club's own outlets, plus they have to write their notes for the programme. So many people want a slice of them – and they want their slice to be as honest, real and open as possible. No one wants the safe and clichéd retelling of events ('It was a game of two halves' etc.), but due to the sheer quantity of time spent in front of a microphone both ahead of and after a match, it's perhaps inevitable that their words are often flat and lifeless.

People laugh about the nonsense and the deflecting tactics managers employ in interviews, but it's not really a laughing matter. Ultimately, you want your team's boss to come out and say what he actually thinks. But there's no overwhelming urge within the managerial fraternity to do just that. And among their number are some who treat us like fools or buffoons who can't read between the lines. But we all can. We can look bluntly at these individuals and we can see right through them.

But fans never get the opportunity to go in front of managers and interrogate them as to why they often speak such nonsense. At best, they can try to hold their manager to account on social media or on a phone-in radio show. These days, fans hang on every word a manager says, dissecting every syllable. Fifty years ago, a manager would do an interview and people would have forgotten about it within a day. Yesterday's news and today's chip paper. The accountability is now 24 hours, right around the clock. It never sleeps. At any point of the day or night, a keyboard warrior is busy questioning the latest utterance by the manager of their favourite team. Everything is documented and easy to find online.

The result of this intense scrutiny is that fans can get let down by words they take at face value. A key example of this is the case of Brendan Rodgers and Celtic Football Club. During his time as manager at Celtic Park, Rodgers came out with all the things that the faithful wanted to hear.

'I was born into Celtic.'

'There is not a place I could be in this world right now where I'd be happier in my football life and my personal life.'

'I don't see Celtic as a stepping-stone. I want to be here as long as I can.'

'I'm in the best job in the world.'

Not for one moment am I saying that Brendan Rodgers wasn't a phenomenally successful manager during his time in Glasgow. Seven successive major trophies in 33 months is an astonishing return for anyone. It's just that all this silverware didn't seem to be enough to satiate Rodgers' ambition and he left to take the reins at Leicester City instead. That was a curious move for anyone currently employed in the best job in the world, especially when an unprecedented treble-treble was very much on the cards. Why would you leave with the prospect of that record success on the near horizon? More specifically, why would you go having made what had appeared to be hand-on-the-heart personal allegiances to the particular ship you have now so willingly jumped from?

I wouldn't say that those words from early in Rodgers' Celtic reign were throwaway, but they clearly weren't completely thought out. Was he being honest with the fans? Or with himself? Yes, he went on to preside over one of the most fruitful periods in the club's history, but his legacy is now tainted by the timing of his departure and those words which came back to haunt him. He left mid-season, on the cusp of that extraordinary record, when he could easily have seen the season out, secured the ninth and final trophy before admitting 'You know what? I've had an amazing time, but I think I've done as much as I can.'

The fact that he quit his boyhood club for a then middling side down south made those loyalty statements ring hollow. It's probably easy to say he brought it on himself, but he did, didn't he?

> Statements of loyalty often ring hollow. Why would a manager make such committed public comments which later return to bite them on the backside?

Why would you make such committed public comments which later return to bite you on the backside? When he could have departed with total respect, he left under a huge cloud.

José Mourinho is a manager unconcerned by the disparity of what he might have once said and what he thinks – or, at least, what he says he thinks – now. In 2013, during his second spell in charge of Chelsea, he declared: 'I don't want to win the Europa League. It would be a big disappointment for me.' By the time he was the boss at Old Trafford four years later, his tune had radically changed and he called the tournament an 'important' one.

But Mourinho speaks without fear of being outed for contradicting himself. He should be a spin doctor. He can say it any which way he feels. Try to question him and he'll simply tell you how many trophies he's won until it makes sense.

So how do you get managers, especially in the heat of a battle just fought, to speak straight and true? Certainly they would all benefit from that 20-minute period of immunity, which would allow them to get everything off their chest and vent their spleen. No holds barred. Anything goes. They could say what they want to say and what we want to hear.

But, if you don't think that will work, I've another suggestion to raise the levels of truth coming out of a manager's mouth. At every press conference and at every post-match interview, he would be required to be connected up to a lie detector. Other than injecting him with a truth serum, this is the only way we can measure the degree of honesty in his words. No more could a manager deny seeing an incident. No more could he argue against the clear malice of a late tackle by one of his own players. And no more could he faithfully claim that his new appointment was the job he'd been waiting for all his life.

While hooking them up to the mains – and possibly administering a slight electric shock every time they uttered an untruth – is probably a bit harsh, in the stats-heavy world of modern football the results of the lie-detector tests would be made public and a league table of double-talking managers compiled. Those are the kind of stats that people would patiently wait for while being totted up. They might hate the delays of VAR, but they'd happily hang around to see who was crowned king of the truth-benders.

For managers tempted down the route of disingenuousness, half-truths and verbal smokescreens, advice comes from one of the most straight-talking managers ever to grace the Premier League – one Sean Mark Dyche. 'I don't spin. I'm not trying to work an angle,' he explained to the author Michael Calvin. 'If you want to bullshit people, you'd better remember your bullshit. But if you're going to be honest, you don't have to remember anything because you've just told it how you see it.'

Amen to that.

MY TOP TEN **UNDERRATED PLAYERS**

Some players hog the headlines, while others often find themselves not getting their due respect. Here are those unsung heroes deserving of more limelight…

10 MUZZY IZZET

If people look back at the Leicester team in which he made his name, they probably think of the three big centre-halves or of Emile Heskey and Tony Cottee up front, or Neil Lennon and Robbie Savage in midfield. But Izzet was a bright spark in the middle of the park. He offered something a little bit different. He was a clever footballer who didn't get the credit he deserved. He was an unassuming sort of bloke, as well, so I'm not sure he actually wanted the credit. But he was a really terrific footballer who could have played for one of the big boys.

9 ARTHUR NUMAN

At Rangers, Numan was a superbly consistent player who could do everything. He was a nice passer of the ball, he could read the game well and he was athletic. But he was rarely picked out to take the plaudits, whether for Rangers or for the Netherlands. In the era of Dutch football that produced the likes of Bergkamp, Kluivert, Davids and van Hooijdonk, Numan largely went under the radar. The reliable ones often do.

8 JEREMY GOSS

Although known as 'God' among his Norwich team-mates, he failed to receive the credit he deserved from those in the stands. While he didn't have the vision and precision of his midfield team-mate Ian Crook, he had the lungs and the heart to complement him perfectly. Goss did the hard yards and was a specialist when it came to spectacular volleys, as the goalkeepers of Bayern Munich and Leeds United will testify.

7 PADDY CRERAND

If you asked people to name Manchester United's 1968 European Cup-winning side, they'd come up with Charlton and Best and Stiles and Kidd and Stepney first. Paddy Crerand's name would be way down the list, but his tenacity in the tackle was crucial to that Manchester United team, giving extra bite to the midfield, while his measured passing fed their more creative talents. It's between him and Darren Fletcher as United's most underrated player. I think most fans who saw Crerand play would plump for him.

6 SON HUENG-MIN

People bang on about the likes of Harry Kane and Dele Alli, but Son's been phenomenal in that Spurs jersey. He's the one who's happy and willing to play different roles in different positions – and has been totally reliable too. A refreshing type of player who will have the total respect of the dressing room but who perhaps hasn't been the recipient of enough plaudits from the club.

5 ROB LEE

The likes of Andy Cole, Alan Shearer and David Ginola arrived at Newcastle during Kevin Keegan's reign. These were the stars of that side, the big names that roll off the tongue. But the glue that was holding the team together in the middle of the park was Rob Lee. An old-fashioned, box-to-box midfielder, he had an iron lung and was the heartbeat of a brilliant Newcastle team.

4 MICKY HAZARD

Mainly known for his time at Spurs and Chelsea, Hazard was a brilliantly inventive and creative midfielder, one who, in another era, would have earned the kind of plaudits handed to his Spurs team-mate Glenn Hoddle, in whose shadow he often found himself. He made goals but he also scored some belters. I played against towards the end of his career when he was at Swindon and I've faced few cleverer players than him. The fact that he never represented his country at any level is, to my mind, nothing short of criminal.

3 TIM SHERWOOD

I used to clean his boots when he was a young pro at Norwich. Sherwood was a really fantastic footballer – really intelligent. He could see a pass, he could make a pass, he was aggressive, he was strong in the air and had great leadership qualities. The fact that he captained Blackburn to the title tells you what Kenny Dalglish thought of him. But despite being supremely influential at the clubs he played for (he went on to play for Spurs, Portsmouth and Coventry), he was rather overlooked throughout his career. He won three England caps, but should have had many more.

2 JORDAN HENDERSON

He was the long-term successor to Steven Gerrard and inherited the Liverpool captaincy on his predecessor's retirement. Those were big – probably impossible – shoes to fill and the truth is he isn't as good a player as Gerrard. But in the way he's carried himself, in knitting everything together, he's proved himself to be such a key part of the Liverpool side. He plays in different positions and plays them all well, in addition to being a great leader. He's only now getting the respect which he probably warranted earlier.

And my all-time underrated player is...

1 JOHN ROBERTSON

He never got – and still doesn't get – the credit he deserved. But Brian Clough loved him and that says it all. Before Nottingham Forest's second European Cup final – this time against highly rated Hamburg and their right-back Manny Kaltz, regarded as one of Europe's finest – Clough said 'We've got a little fat guy who will turn him inside out'. Robertson scored the game's only goal. Clough knew...

11

Put Away the Smartphones at the Match

There's a wonderful photograph – taken by Stuart Roy Clarke, a football photographer renowned for turning his lens away from the pitch and towards the crowd – called 'Looking Up'. It was taken at Roker Park in 1996 and poignantly captures a moment in a match against Coventry City when several dozen Sunderland fans are gazing out on to the pitch transfixed, presumably by the trajectory of a high ball. All of those within shot – mostly young lads, all of whom are in Sunderland shirts – are in deep concentration, their mouths open in anticipation of what is about to unfold on the field of play. They are all in the moment, and deeply so. Nothing could possibly distract them. They are spellbound.

Spin forward 20 years to view another image depicting fans at a match – although this time it's not a beautifully composed photograph but a paused image from a BT Sport transmission, one that would swiftly do the rounds on social media. It's the second leg of a delicately poised Champions League quarter-final and Manchester City's Sergio Agüero is about to take a penalty against PSG. But the main focus of the image isn't the Argentinian striker, nor is it the PSG keeper. Instead, the fans behind the goal are taking centre stage.

Like the Sunderland photograph, it tells a story of its own particular time. Of the 30 or so people in the shot (again, mainly young lads), around half of them are holding up their phones to film what happens next. Unlike the Roker Park faithful, they are not spellbound. Rather than getting overwhelmed by the excitement of their team potentially grabbing the goal that may take them into the semi-finals, each has had the presence of mind to whip their phone out of their pocket to document the spot-kick. Perhaps the sight of all of those phones before him put Agüero off. He knocked the penalty wide.

It would be difficult to find a more striking visual manifestation of the change in football over the two decades than putting those two images side by side. If you could travel back in time to show the Sunderland boys the scene at the Etihad, they wouldn't be able to compute. They wouldn't understand. Why do those lads have strange devices in their hands? Why are they filming the action that's just a few yards away from their position in the first few rows? And why aren't they watching the action with their own eyes?

Theirs would be a combination of confusion and indignation that I can certainly identify with. If I wanted to watch a game, there's not the remotest chance of me getting my phone out to take some pictures. I'm more interested in the game. Who on earth wouldn't be?

As the Sunderland photograph shows, football is theatre, with the audience ready to be dragged through the full range of emotions over the course of 90 minutes – from hope to despair, via anxiety and anguish. To let yourself become absorbed, to surrender to the moment, takes conviction and commitment. You can't let yourself be distracted by the little gadget in your pocket. Your hardened football fan would be flummoxed by the notion. Football is all. When the match is in progress, nothing else can interfere. Or, rather, nothing else *should* interfere.

Different times have produced those different pictures. Back in 1996 – and for decades and decades before – for the working football fan, the week would pivot around the match on Saturday. The stadium became a place of worship for a large congregation, all there to show their true faith. That faith is less than devout these days. Perhaps life is now so multi-layered that there are several other pivots in people's weeks.

> There's absolutely no excuse for watching events unfold on a small screen. Instead, they can watch it on a bigger one: the widescreen experience called real life

I've never felt the urge to document and record. When I'm on holiday, I want to enjoy the holiday and not spend my time constantly taking pictures by the pool. I'm not sure what drives these particular match-goers to film, and later upload to social media, their wobbly footage. It's not as if the results are worthy of a Martin Scorsese or a Steven Spielberg. Haven't they looked around the ground? Can't they see all the television cameras in position, ready to film every aspect of the match in sparkling high definition and from a multitude of angles? How does the fuzzy and distorted footage these fans have shot hope to compete with the skill and artistry shown by a top football broadcaster?

Any acknowledgements that these amateur film-makers might receive from fellow fans for uploading the footage for public viewing can't remotely compete with the pleasure of watching the incident itself at the time with the naked eye. Their memory isn't of witnessing that cup-winning goal in the flesh, one which they can describe to their grandkids in vivid detail in their later years. The memory that they'll keep is of holding up their phone and later rewatching the goal on a tiny screen.

'Tell me about that goal again, Grandpa.'

'Well, Christian Eriksen got the ball halfway into the opposition's half and he was such a creative player that, whenever he was in possession, I would always reach for my phone in case something special happened. I quickly put my phone into camera mode and started tracking his run. Then he clipped it forward to Harry Kane whose scissor kick put it into the bottom corner.'

'What was his celebration like, Grandpa?'

'I didn't really see it. I dropped my phone and missed him celebrating right in front of us.'

'And was that a definite red card for the opposition's right-back, Grandpa?'

'I don't know. I was taking a selfie with the mascot at the time.'

A pause. 'What's a selfie, Grandpa?'

Hopefully our current times will be a blip in history. Perhaps, if the phone becomes an outmoded item of technology in decades to come, future generations will go back to basics, realising there's absolutely no excuse for watching events unfold on a small screen. Instead, they can watch it on a bigger one: the widescreen experience called real life.

At the cinema or the theatre, people are requested to switch off their phones as a mark of respect both to the rest of the audience and to the film-maker or playwright who's created the work that they're watching. Should football be any different, just because it's a noisier, more boisterous affair? In this respect, football is similar to a music gig. Like certain sections at a Premier League ground, there will be a proportion of gig-goers who feel that the hefty amount of wedge they've paid for a ticket is offset by the footage they've captured on their phone. It's proof they were there, I suppose. But what the hell's wrong with just watching a football match or a gig? Why annoy the people next to you and behind you who are trying to experience the event the way it's supposed to be experienced?

Fans go to matches to be able to say, 'I was there, I saw that', not 'I was there, I *filmed* that'.

The reason for taking a seat in the stand is to see events unfold, perhaps even history be made. But there are too many people who are more interested in operating their selfie sticks, and seeing where they're sitting and who they're sitting next to. Football tourists, you could call them. Rather than watching the actual action, it's more a case of 'We're here and we're telling everybody about it'. Well, don't. Just watch the action you've made a sizeable financial outlay to see. You seem to have paid good money not to become absorbed in the action going on right in front of you, but for the right to film it badly on a phone.

When you watch football on television, you even see people filming throw-ins. What the hell's that all about? They can only be doing so in order to upload it to YouTube and say 'I was there'. What is the need to document and report on every aspect of their life? Why don't they rely on the highly sophisticated organ that resides in their head, one capable of forming and storing millions of memories? It's called the brain.

There's a serious point to be made here too. The more members of the selfie brigade who go regularly, and who perhaps even buy a season ticket, the harder it is for the more diehard fan to attend. The latter are missing out on seeing their team, on seeing their heroes up close and personal, while those less-than-committed supporters seem more interested in being there just to be able to tell their friends. That can't be right.

Of course, phones aren't only used at football matches to take selfies and film the action. They offer distractions in other ways. It used to be that you'd only know the latest scores of the other games taking place when the Tannoy announcer ran through them at half-time. Fans now are often aware of exactly what's happening across the country; they can even stream another match to their phone if the one they are at is less than thrilling. And now they use their smartphones to find out what's happening in the stadium when there's a VAR decision because they've been left in the dark. What's being checked? Did the referee get it wrong? They have to find out from other sources, via their phones, exactly what's going on a few yards in front of them. The sooner that VAR sorts out the communication issue inside the stadium, the sooner that phones can stay in pockets. But until that time, you can't blame these fans for reaching for their phones. It's just that being told what's going on in front of them should be an integral part of the price of admission.

So what's the cure? Obviously we can't issue a wholesale ban on smartphones in football grounds. Nor can we insist on a phone amnesty as fans go through the entrance, where they have to surrender their phone until after the game, much as a child might have theirs confiscated in the classroom until the school day is over. Imagine trying to enforce that on 50,000 Newcastle fans at St James' Park.

The least we could try to do is to impose the rules of the theatre or cinema within football grounds, with stewards empowered, like ushers, to ask those not adhering to the house rules to desist. Persistent offenders would be asked to leave. That doesn't sound wildly inappropriate. Football is theatre, after all.

I suppose it is a case of each to their own, with everyone free to define the fan experience how they please. But this still doesn't make it right in my eyes. We need a shift away from the narcissism of the selfie generation that's seeping into our stadiums. The phone-happy fans should either get on with the business of watching the match and supporting their team or surrender their seat to someone who will.

I want to see more photographs like that one at Roker Park and fewer like that Etihad picture. For the couple of hours that you're at a match, you should be fully focused on what's occurring on the pitch. It's a place of escape, after all. Phone switched off. Eyes to the front. Undistracted, absorbed.

If not, why are you there? Why don't you want to be consumed by the moment, lost to the beautiful game of football?

PART THREE
IN THE MONEY

There's one thing that has reshaped and redefined modern football to a greater extent than anything else. It seems to affect and influence every decision that is made within the game. And too often it appears to be the overriding motivation.

Money.

Everywhere you turn within the upper echelons of football, you're met with the smell of cash. Some might even call it a stench. Money is what turns the industry's wheels faster than ever, whether the source is billionaire club owners, broadcasting rights or plentiful sponsorship deals. There is gold to be mined in this here sport. The recipients of this windfall are doing just fine. Buoyant, in fact. Transfer fees going into clubs' coffers have never been higher, players' wages have never been higher, agents' commissions have never been higher.

But while the inflation within football is right across the board, not everyone can cope with it. For instance, hopelessly devoted fans have never paid more than they currently do to watch their beloved team, nor have they ever forked out so much to prove this devotion through the purchase and wearing of a replica shirt.

For too many parties within football, the primary concern is money (and the rapid accumulation of it), rather than the pursuit of glory. And, yes, while any and every industry needs to be financially solvent, the level of greed shown in certain quarters needs to be reined in. Wings should be clipped and some measure of equilibrium restored. The gap between football's haves and have-nots is widening with each passing season; the salary of a top-flight superstar can easily dwarf the transfer budget of an entire lower-league outfit. While the big boys have become fat cats, clubs just a couple of divisions away are struggling to pay the wages of staff and players. It's heartbreaking to see these extremes in such close proximity. For the good of the game, the playing field needs some levelling.

Something needs to be done to stop that gap stretching further – and ideally for it to begin to narrow. We need to create a culture where no one is priced out of the game, where exploitation has no place and where those seeking to simply make a fast buck don't prosper.

We need to be better than that.

12
Make It Tough to Own a Football Club

'I didn't even know there was a football team called Bury, to be honest with you. I'm not a football fan.'

These weren't the words of a day-tripper visiting the Lancashire town for the first time and stumbling across a match at Gigg Lane. This was the unembarrassed and shameless admission – as told to the nation on 5 Live – by the owner of this particular football club. The custodian. The ultimate authority. The man in whom all those fans are supposed to faithfully trust. 'I never went to Bury. It's not a place I frequented, so for me to walk away from Bury and never go back there is a very easy thing to do.'

Steve Dale took over at Bury at the end of 2018, paying the princely sum of £1 for the financially stricken club. At the time, he suggested this was a philanthropic venture for him, talking about 'community initiatives' and helping 'those less fortunate'. Eight months later, though, Bury were expelled from the Football League, the first club to suffer this particular ignominy since 1992, and Dale's true colours seemed to be revealed in that 5 Live interview. He turned out not to be the club's custodian and was seemingly disinterested in protecting and strengthening it for future generations.

You saw the faces of the Bury fans on the television when they realised what the fate of their beloved club was going to be. OK, it's not a mega-club like Manchester United or Liverpool, but it meant a hell of a lot to the people of Bury. It was one of the old traditional clubs of the north-west with a history as long as your arm. And it was put in a position where a new owner came in, promised the world but didn't deliver.

For him to get to that position, though, the EFL (English Football League) really need to take a long, hard look at themselves and ask whether the mechanism allowing new owners to take over is genuinely fit for purpose. In Bury's case, it clearly wasn't. They really have a lot to answer for.

Just the fact that this guy can come into a radio station, as brazen and blasé as he likes, and make that statement about his total lack of connection to the town whose football club he owns is extraordinary. The EFL said that he had 'passed the onus test but had failed to provide evidence of the source and sustainability of funding'. Now I'm no bank manager or

> The fact that this guy can come into a radio station, as brazen and blasé as he likes, and make a statement about his total lack of connection to the town whose football club he owns is extraordinary

financier, but surely checking that a potential purchaser has sufficient cash in the bank – or, at least, proven and trustworthy backers – has to be the bottom line before any takeover is finalised.

But, when you dig into the details, you find that the rules in place at the time of Dale's ownership stated that this funding must be proven within ten days *after* a takeover. Horses and stable doors come to mind. Despite not coming up with the evidence of his financial security, Dale wasn't censured. As the *Guardian* journalist David Conn has explained, 'a major flaw in the rules is the lack of appropriate sanction for an owner who flouts them: the takeover cannot be denied'. So you can take over a football club without the necessary money, fail to show you have that necessary money, but still carry on regardless. And it was the club itself that took the punishment, not the man, having matches suspended and then, ultimately, being expelled.

If someone from the other side of the country, with no prior links to the area, starts sniffing around a football club, trust your instinct and be suspicious, particularly if that person can't point to the town on a map

For Dale to have been able to take the reins suggests the club ownership bar is set way too low. The checks seem to be left wanting when it comes to their vigorousness. The duty of care resided with the EFL and it simply wasn't good enough. The FA could be seen as culpable too: its chief executive, Greg Clarke, admitted that the first time he spoke to Steve Dale was actually *after* the expulsion had been confirmed. More horses, more stable doors. And it wasn't as if warning shots hadn't already been fired concerning Bury's financial management. In 2014, the previous owner took out a loan against Gigg Lane with a crippling 138 per cent annual interest rate.

But will Bury's experience stop other clubs going the same way? These clubs are the lifeblood of the English football structure and yet questions have to be raised over the league's ability to safeguard its members from such dubious characters in the future.

If someone from the other side of the country, with no prior links to the area, starts sniffing around a football club, trust your instinct and be suspicious, particularly if that person can't point to the town on a map. There are fewer concerns if they're someone with demonstrative connections to both town and club; the whiff of suspicion doesn't linger at their heels – although the same checks should obviously be applied.

The whole community has a moral stake in the local football club, if not a financial one. For something this important, the bar has to be set high when judging if someone is fit and proper to take over a football club. An institution is being placed in their care, a culturally vital community asset that must never be handed over to any Tom, Dick or Harry. They have to be able to navigate and successfully complete a process that has credibility. Steve Dale never seemed a credible option, but he appeared to pull the wool over the EFL's eyes.

While Bury failed to sidestep expulsion, 12 miles west of Gigg Lane, Bolton Wanderers stayed in League One by the skin of their teeth, thanks to a new consortium taking charge in August 2019. The previous owner, Ken Anderson, had taken over after serving the maximum eight-year ban on being a company director following no fewer than eight of his companies going bust. Sure, he'd done his punishment and served his time, but doesn't a business history such as that start alarm bells ringing? Once bitten, twice shy… But *eight* times? That's your entire leg being bitten off, isn't it?

The question from Bolton fans must have been: 'How did anybody not see this happening?' And it's the fairest of all questions. If you were given a sheet of paper on which the Bolton owner's previous record in business was set out, the club's fans would be wondering how the hell they got where they are. Anderson has been described by Forest Green Rovers owner Dale Vince as 'a rogue chairman, a slippery character and untrustworthy'. In 2019, the wages of Bolton's players and staff went unpaid for four months.

I suppose the baffling thing about all this is that when somebody wants to take over a football club, we all assume that they will have the best interests of the club at heart. That's the dream of any football fan whose club's ownership is changing hands. They presume that the new owner is coming in with both a desire and an intention to build the club back up from whence it came, that he has both a plan and a willingness to invest. But Steve Dale is not alone. Over the years, there have been so many owners who have gone into football clubs to the detriment of all concerned. You have to question their intentions. The only conclusion is that they are in it purely for financial gain.

The kind of figure that Blackburn Rovers' former benefactor, Jack Walker, was is a rarity. He was born in Blackburn, a self-made man who loved the club and who gave plenty back to it, building the stadium and building the team. He backed the manager and gave the fans hope again, through his adoration of Blackburn as a town. And he brought success back to east Lancashire. A combination of financial power and fanatical passion, he was an astute businessman but never saw the football club as a vehicle for making money for himself. It was about giving something back to the people of Blackburn, giving something back to his hometown. That was his overarching motive. How often can you say that about club owners these days?

Identifying an owner's – or prospective owner's – motivation is key. It's absolutely fundamental. Look at the Glazer family at Manchester United. Why did they buy it? Because they love the club? Because they have deep ties to the area? That didn't seem to be their intention when they came in. Yes, they've backed various managers financially, but we sort of know why they're there, don't we?

While the intention of Liverpool's own American proprietors will obviously also be financial to an extent, they are at least visible in a way that the Glazers never really have been. Over at Chelsea, Roman Abramovich has come in for flak for arriving in England with full pockets and splashing it around, but the proof is in the pudding. He has been a highly successful owner.

He might not be everyone's cup of tea, but that won't concern the Chelsea fans. They've seen him attend a high proportion of games over the years, a presence that breeds trust. He's not been an absent landlord. Plus, the Stamford Bridge trophy cabinet has never been as crammed as it's been during his regime.

> Roman Abramovich has come in for flak for arriving in England with full pockets and splashing it around, but the proof is in the pudding. He has been a highly successful owner

Perhaps if the Glazers had made more of an effort on the PR front, rocking up at games and showing a real interest, things would be different at Old Trafford. But this is a family that has always seemed to be on the outside. The United fan base hasn't felt the love from them – to the extent that a section of them broke away and formed their own club, FC United of Manchester, the so-called Red Rebels. This is a really important duty for owners and I think there would have been greater sympathy for the Glazers had they not appeared distinctly aloof.

Incoming owners – particularly from abroad – are unlikely to have anything resembling a lifelong connection to their new club and won't know the ins and outs of its entire history. But they should make the effort to immerse themselves in as many aspects of it as possible, to soak up the club's heritage and culture. The fans are always going to show more love themselves if they can see an effort is being made. The mutual respect between Leicester City's fans and the Thai ownership is transparent proof of this.

There can be no more complacency around the subject of football club ownership, no more easy-to-circumvent regulations that have all the effectiveness of a chocolate teapot

These owners are usually successful businesspeople, clever people who have built their fortunes using their sharp business brains. But football is totally different to most other industries. You have to get the supporters onside, and neglecting the fans has often been an owner's downfall. I can't ever see the Glazers winning the support of the United faithful; they're always going to come under scrutiny. When they do come to settle up, there will be a lot of United fans relieved that that day has finally come.

Often there is hope when a new owner comes in. Newcastle fans wanted Mike Ashley to invest in the team and his arrival was met with excitement and the hope that they were going to be a truly competitive force again. But he's remained financially prudent, running Newcastle as a business and only as a business. The fans' frustration has been understandable and his ambition has frequently been questioned. They thought he was going to be their Abramovich figure, ready to spend his way to the Champions League. He wasn't. Abramovich's ambition has been ferocious and his primary motive – amassing silverware – can't be doubted. Ashley's motives, on the other hand, have been under constant scrutiny for years.

For a highly successful businessman, Ashley has been far from a PR success. He rarely undertakes interviews and generally keeps his distance. And, as shown by rebadging St James' Park as the Sports Direct Arena for a period of time, there has been little considered thought about the history of that grand club. In my view, the renaming was a truly vulgar act and a red rag, an absolute red rag to a bull. The fanbase was apoplectic about the arrogance behind that decision. It was such a spectacular own goal. Had he retained any level of respect from the Newcastle fans, that was lost in one fell swoop.

When a new owner comes in to take control of a club, the first question the fans will ask is, 'What is he going to do for us?' That's the principal thing they'll want to know. 'What are his intentions? How is he going to take us forward?' If the fans can ask the tough questions, so can the authorities. 'He may be a billionaire, but he might just be a phoney too?'

Sadly, there aren't too many billionaires down in the lower leagues. They've had their fair share of phonies, though. And, as tragic as the circumstances surrounding Bury have been, they must, *must* be learned from. There can be no more complacency around the subject of football club ownership, no more easy-to-circumvent regulations that have all the effectiveness of a chocolate teapot.

To avoid another historic club being removed from the sainted 92, the fullest diligence needs to be observed when assessing a prospective owner's suitability, especially the financial aspect. The rules – introduced by the FA and administered, in the top four divisions at least by the Premier League and the EFL – must be as tight as can be. The survival of a club, and the possible end of its history, depend upon it.

Owners come and owners go, but the fans are the one true permanent fixture of a football club. So why shouldn't they be involved in judging the suitability of the latest temporary proprietor?

In Germany, significant fan representation on the boards of clubs keeps the owners in check. In fact, since 1998, Bundesliga clubs are unable to play in the league if a private investor owns 50 per cent or more of a club. The '50+1' rule means that a club's members – that is, its fans – retain the majority stake. The stability this provides, where a club isn't susceptible to the lies, deceit and dodgy dealings of an unscrupulous owner, has to be an example that the vulnerable clubs of the lower leagues in the UK could learn from.

But, among all of the imaginative thinking and robust regulations required to avoid a repeat of the Bury calamity, one fundamental box has to be ticked when assessing the suitability of a new owner: check that person has actually visited the town before.

13

Stop Fleecing the Fans

I'll tell it straight. When it comes to ticket prices, football clubs have abused fans.

For your family to go to a top-flight game, you're talking a small fortune, wherever you go in the Premier League. And that's before you factor in petrol and car parking and burgers and this, that and the other. Is it right? Absolutely not. And how is it fair that the rise of ticket prices over the past couple of decades has been so out of kilter with the rate of inflation? It's not even close. For instance, an averagely priced seat at Highbury cost £21 in 2000. A comparable seat at the Emirates will, 20 years later, set you back £71.

Football is a working-class game, so how can the lifeblood of the game – the people who spend all their hard-earned money supporting their club – be outpriced and not able to go? It's become a rich person's sport. And it absolutely shouldn't be. That's not what football was founded on. And as a result, it's losing its identity.

The working class have to put up with watching football on the telly or listening to it on the radio. They can't afford to go and support their team. Or, if they do, something else in their lives has got to give. They're being stretched. Clubs are making it uncomfortable for the average football fan to do what they've always wanted to do and always loved to do. It's been taken away from them. It's a case of 'If you're rich enough, you can come and watch'. As a result, football is losing its sense of community. Plenty of local people still support their local club, of course, but rather than it being a weekly pursuit, it's now perhaps a once-a-season treat.

Football clubs might argue that, in the Premier League at least, they have no problem filling the seats. That's an argument, sure, but it's an argument that shows they have no issue with changing the culture of the game. Much of the working class has now been priced out by their beloved clubs. And the clubs are charging these prices simply because they can! It doesn't get any worse than that, really. The support that people have shown their club throughout the years and across generations – and the heart and soul they've put into that – is just being manipulated by clubs' sheer greed. Clubs know the market. They know what they can get away with charging.

These are not the usual rules of commercial engagement. But a football club is not a supermarket. Supermarkets are in competition with each other for your custom and will slash their prices accordingly. Football clubs don't compete in this manner. Fans aren't going to swap their club for the one just down the road in the way they might switch supermarkets. And clubs know this full well.

And then there's the prickly subject of categorising games – of charging more for certain matches, depending on the quality of the opposition. Taking Arsenal as the example again, for season 2019–20, the Gunners set the top price for a Category C match at the Emirates at the £39.50 mark for non-members. When Liverpool or Manchester City come to north London, parking your backside on the exact same seat costs £97, way more than double the price.

Not all top-flight clubs categorise games. Burnley, for instance – a club that's very connected to the local community, with a stadium close to the town centre – doesn't feel the need to fleece its regulars whenever a high-flying side rocks up at Turf Moor. Their ticket prices are fixed, no matter the opposition. A match is a match is a match, after all. A club doesn't receive more points for beating a top-six side, so why should they receive more cash from their hard-working fans? It's about loyalty and longevity.

It's not rocket science. Certain non-league clubs – including Kettering Town, Gainsborough Trinity and Dulwich Hamlet – have this loyalty and longevity at the forefront of their minds when setting season-ticket prices. They simply ask a teenager to pay their age. So a 14-year-old will fork out the un-princely sum of £14 to watch all their team's home league games for an entire season, a 15-year-old pays £15 and so forth. That's how you create fans for life.

> Fans aren't going to swap their club for the one just down the road in the way they might switch supermarkets. And clubs know this full well

Aside from outlawing the categorisation of matches, ticket prices in general should be capped. I believe football clubs owe it to their supporters to do so. There is currently a £30 away ticket cap in operation across the Premier League, so the principle has already been established. Now it should be the turn of the home support to feel the benefit.

Yes, it would create a shortfall in a club's income and that would have to come from somewhere. But Premier League clubs certainly now generate enough money to actually give something back to their support.

The shortfall could be covered by a reduction in the outrageous salaries the players are on. Clubs shouldn't be paying the vast amounts of money that they do at the top level, and then taking it out on the supporters' pockets. This is essentially what they are doing. They're taking it off the working classes to fund these wages.

After all, is it morally right to give a player a contract for £350,000 a week and up the ticket price by another £6? Of course it isn't. That's going to affect whether a person in a low-paid job can go and support their team year in, year out, or whether they can take the kids. But football clubs don't really care what the right thing to do is. It's all about generating money. And they do it because they can. They're turning their backs on their fans and their history, on their lifeblood.

I mean, how much money does a player actually *need*? You hear these figures – £300,000 a week, £400,000 a week. Really? There has to be a level that players could earn at and that we could all agree was a pretty reasonable amount.

Setting extortionate ticket prices seems to be a particularly English disease. Clubs in the other four major leagues in Europe don't feel the need to behave this way. Just compare the Premier League with the Bundesliga. For the 2019–20 season, the average price of a Premier League season ticket was £698. The lowest available season ticket was offered by West Ham at £350, while the most expensive, for Tottenham's new stadium, came in at an eye-watering £1,995. By contrast, the cheapest season ticket in the Bundesliga for the same season was at Wolfsburg for £200, while the most expensive was Eintracht Frankfurt's at £740. So a marked difference there.

Here's the rub, though. Those Bundesliga figures are for *seated* season tickets. With German top-flight stadiums having terracing, if you're happy to stand to watch your team all season – and, of course, most fans are – there are some absolute bargains to be had. Bayern Munich are actually the joint-cheapest club when it comes to standing season tickets, with theirs costing just £130 (as do Wolfsburg's). That works out at less than £8 for each of the 17 home games – an extraordinary bargain to see one of Europe's finest teams week in, week out. That's also the price you'd pay to go and see a match in English football's eighth or ninth tier, giving you a sense of the gross inequality between countries. Plus, German season tickets often include free travel on local transport to and from the game. It represents brilliant value for money.

And while the Bundesliga is the cheapest of the big five European leagues – and, not coincidentally, the one with the highest attendances – the others

> Why do clubs take advantage of their most loyal fans? You can only say it as it is. It's greed, it's avarice

are far from extortionate. The average season ticket price in La Liga, Serie A and Ligue 1 is less than half that in the Premier League. We are in a league of our own when it comes to the price of admission.

But these top European clubs can still attract the best players and can pay sky-high weekly wages. They're simply not reliant on squeezing money out of their supporters to do so. These clubs clearly care more about their supporters than English clubs do. That can be the only answer. We are the cradle of football, but we're the ones doing a disservice to the people who've made the sport what it is. I know they have to balance the books, but there are ways and means to do that. Why do they take it out on their own supporters? Why do they take advantage of their most loyal fans? You can only say it as it is. It's greed, it's avarice. Why else would clubs do it?

Of course, before they've coughed up the entrance fee, fans may well have paid a visit to the club shop. Once inside those doors, it becomes clear that a club's licence to print money extends beyond ticketing. Welcome to the obscenely expensive world of the replica shirt.

In February 2019, I went to Madrid to cover Atlético Madrid's Champions League last-16 match against Juventus for BT Sport. While I was there, I thought I'd pick up a nice red-and-white Atlético shirt for my daughter. When they asked me for 60 euros at the till, I was flabbergasted. This was a shirt for a seven-year-old. Not the full kit. No shorts, no socks. It wasn't a jacket. It wasn't a coat. Just the shirt. A nice shirt, I'll admit, but just a shirt nonetheless. Sixty euros! (And she only wore it twice!)

Shirt sales are seriously big business. It's a cash cow that's continually milked without shame. In 2016, Manchester United sold a staggering 2.85 million shirts across the world. Their sales have since been overtaken by Liverpool; obviously the more successful a team, the more willing its fans are to demonstrate where their affiliation and allegiance lies. But they're all paying through the nose to do so.

They play on the heartstrings of the hopelessly devoted completists among their fans who feel they need the full wardrobe of current shirts

The prices of Liverpool's shirts are no more than those charged by most, if not all, Premier League and European clubs. But that doesn't make the financial hit any easier. Liverpool's standard men's home 2019–20 shirt retailed at £64.95, while the elite version came in at the £95 mark. What were people getting for this additional 30 quid? The latter is the version worn on match days by the club's superstars and features such vague extras as 'enhanced player performance' and 'a more athletic structure'. Quite why the less-than-athletic citizens of the Kop would need these enhancements is beyond me. Ain't no one going to mistake them for Salah or Firmino.

Other versions of the standard home shirt are available too. The ones marking them as European champions and Club World Cup champions cost £74.99 and £79.99 respectively, thanks to the addition of those all-important extra logos. These versions play on the heartstrings of the hopelessly devoted completists among their fans who feel they need the full wardrobe of current shirts. It's not unlike a band releasing a compilation of greatest hits who, to ensure they get the hard cash of those who already own these tracks from previous albums, include a brand-new song on the track listing. The loyal fan can't leave a gap in their collection. Full price is paid just for that one new song. And it's unlikely to be even half as good as their best material.

Clubs only actually need two kits. That's all they used to have back in the day and the maths worked out perfectly well. Let's stay with Liverpool, for instance. They used to have their red home kit and a yellow away kit. If they still had that two-kit set-up today, there'd be no problem whatsoever. There would be the obvious colour clashes – when playing at Manchester United or Arsenal or Sheffield United or Southampton or Bournemouth or Crystal Palace – but that single away kit would suffice; no Premier League team plays in red *and* yellow.

The issue is that nowadays clubs often elect to wear their away kit when on the road, regardless of whether there's a clash with the home side's colours. So when Southampton venture up the M1 to the King Power Stadium – and despite their traditional red-and-white stripes not remotely conflicting with the royal blue of Leicester City – they'll don the black and yellow of their away strip. Furthermore, had this away strip been blue in hue, there's a strong chance that the third kit would have been reached for. It's the occasional use of a third kit that means clubs can legitimately sell it at top dollar. As it's a strip they do actually use, the marketing department can justifiably ask those most loyal to the club to stump up another wad of cash.

But it doesn't even end there. With not-so-subtle timing, four days before Christmas 2019, Chelsea announced the launch of a *fourth* kit, a commemorative kit that saluted the 50th anniversary of their first FA Cup triumph. It replicates the kit worn by the victorious players back in 1970 and would be worn by the current team on the 2020 FA Cup trail. And, yes, it was very attractive, particularly the yellow socks and the absence of advertising on the shirt. A handsome retro affair it certainly was.

But, really, a *fourth* kit? That's another clear example of exploitation, that really is. It takes the biscuit. In fact, it takes the whole packet. You can ask yourself if they can legitimately do this, and of course they can. Such a kit would almost certainly be a huge money-spinner. The justification comes through the regular pinging of the tills.

And putting out a retro kit is a clever move. Were it an anonymous design that was nothing other than a blatant attempt to squeeze yet more money out of punters' pockets, that might have been a step too far. They might well have been in receipt of fan discord and negative press. But the retro element, tying in with a particular landmark occasion in the club's story, suggests it's a one-off. It also marks any purchaser of it as a true Blue, someone who knows the heritage, someone who knows the history. Kudos goes to the person who wears it at the next home game.

But where would commemorative shirts end? A club's first FA Cup triumph is a significant milestone and one that – once, or if, you get over the concept of a fourth kit – is worthy of saluting. When they've run out of commemorating particular trophy wins, where next? Putting out a replica kit of that season they avoided relegation on the last day? The kit worn when they were runners-up in the Zenith Data Systems Cup? That time they reached the last eight of the Johnstone's Paint Trophy?

If a club is so proud of a particular moment in its history and wants to commemorate it with putting out a replica kit, it should just give them away. Do something for the fans who give them a lifetime's support, rather than finding another way for them to pay. It's not that it would be the club giving away a £65 shirt for free. It's been reported that the typical mark-up is around 1,000 per cent, shared between the club and the manufacturer. Giving one of these away to, say, their ticket-holders wouldn't break the bank of any Premier League club, but what it would do is reward the fans for their support. If that's a concept too tricky for the marketers to handle, at least give this fourth shirt away as reward to those paying full price for one of the other shirts.

The profits certainly allow for this gesture of goodwill. A margin of 1,000 per cent would delight

Releasing a fourth kit is another clear example of exploitation. It takes the biscuit. In fact, it takes the whole packet

any and every captain of industry. If, on one of their weekly tasks, one of the teams on *The Apprentice* came back into the boardroom with a profit return of this size, Alan Sugar would be thrilled. He might even break into a smile. That would be a team that certainly wasn't getting fired that week.

Lord Sugar would surely also appreciate the loyalty of the market that these marked-up goods are serving. As I mentioned earlier, a club's kit is not a generic product being manufactured by a dozen other companies, a dozen other competitors. This is not flogging washing powder where, if the customer felt the price was too high, they'd simply move to another brand. The beauty of selling to football fans is that they're a captive audience that shows lifelong loyalty. As the market of one particular football club, they're not going anywhere. It's a closed shop.

Both individually and collectively, the clubs know this and they all charge broadly the same price for shirts. They might be rivals but they still exploit their own in the same way. They're all pretty sharp. There are no pangs of guilt. None of them put their head over the parapet to start charging much-reduced prices. As long as the club down the road is selling theirs at a similar price point, there's little dissent from the supporters. There's no 'Hold on, Rovers down the road are selling their shirts at 40 quid but I'm paying 65…'

> The beauty of selling to football fans is that they're a captive audience that shows lifelong loyalty

We all understand that merchandise is important, whether for supporters to show their allegiance and identity, or for clubs to further bolster their bottom line. But the pricing of it shouldn't be to the detriment of the common football fan. The onus is on clubs to look after what they regard as their lifeblood. There's not a chairman around the country who doesn't talk the fans up, who doesn't understand the necessity of building the fanbase.

But if clubs are going to charge full whack for the gear, they should at least be honest about it. They could acknowledge that buying a single shirt – let alone the full set of three or four, plus perhaps an equally expensive training top – is a significant outlay to many fans. They wouldn't buy any other kind of shirt for a similar amount of money. Supporters know they're being ripped off, but it's become one of those things that they accept, another burden of being a fan to add to all their other grievances and hardships. It would certainly help if clubs at least thanked them more vociferously for spending their hard-earned wages in the club shop or website, while explaining that it's effectively an investment in their team, to help buy players who will hopefully fire the club back into those days of glory.

In an ideal world, though, fans wouldn't be exploited by the club to whom they devote so much of their time, money and thoughts. It's very hard to halt market forces, especially when the replica shirt market turns over such a pretty penny. But there are ways. As well as insisting that clubs only have two kits in any season, the footballing authorities could also put a cap on a shirt's retail price. Somewhere in the region of £40 would still offer an impressive profit margin to clubs while making it much more affordable to those in the stands week in, week out. Plus, it would be a long overdue PR exercise, with any feelings that fans harbour of being ripped off diminishing and dissolving.

And I can tell you that being ripped off isn't a pleasant feeling. Handing over that 60 euros in Madrid still hurts.

14

Mercenary Players Need to Tell the Truth

Let's get this straight from the start. Footballers heading overseas, where they're rewarded with significant monetary gain, is nothing new. Playing for the highest bidder is not a product of the modern age.

In 1952, Tom Finney was approached by Palermo with an offer of an annual salary of £10,000. The decision whether or not to sign wasn't his to make. Preston North End turned down the Italian club and the winger remained tied to the £20-a-week maximum wage imposed by the sport's governing bodies. But if he received any criticism for even considering the approach, Finney was rational in his outlook. 'I have yet to meet any working man who would turn his nose up at a huge salary. Who would look their boss squarely in the eyes and say "Well, thanks for the offer, but I will have to decline because I really don't think I'm worth it"?'

Finney wasn't the only one whose head was turned by Italy. A few years later, several British players – including Denis Law and John Charles – moved to Italian clubs. Jimmy Greaves was also one of them, swapping that weekly £20 he'd been earning at Chelsea for £130 at

AC Milan. He was, though, honest and transparent in explaining his motivations. 'I got involved with Milan for mercenary reasons,' he later wrote in his autobiography. 'Money was the only motive.' Lira had been the lure.

If money was a prime motive 60-odd years ago, it's unsurprising that, in today's cash-drenched times, it continues to be a major enticement to today's footballers. The former Tottenham full-back Benoît Assou-Ekotto has been particularly candid about this. 'I don't understand why, when I say I play for the money, people are shocked. "Oh, he's a mercenary." Every player is like that.' Emmanuel Adebayor would certainly agree. 'A lot of people say I always play for contracts. At the end of the day, we are all footballers. This is my life. This is my work.'

It's all about the money. We all know it. We would all be lying if we said we wouldn't be tempted by a humungous wage increase

> If a player wants to go and play in China or Qatar, they should just be upfront about why. Just tell us that the cash being offered is simply irresistible

from elsewhere. So why do we frown at a footballer who makes that decision? What gives anybody the right to be judge and jury? Footballers are entitled to move wherever, however and whenever they like, just like anybody else in any walk of life. And if they're chasing the money, I don't begrudge them that.

But there is just one teeny-weeny detail that does get my back up. Just tell us straight that you've gone for the dosh. Please spare us the fairy tales and the embarrassing bull. Greaves and Assou-Ekotto and Adebayor weren't remotely disingenuous in explaining their motivations as footballers. But most others are. They shouldn't try to kid us. If they want to go and play in China or Qatar, they should just be upfront about why. Don't say that it's a better league than the Premier League. Just tell us that the cash being offered is simply irresistible. Give us the truth. The case of Marko Arnautović is the most glaring example of this. When the striker first informed West Ham that he wanted to move to China, his brother, who is also his agent, went public, explaining that his sibling wanted 'to go to a new market and challenge for titles'. No mention was made of the eye-wateringly large sums of money being set as bait. When he did finally leave for Shanghai seven months later, it was reported that his weekly wage had nearly doubled overnight and was now in the ballpark of two hundred grand. Just a coincidence, of course. A fortunate by-product. It was always just about the trophies.

You have to question a player's ambition. Heading to an inferior league when you're still in your physical prime makes no sense to me

Maybe I'm wrong, but I don't think Arnautović would have known much about the Chinese Super League. I bet he didn't even ask where his prospective new club was based and who the manager was and what other players they had in the squad. Do you think that really came into any part of the negotiations? It would more likely have been 'How much? Yeah, OK, deal done.' Maybe he did go over and do a recce, but I think when the cheque is that fat, then there's not a lot to think about.

At 30, though, Arnautović could still have offered plenty to a club in one of Europe's top leagues and tried to win silverware of a more prestigious nature. Instead, his career is now beginning its descent instead. He's not the only one. Chelsea winger Ramires was only 28 when he downgraded for the Chinese Super League; his Stamford Bridge team-mate Oscar was just 25. Why wouldn't these players want to challenge for real honours in the world's best domestic leagues? In years to come, the Chinese Super League might rival the great leagues of Europe, but not right now. Just ask Carlos Tevez, who described his 16-match spell in Shanghai as being 'on vacation for seven months'.

You have to question a player's ambition, of course. I can understand players in their mid-thirties fancying some time playing in the Middle East to earn a nice little nest egg. Both Pep Guardiola and Xavi made the trip from Barcelona to Qatar at that time of their lives. But heading to an inferior league when you're still in your physical prime makes no sense to me.

I mean, just how much do these players want to earn? We're talking astronomical amounts here. But players can have the best of both worlds. If you're already a Premier League player on a hundred grand a week, that's more than £20 million over the run of a four-year contract. And you have the privilege of playing in what many people regard as the best league in the world, plus the chance of taking part in the Champions League or the Europa League. That's not a bad life, is it? Why would you throw that all away for the Chinese Super League which, at the moment, is perceived to be all about the money and not about the glory?

This is money that you're unlikely to ever spend, but you could be saddled with a lifetime's regret for making that move. I do think that these players will experience some regret over their decisions. When they sit down on their golden thrones or whatever they've bought with their extortionate wages, they may well be thinking *Could I have stayed and achieved more in the bigger, more reputable leagues I was brought up on?* I think that could well be the case. Everybody has regrets. And, in football, you're a long time retired.

Nobody begrudges footballers earning money and trying to make their family secure. Just don't tell us you're ambitious and then get on a plane to China, when you're already playing in one of the best leagues. You're not kidding anybody, so tell us why you're going. Fans will question your hunger, yes, but they won't question your honesty.

Players further down the ladder, in League One and below, must be envious of those top players making that career choice. They themselves are making years and years of sacrifices trying to reach the top, but see these superstars in their prime and their pomp who, out of sheer avarice and greed, don't want to make the most of their talent. They just want their already comfortable bank balances to be further plumped up. This must frustrate the hell out of lower-league players who would give their right arm to have an opportunity to play in the Premier League.

When I went from Norwich to Blackburn, was money a motivation to me? I have to admit that, yes, it was nice that my wages went up. I was on about £1,000 a week at Norwich and went up to £12,000 a week at Blackburn, which was a considerable increase. But, honestly, that wasn't my first motivation. With the greatest respect, Norwich were never going to win the Premier League, while Blackburn had finished runners-up to Manchester United the previous season. They were becoming the team of that particular moment.

There are various reasons why players move. Some players get stale and they want a fresh challenge. Some prefer the manager that another team has, or they might have friends in that other team. But people are only human and the money element comes into any job. If a guy's working in insurance at one company in one city and gets a job offer in another city for a 25 per cent increase on his wages, then he's going to take it. Nobody would necessarily call that person a mercenary. But I think it's a slightly different case in terms of some of the mercenaries in football. It's an industry like no other. There are hopes and dreams and loyalty involved.

With the greatest respect to all the other jobs you can have, when you're growing up your aim isn't really to become an insurance salesman. You don't dream about that. But when you're three or four years old, you get your first football shirt, you get your first football, your first boots, and for many it becomes your dream to play and win trophies. I was like it myself – I painted a picture when I was at first school and wrote that I wanted to be a professional footballer. I mean, it was a bloody awful picture, I had enormous ears and a big nose, but…

There's a frustration from fans who see a player with supreme talent put money over ambition. I played at the highest level and I too find those priorities strange. Would I have ever gone to Asia to play while I was in my pomp? I'd be lying if I said that was

> Would I have gone to Asia in my pomp? A deal in China versus playing Premier League and Champions League football? There would have been only one winner

difficult to answer. A deal in China versus playing Premier League and Champions League football? Sorry – there would have been only one winner.

Perhaps other players are more easily bought. Perhaps the exodus will continue. And what's to stop leagues whose clubs have seemingly bottomless pockets from offering more and more money to the top players from Europe and South America? Where will it all end? How can it be contained?

If it hasn't already spiralled out of control, one way of ensuring that it doesn't do so would be for FIFA to impose a worldwide wage cap. This would go some way to ensuring that players switch clubs for purely footballing reasons, not financial ones. In such a scenario, a player would then be way more likely to choose a Serie A club over a Chinese one if he were being offered the same terms by either club. Or if something incredible was happening in China by that stage, maybe he'd go there. But for the right reasons. With him being paid the maximum amount he could be, the pursuit of meaningful, prestigious trophies in competitive leagues would become the true, undeniable challenge – the purpose of his career. And we would continue to see the best players playing for the best teams in the best leagues. That has to be the ultimate objective, doesn't it?

A wage cap might be difficult to impose on global football, but there's been one in the NFL since 1994 and you never see a poor NFL player. Their standard of living isn't in jeopardy; nor are they focused on accumulating obscene wealth. They simply get on with task at hand: achieving sporting glory. It's the same across American sports, with salary caps also in operation at the highest levels of baseball, basketball, ice hockey and soccer.

As if to prove it's not such a revolutionary – and potentially unworkable – measure, in December 2019, the Chinese football authorities announced the imposition of a salary cap on all new contracts issued by Chinese Super League clubs. The days of the likes of Arnautović and Ramires and Marouane Fellaini heading to China to make themselves rich beyond their wildest dreams now seem over. The cap limits a foreign player's weekly wage to the pre-tax equivalent of £42,000, compared to the average Premier League wage packet of £61,000.

In the end, it comes down to whether a salary cap put in place right around the world would be good for the game. And of course we all know it would. A return to the maximum wage! Although we should probably set it a little higher than the twenty quid a week that Jimmy Greaves was running away from...

MY TOP TEN **BEST-VALUE PLAYERS**

So much money is spent on transfer fees – some recklessly, some wisely. Here are the players who I regard as having made the best pound-for-pound impact for their new club…

10 N'GOLO KANTÉ
Caen to Leicester City, August 2015, £5.6 million

There's a case to include a couple of other bargains from that title-winning Leicester side (Jamie Vardy and Riyad Mahrez), but for me it's got to be Kanté. He was the main cog in that team, the engine. He seemed to have an iron lung – I don't think he stopped running all of that season. When he moved to Stamford Bridge, Chelsea had just had their poorest season for 20 years. One year later and Kanté was collecting his second successive Premier League winner's medal. Coincidence? *Mais non.*

9 ALAN SHEARER
Southampton to Blackburn Rovers, July 1992, £3.6 million

When he signed for Kenny Dalglish, his scoring record down on the south coast was far from prolific, let alone astounding. A modest 23 goals in 118 league appearances didn't remotely suggest he'd become the Premier League's greatest-ever marksman. But everything clicked once Shearer came under Dalglish's guidance at Ewood Park, his 34 goals firing Blackburn to the title in 1995. It's going to take a very special player indeed to eclipse the 260 Premier League goals that England's greatest striker notched up.

8 FRANK LAMPARD
West Ham United to Chelsea, June 2001, £11 million

Lampard was far from the finished article when he made the move westwards across the capital, but he blossomed into a truly world-class footballer during 13 trophy-laden years at Stamford Bridge. Whether creating goals or prolifically scoring them (he remains the only midfielder to have notched up more than 150 goals in the Premier League), he surely represents free-spending Chelsea's best piece of transfer business ever.

7 SERGIO AGÜERO
Atlético Madrid to Manchester City, July 2011, £38 million

He made an instant impact with City, his 30-minute debut as a sub producing two goals and an assist. Since then, he's proved himself to be a supreme finisher, with the Argentine having overtaken Thierry Henry when it comes to amassing more goals than any other overseas player in Premier League history. And, of course, that last-gasp, title-winning goal paid back his not-inconsiderable transfer fee in one stroke. In the words of Martin Tyler – Agüerrrrroooooo!

6 VINCENT KOMPANY
Hamburg to Manchester City, August 2008, £6 million

I played against Kompany for Celtic in the Champions League when he was a 17-year-old central defender at Anderlecht. I came off the park thinking, *Who is this kid? He's going places.* He was an absolute, indisputable bargain. The impact that he had at the Etihad is there for everybody to see. He dragged City from being a nearly team to a winning team who played beautiful football. The fact that almost as soon as he left the club Liverpool accelerated away from City as the main force in English football says it all.

5 VIRGIL VAN DIJK
Southampton to Liverpool, January 2018, £75 million

People will look at the price tag and think that I've taken leave of my senses. And, yes, while £75 million represents one of the most expensive transfer fees in history, the Dutchman has been worth every single penny. He proved to be the missing piece in the Liverpool jigsaw, the missing link. When he moved to Anfield, it was his presence that took them to the next level. Without him, you couldn't see them having the maturity to win the Champions League. Their weakness was their defence. With van Dijk (and another bargain, £8 million Andy Robertson), it certainly isn't now.

4 THIERRY HENRY
Juventus to Arsenal, August 1999, £11 million

Henry didn't hit the ground running when he arrived at Highbury, but all of a sudden – after failing to score in his first eight matches – he found his confidence and finished that first season with 26 goals. He had turned from an ugly duckling into a beautiful swan, arguably the best player the Premier League has ever known. The goal he scored against Manchester United – where he had his back to goal, flicked the ball up and volleyed it over Fabien Barthez's head – was sublime.

I know he was in a good team, but he was the main man in that team. And an absolute snip at £11 million.

3 PETER SCHMEICHEL
Brøndby to Manchester United, August 1991, £505,000

Name a more influential goalkeeper in the Premier League era than Peter Schmeichel. He changed the art of goalkeeping as we knew it in this country. The jury was well and truly out on him when he came over from Scandinavia because of his style, but the great Dane subsequently took the role of the goalkeeper to another level. And, of course, he was a key vertebra in the spine of that highly successful Manchester United side.

2 ERIC CANTONA
Nîmes to Leeds United, April 1992, £1 million; Leeds United to Manchester United, November 1992, £1.2 million

Iconic is an overused word, but it's rightfully employed when used to describe Eric Cantona. He's still surely the most unpredictable player to have ever graced the Premier League, but spearheaded both his English clubs to the title. His impact at Old Trafford was extraordinary, bearing in mind the legends to have worn the red shirt: four titles and two FA Cups in less than five years. He had it all – he was strong, he scored fabulous goals, he was fiery and, like all great mavericks, you never knew what to expect from him. It's actually almost unsurprising that he went into acting when he retired; when he graced a football pitch, it was pure theatre.

And the best-value player ever is…

1 HENRIK LARSSON
Feyenoord to Celtic, July 1997, £650,000

When, in his first game for Celtic, Larsson gave the ball away and Chic Charnley scored for Hibs, Celtic fans were thinking, *Blimey, who's this dud?* A full 242 goals in the green and white later and the Swede's impact on European football is beyond debate. When he eventually decided to leave Celtic Park, around 30 clubs expressed an interest in signing him. Barcelona won his signature and he went on to achieve great things with them in the Champions League. He then pitched up at Old Trafford towards the end of his career. The fact that he got a standing ovation from the likes of Ferdinand and Giggs and Ronaldo after his final game shows the deep respect his top fellow pros had for him.

15
Stop Clubs Selling Stadium Naming Rights

Football traditionalists have taken rather a pounding in recent years. At best, someone who identifies themselves as such can be called 'old school'. At worst, they're seen as a dinosaur: slow, plodding and out of step with the times.

When it comes to certain aspects of football, though, I'm happy to nail my colours to the traditionalist mast. I like tradition. I like history. I love all the old photos. I love the old stadiums. And I especially love the names of old stadiums.

These names carry generations of history with them. They feel permanent, unshifting. I feel a warm glow of satisfaction that my place of work felt so grand from its name alone: Carrow Road, Ewood Park, Stamford Bridge, Celtic Park, St Andrew's, Villa Park… And I love the fact that my kids know exactly which teams play at these grounds, as their great-great grandparents would have. This is tradition being upheld.

Since selling the naming rights to football stadiums came into practice in the late 1990s, this tradition has been chipped away at.

And, no, I don't approve. Selling off a chunk of your club's history really shouldn't be allowed to happen. Fans deserve better. Half of the experience of being a fan is looking back over the years – remembering, recalling, comparing it to now. Fans are proud of the past, of seeing the evolution and the journey of their team over the decades. This is why clubs open museums. It's why, as club ambassadors, former players lead guided tours of their old stomping grounds. And it's why these same club legends are in high demand on the after-dinner speaking circuit.

But in selling off the name of their ground – quite often, their old, very historic ground – to the highest bidder, clubs are loosening the connection to the past. It cheapens the game, it really does. It's an echo of the game's governing bodies taking the corporate shilling and adding a sponsor's name to a historic trophy. I'm thinking specifically here of the League Cup and the never-ending list of sponsors whose names have been attached to it over the past four or so decades: the Milk Marketing Board, Littlewoods, Rumbelows, Coca-Cola, Worthington's, Carling, Capital One and Carabao. The competition undoubtedly suffered from, and was tainted by, taking a sponsor in the first place. Switching this sponsor regularly compounded it. Again, history and heritage are the losers.

I used to love playing at the old grounds, many of which have succumbed to the demolition crew's wrecking ball: The Dell, Highfield Road, Highbury...Highbury has to be one of my favourites. The history oozed out of the brickwork. It was a terrific ground. Something was definitely lost when they moved across the railway tracks to Ashburton Grove. I think if you asked the average Arsenal fan aged 30 and above whether they'd take Highbury over the Emirates, there would be no doubt about the answer. Yes, I understand the whole argument about increasing capacity and improving people's chances of getting hold of match tickets, but compared to atmosphere-rich

Highbury, the Emirates doesn't come near. It feels like a corporate venue designed to attract the prawn-sandwich brigade, as the sky-high prices that Arsenal charge seem to suggest. It might only be a few hundred metres away from Highbury, but emotionally and spiritually it's so far removed from the North Bank and the Clock End.

The fact that Arsenal sold the naming rights to the new stadium made things worse. Had they resisted and simply called it something like 'New Highbury', then at least some kind of connection to the recent past would have been maintained – even if that wouldn't have improved the atmosphere.

And don't get me wrong. I'm not against new stadiums per se. I think Tottenham's new ground is magnificent, with that White Wall of fans, inspired by Borussia Dortmund's formidable Yellow Wall. And – at least for the time being – they've not renamed it in the image of a multinational corporation. Well, there's a reason why they haven't sold the rights off to the highest bidder, as their ever-shrewd chairman Daniel Levy has revealed: 'We are only going to do a naming rights deal if we get the right brand, in the right sector, on the right money. If we can't meet those three criteria, then we won't.' The right money is believed to be an immense £375 million over 15 years, a world record were it to be realised.

In selling off the name of their ground – quite often, their old, very historic ground – to the highest bidder, clubs are loosening the connection to the past

The practice is not going away. Elsewhere in the capital, it's been reported that the London Stadium and West Ham are jointly pursuing a sponsor for the ground. Meanwhile, Everton have announced a £30-million naming rights deal with former Arsenal shareholder Alisher Usmanov for their new stadium once it's completed.

I appreciate that building an ultra-modern, high-capacity stadium is a serious construction project that requires a vast amount of capital. And I also recognise that the chance to recoup a significant chunk of that in return for simply giving it the name of a cash-paying sponsor is not unattractive. But clubs have built stadiums for future generations and I believe they need to name them for future generations too.

> I appreciate that building an ultra-modern stadium costs a pretty penny. But clubs build them for future generations and I believe they need to name them for future generations too

Sunderland didn't feel the need to tarnish their rich heritage by flogging the naming rights to their new stadium when they moved in in 1997. And what a fabulously evocative name they gave it, too, one that referenced the Davy lamps used in the area's coalmining industry. I hope they never sully the Stadium of Light by adding a sponsor at any point in the near future. Or ever, in fact. When Southampton took the keys to St Mary's in 2001, the plan was for it to be called the Friends Provident Stadium before fan pressure insisted that St Mary's be added. Good on them. It's been pleasingly sponsor-free since 2006. St James' Park has been sponsor-free since October 2012, after Mike Ashley's short-lived and embarrassing project to rebrand it as the Sports Direct Arena.

To be fair, once some clubs chose to put a price tag on their history, you might have expected a torrent of others to follow suit. So fair play to those many clubs who remained deaf to the overtures of corporate marketing departments. So Molineux is still Molineux. Turf Moor is still Turf Moor. Bramall Lane is still Bramall Lane. These are names as old as the hills, wonderfully unglamorous in what is often touted as the world's most glamorous league.

After all, it's not as if the amounts being paid for the rights is always particularly astounding. Leicester City's deal with the Thai duty-free empire King Power reportedly nets them a modest £3.2 million a season, while Brighton's original deal with American Express was rumoured to be worth only £4.5 million over ten years. You have to ask yourself whether this comparatively moderate level of income is worth risking any potential damage to the reputation of the football club.

Obviously the better-heeled clubs at English football's top table, those whose coffers are plumped up with fast-flowing TV revenue, have less pressure to sell the naming rights. Hence Anfield, Old Trafford and Stamford Bridge continue to be known as they always have been. Further down the pyramid, the contribution to a more minor club's cashflow from naming rights money is likely to be a significant deposit in their bank account. I can understand that. It's very tough beyond the Premier League and the Championship. But they could at least find some sponsors without such depressingly prosaic names. These grounds represent the fields of dreams for each club's supporters but, once the deal is signed, their official names are decidedly humdrum – not the stuff of dreams at all.

For instance, Colchester United play at the JobServe Community Stadium, while Peterborough's famous old London Road ground now answers to the Weston Homes Stadium. How very romantic. And, until recently, Cheltenham played home matches at the unalluring-sounding LCI Rail Stadium; the home end there is still known as – or, rather, its official name is – the Speedy Skips Stand. Toto, we're a long way from the Premier League now.

Sometimes you wonder about the wisdom of a naming rights deal for sponsors at the lower-league level. If you're not a familiar product name, and if it's not immediately clear what goods you manufacture or services you provide, the benefits seem rather hidden to me. For instance, Rotherham's newish ground, the New York Stadium (named after the area of the town in which its built and not because it's sponsored by a bagel bakery), is now known as the AESSEAL New York Stadium. AESSEAL, anyone? No, me neither. I just had to look them up. They're a manufacturer of 'mechanical seals and support systems'. Ah, OK. I'll be sure to go to them the next time I need one of those.

(Very occasionally, however, some fun can be had with a renamed stadium. Here, I doff my cap to Livingston supporters who, when referring to their team's stadium, the Tony Macaroni Arena – they are sponsored by the Scottish chain of Italian restaurants – choose instead to call it The Spaghettihad. Pure genius.)

It's hard to change our ways. And I'm not entirely sure why we have to. Why can't we just refer to these stadiums in the way we always have? Why do we have to unwillingly popularise a company's name every time we mention a particular ground? Bournemouth's Vitality Stadium will always be Dean Court to me. Similarly, Leyton Orient play at the ground currently known as the somewhat anonymous Breyer Group Stadium. That'll be Brisbane Road to the rest of us. As a history enthusiast, when I look back at my own career, I'm glad I played at Carrow Road and Ewood Park, and not the McDonald's Wimpy Vodafone Stadium.

It's not as if there aren't other sponsorship opportunities for football clubs to explore, especially for those flying high in the Premier League. Take Liverpool, for instance. They currently have numerous 'official partners', brands that want to be associated with a team experiencing tremendous success. They're paying to be a part of that. Other than the income they provide, their contribution to the cause is rather tangential, as a rundown of Liverpool's official partners confirms. Their names might not appear on the first-team shirts, but the club is supported financially by companies that manufacture cars, tyres, beer, vodka, jeans, phones, moisturiser and pushchairs. The list of official partners even includes an Alpine ski resort.

None of those products have any direct connection to football, but the revenues they bring into the club allows reinvestment into players and infrastructure. If that's where the money goes. When a team is underperforming but cash isn't being transferred into the recruitment budget, that's when the club can come under fire. If the high-ranking executives are prioritising securing partnership deals over swiftly dealing with on-field matters, that's when the natives will be getting restless. The perception will be that, in the boardroom and along the back corridors, business matters outtrump those of a footballing nature.

Why can't we just refer to these stadiums in the way we always have? Why do we have to unwillingly popularise a company's name every time we mention a particular ground?

All the while that the footballing side is moving along swimmingly, as at Anfield in recent times, there's no disquiet about commercial activity. It doesn't come on to fans' radar in that scenario. If the team are playing well – or brilliantly, in Liverpool's case – the executives have it easy.

Aside from shirt sponsorship, a stadium's naming rights represents the most visible form of a football club's corporatisation. It's there in big ugly letters on the entrance to the ground and on all the road signs nearby. It's this – rather than the comparatively invisible 'official partners' – that's eating into football and its to-be-cherished traditions.

So while other sponsorship keeps a club's income ticking over, let's ditch the idea of flogging off the stadium name. Those who've banked the cheque are only the temporary custodians after all, individuals whose motivation isn't the position and reputation of the club in several decades' time. The short-term financial gain they're happy to accept will never compensate for the damage done over a longer period to that club's integrity. And it's a dent in the integrity of football itself too.

Put simply, selling stadium naming rights is an avenue for clubs which must have a permanent roadblock put in place. I would recommend that once all current and existing deals have expired no club should be able to enter into another such agreement. Each club then has to lodge the permanent, sponsor-free name of their stadium with the FA which, once done, cannot be altered. It would be the football equivalent of registering your newborn baby's name at the register office.

Say goodbye to the Emirates. And hello to New Highbury.

16

Tighten the Rules on Who Can Become an Agent – and on How Much They Can Earn

There are certain professions that get a bad press because particularly bad apples have tarnished the reputation of the entire trade: estate agents, second-hand car salesmen, tabloid journalists…Add to this list the noble vocation of being a football agent.

I don't have a problem with agents. OK, let's clarify that. I don't have a problem with the idea, the *principle*, of agents. If you're a young player and you're going into a contract negotiation, why would you be expected to know about the ins and outs of contracts, all the clauses, sub-clauses and sub-sub-clauses? To get the best deal for you there and then, and the best deal for your long-term career, you'll almost certainly need advice and guidance from a trustworthy representative.

The issue I have is that over the years there have been certain agents who have fleeced players. They've taken too much money from them.

They've taken them to the cleaners. Did they give their clients the best advice? No. Did they have the players' best interests at heart? No. Was it all about making a fast buck? Absolutely.

Agents are just like everybody else: they're trying to make a living. Some are better than others. Some have their players' best interests at heart, while others will be just purely thinking about themselves and their bank balance. But I suppose that's like it is in any walk of life, in any other industry or profession. There will be honourable people and there will be less-than-honourable people.

But agents – whether honourable or not – increasingly run the game these days. They dictate the terms on which the business of football operates. This isn't healthy. For instance, the close proximity of certain clubs and certain agents is having a huge impact on the game (especially when some clubs seem only to deal with particular agents). And I don't think the situation where the same agent can work for both the player and the buying club in the same deal is one that makes any sense at all. To the outsider, to the layman, there seems to be a conflict of interest here. Rather than solely being the player's adviser, these agents are also performing the same role for the organisation that wants to recruit that player. So whose best interest is being looked after in this scenario? And how much power is this giving the agent?

But agents are entitled to act in this way. It's not their problem. The rules allow them to get around what appears to be an obvious conflict. And until there's a law in place to say that they can't work for the club as well as the player, then they're going to carry on doing just that.

The agent isn't necessarily always at fault and yet – collectively, as a profession – they are the ones to be demonised. The ones who are deemed as unscrupulous are, at least, upfront. An experienced player will know what they're getting and it's up to them to control the situation, to steer the relationship.

It's a different matter with younger players who are still wet behind the ears. It's very difficult for them. I'll use myself as an example. I was a young man with no real knowledge of football and its workings. I got into the game late, because I wasn't good enough as a youngster to be signed on schoolboy forms and ended up having a trial at Norwich during my GCSE year. I went into the club on £29.50 a week, with digs and a bus pass, for that first year. For my second season, I moved up to a full £35. My first professional contract was only £175 a week, but I was in Norwich City's first team by then and I would have taken whatever I was told to take. It wasn't about money necessarily. I was still signing contracts within Norwich and I was just happy to be getting an improvement each time. I had progressed into the first team and all I was thinking about was football.

Of course, when I moved to Blackburn that changed. At that point, I did feel that I needed an agent. My first real introduction to the profession was meeting Eric Hall when I was still at Norwich. He was the most visible and well-connected agent in English football in the 1990s, someone who was often on the television or in the papers, unlike the more inconspicuous nature of the profession these days. He was known by his 'Monster, monster' catchphrase and was fond of calling people 'schmucks'. He was a funny guy with a good heart. I liked him, but I never signed terms with him. My dad put a stop to that.

Instead I signed up with a guy from the PFA (Professional Footballers' Association) to represent me, as my dad thought that having the players' union batting for me was the most sensible route at the time. I liked the security of someone negotiating who clearly knew more about contracts than I did. I always used to work on the premise that I would listen to the agent, but would tell him exactly what I wanted. This probably is a totally unremarkable approach, but this way I felt I would still have control of the situation. The final call was always mine.

But I don't necessarily think that that's the case with all players – that they have control over their own affairs. I always felt that it wasn't the agent's responsibility to make the final decision: it was my responsibility. So, when it came to contract renegotiations, it was still my decision whether I was happy with what I was being offered. Ultimately, the player has to work things out for himself.

On 1 April 2015, FIFA de-regulated football agents, having found it too difficult to police all football transfers across the globe, many of which were arranged by non-qualified agents. Instead, it lobbed the ball into the court of individual football associations, with whom individuals now merely had to register. No longer did prospective agents have to sit the notoriously difficult entrance exam, which only around 6 per cent of those sitting it passed. No longer did agents need to take out indemnity insurance. And wannabe representatives didn't have to have any handle on legal matters whatsoever – no knowledge of contract law or anything. Since deregulation, all a prospective agent needs in order to work in the profession is no criminal record, no history of bankruptcy and £500 to cover the registration fee (plus £250 for every year thereafter).

This lifting of legislation changed the agenting landscape. Prior to April 2015, 518 agents were registered with the FA in this country. Within a year of deregulation, that figure had nearly trebled to 1,516. So we're at a juncture where agents carry more power within the game than ever before and yet pretty much anyone can be the one wielding this influence. A kid could be flogging handsets in a branch of Carphone Warehouse today, but tomorrow could be advising a teenage footballer on legal matters. That sounds utterly preposterous to my ears.

The thinking behind deregulation was that, with only around 30 per cent of worldwide football transfers being brokered by licensed agents, too much business was being done in the shadows, in the dark corners, under the counter. By removing the formalities, FIFA opened the floodgates by handing back control of agents to each country's football association, who would publish details of all transfers. By making the ability to become an agent much easier, the logic suggested that the procedure would become a transparent one, resulting in no one needing to circumvent the system.

This is far from a satisfactory state of affairs. A player looking for a new agent will consult the FA's list of agents – those with no criminal record who've coughed up the required 500 quid – and assume that everyone listed on this official document are fine and upstanding members of the community who are also fully conversant with the twists and turns of contract negotiation. They'll assume their new agent knows exactly how the system works. But, with agent numbers trebling in that first deregulated year and growing since, there will be more than a small smattering of agents who don't know what's involved, who are bluffing their way through, who don't have a clue. And players need more help in identifying the chaff among the wheat.

In a multibillion-pound industry, often employing young, starry-eyed, potentially vulnerable kids, it seems madness to not have regulations in the form of fit-and-proper-person tests to show that these individuals are capable of representing players and clubs. They must prove that they have reached a level of competence. The careers and hopes and dreams of talented young people are the collateral damage otherwise. To me, it just seems so obvious that there needs to be an entrance exam before someone can declare themselves to be an agent and can operate as one. After all, in any job you have to do the training, don't you?

My son's at university at the moment. He wants to be a physio so he's studying physiotherapy and is going through a set process to become one. Why doesn't that happen with football agents? Why wouldn't football make it their business to do so? Under the present set-up, the clear opportunity exists for brazen pirates and cowboys to chance their arm. And there are pirates and cowboys – you can't get around that. And these shifty individuals aren't giving the decent agents, of which there are plenty, a good name. It's very unfair; there are a lot of good agents out there.

The problem comes with the ones who are less than scrupulous, the ones whose motivation isn't necessarily the long-term welfare – and career trajectory – of their client. I don't blame these chancers. With the door being left so wide open for them, you can't hold them responsible for seeing a gap and taking the opportunity to earn a fast buck, to make money for themselves and their family. Some people are very creative and capable of doing so and probably are very good at it.

And there is plenty of money to be made. Within two years of deregulation, English football clubs paid £220 million in agents' fees, a 38 per cent increase on the previous 12-month period. During 2019, £501 million was spent on agents' commission worldwide, 20 per cent up on 2018's figure. It's all heading in one direction.

As we try to get our heads around these eye-watering amounts, the so-called super-agents are becoming very rich people indeed, travelling from transfer negotiation to transfer negotiation by private jet. One such agent, Jorge Mendes, was even bought a Greek island by one of his clients – a player by the name of Cristiano Ronaldo.

Mino Raiola, whose clients include Paul Pogba, Zlatan Ibrahimović and Henrikh Mkhitaryan, appears to have trousered a phenomenal amount of cash from one deal in particular. The authors of the book *Football Leaks* claimed that Raiola stood to personally earn up to £41 million from Pogba's £89-million move from Juventus back to Manchester United. Take that figure in. Say it out loud a few times to let it hit home. £41 million. It's an obscene amount of money for brokering a single deal for a footballer. £41 million. It doesn't get any smaller or sound any more reasonable the more times you say it. Forty. One. Million. Pounds.

These hundreds of millions of pounds every year is money that's leaking from the game, that's not being reinvested in infrastructure or training or leagues. Take that £41 million alone. Just imagine the positive benefits of investing anything like that amount of cash at the grassroots level. You could install a fair few 3G and 4G pitches with that kind of spending power.

FIFA has announced plans to curb the activities and revenue streams of these high-earning agents. While a maximum 10 per cent cut of any deal sounds like it's a move in the right direction, I'd go further. I'd agree 10 per cent, but would cap it at £3 million, regardless of the size of the overall fee. This doesn't feel remotely draconian on my part. It remains

> Under the present set-up, the clear opportunity exists for brazen pirates and cowboys to chance their arm. It's very unfair. There are a lot of good agents out there

a hell of a lot of money for putting together a single transfer. In anyone's eyes, it's still a very nice little earner.

While limiting the level of commission from a deal would help to clip the wings of the super-agents and restrict the influence they have over the game, let's not forget their colleagues further down the food chain. They need close monitoring too. For the sake of the sport – let alone the sake of the innocent teenage footballer taking his first tentative steps as a prospective pro – there has to be some control placed upon who can declare themselves to be a football agent. Simply paying for your name to go on a roll-call of official agents is totally insufficient. Being on this list is no proof of endorsement or qualification.

A player needs the security of good advice from someone who knows their onions, who's been stringently tested on all aspects of the business of football, who has a history of doing right by their clients. And there's only one way to ensure this. Bring back the exam. Make it tough to become an agent. Players deserve it. And football does too.

PART FOUR
THE SEASON

Football fans know the rhythm of a season. From August to May, it's also the rhythm of their lives. The build-up to a game, the lull after it, then the climb back up to the next match. They know the points of the season at which the league games come thick and fast. They know when the league programme gets punctuated by various cup competitions. They know when the hope and despair of the transfer window will distract them. And they welcome the breathing space provided by international breaks, a time to come up for air and take stock.

But while the shape and structure of a football season remains largely what it has been for decades, change is constantly nibbling away at its edges. The governing bodies seem reluctant to sit still, to merely keep things ticking over, to be content with all that we already have. Nothing seems to be enough. New ideas and new innovations are ten-a-penny, but whether the main motivation behind each one is the long-term benefit of the game is another matter entirely.

Contradictions abound. We're constantly told of the enduring magic of the FA Cup and yet more and more clubs increasingly treat it as an obstacle rather than an opportunity. Similarly, managers constantly complain about overpacked fixture schedules and yet the authorities continue to expand existing competitions or dream up new ones.

When it comes to the structure of the season and its competitions, football's governing bodies – both domestically and internationally – can certainly do better than they currently are. And here's exactly how...

17
Put Fans First When Scheduling Fixtures

When Tony Adams pulled ball number 20 out of the pot, one particular corner of West Yorkshire would have been thrilled. Their team, Leeds United, had been drawn away to Arsenal in the third round of the 2019–20 FA Cup. The tie was one for romantics of a certain vintage, allowing them to recall the 1972 final when Don Revie's men, thanks to a single goal from Allan 'Sniffer' Clarke, denied the Gunners their second successive triumph. Due to their slide down the leagues in modern times, it had been 17 long years since Leeds had beaten Arsenal. For the fans of 2020, with their side top of the Championship, confidence was high that they could once again overcome the red quarter of north London. It was a chance for Marcelo Bielsa to test his charges against a team that, of late, hadn't exactly been making any fresh contributions to the history books. A scalp was there for the taking and a grand day out in the capital was in prospect.

This euphoria was somewhat dampened three days later when the schedule for the third round was announced. After the bargaining and bartering between the FA and the television companies was done and dusted, it was declared that the tie – one of the tastiest of the round – would be the flagship Monday-night match. All the other ties would be taking place at various points over the weekend, but Leeds fans would need to take time off work to get to the Emirates Stadium. And with the match kicking off just a few minutes before 8pm, the prospects of getting back to West Yorkshire on a weekday night using public transport meant catching the one available train that left London after the match was over. The 11.33pm out of King's Cross would get its (no doubt crammed) cargo of passengers into Leeds Station at the ungodly hour of 2.36am. As long as it was on time, that is.

For those travelling by road, either squeezed on to coaches or into cars, being back in their own beds by around 2am was the earliest they could hope for – if they had a following wind, took no wee breaks and encountered no motorway closures. Once home, it would be a case of setting the alarm, getting no more than a short, fitful sleep and making sure you weren't late for work the next morning.

Sadly, there is nothing particularly unusual about the logistical challenges faced by those Leeds fans. Five days earlier than the Leeds–Arsenal clash, on the traditional New Year's Day schedule of fixtures, fans of Manchester United faced an identical fate: heading back north after an evening kick-off at the Emirates. There was an extra dimension: with it being a bank holiday, these Mancunians were faced with a Sunday service on the rail network. So too were the Leicester fans wanting to head back to the East Midlands after their Boxing Day top-of-the-table clash at Anfield. As you can see, it's a recurrent theme.

It's the fans who feel the raw end of the deal when the kick-off times for the FA Cup are announced. Their excitement is diluted when they find out that their club isn't going to be one of the teams playing at the sacred third-round hour of 3pm. A midday or 5.30pm kick-off simply isn't the same. It used to be a really special afternoon, even – or especially – for those following it on television. You'd be glued to the vidiprinter, anxious to hear of any giant-killings among the 32 ties around the country. Times have changed and we can't go back in such a wholesale manner because of other demands, some of which are, yes, financial. But if fans were asked to vote for their preferred time for their side's cup tie, it would be a landslide for tradition. No doubt about that.

It's possibly more appropriate these days to call the list of cup ties a running order, as the over-whelming factor in scheduling these matches is meeting the demands of the television companies. I appreciate that I now work in the media and that broadcasters are also football's main paymasters, but there has to be a balance struck between acquiescing to what television

> For the Leeds fans, being back in their own beds by 2am was the earliest they could hope for – if they had a following wind, took no wee breaks and encountered no motorway closures

audiences want and ensuring that a fan's journey home from the game itself doesn't become the kind of survivalist challenge you'd usually find Bear Grylls undertaking.

On that FA Cup third-round weekend that culminated with the Arsenal–Leeds match, just nine of the other thirty-one ties took place in the traditional mid-afternoon slot on the Saturday. That's just 28 per cent. That's simply unacceptable – and a slap in the face for the competition's history and heritage. The remaining fixtures were stretched out to satisfy the needs of various television channels – and not exclusively those of UK broadcasters. The Manchester City–Port Vale tie, for instance, was just one match scheduled at a particular time to meet the requirements of overseas channels. Under the terms of the deal, it wasn't shown live to viewers in the UK.

It's a state of affairs that does beg an obvious question: who is the competition actually for?

There are ways that you can placate both the broadcasters and the fans on that particular red-letter time in the domestic football calendar. A fair few third-round games could still be shown live across the weekend with their now customary varied kick-off times, but the majority of ties should continue to be held on the Saturday afternoon.

There are 32 matches at this stage of the competition, after all, so there are plenty to go around. The traditions of the first Saturday in January must be upheld. That precious kick-off time cannot become the exception rather than the rule.

Make these league officials do a recce of the route. Once you've been stuck behind a tractor on the A17, then you know the meaning of true torture

Whether cup tie or league match (and bear in mind that for the 2019–20 season the Premier League introduced the concept of 8.15pm midweek kick-offs), there's an ever-present tension between accommodating a club's loyal following, who diligently shadow their team's every move, and those organisations whose financial input has created the current high-cotton days of football at the top level. It's a pull and push between the armchair fan and the supporter who's at the ground in the flesh. And at the moment, it's not the travelling fans who are getting the upper hand.

Once upon a time, every football fan knew when and where they needed to be. Whether home or away, it was either 3pm on a Saturday or 7.45pm on a Tuesday or Wednesday. Certain days were always sacrosanct, Thursdays in particular, until the emergence of the Europa League. Now the Premier League has started stepping over that particular threshold, happy to offer games in our flagship division on any and every day or night of the week.

To emphasise this, the very first Premier League match of the 2019–20 season was a Friday-night fixture, with newly promoted Norwich City travelling across the country to Liverpool. Now, I don't know whether the administrators who set that as the opening match are aware of the geography of the British Isles, but that journey is a challenging expedition at the best of times, let alone on a Friday evening at the end of the working week. Have these people never driven from Norfolk to Merseyside? Let me tell you, it's 250-odd long, long miles that represent the road to hell. One beautifully smooth motorway linking A to B it is not.

If you made these league officials do a recce of the route, driving up from Norwich on the A47 and the A17 and beyond, I can assure you that they would never, ever, ever put that fixture on a Friday night again. Long car journeys are hard enough to endure, what with the hiked-up petrol prices and overpriced confectionery of service stations on A-roads and motorways. But once you've been stuck behind a tractor on the A17, then you know the meaning of true torture. Having now suffered that particular Friday-night hell, Canaries fans won't want to repeat that trip any time soon. It was a rude awakening for them, to which a 4-1 defeat added extra pain. Welcome back to the Premier League.

To get the full picture, these administrators should also try doing the same journey by rail. You either go via London, which is ridiculous, or you get on a crappy, two-carriage train that goes cross-country, seemingly at a maximum speed of 27mph. And it's the dirtiest train, it really is. You have to travel on it wearing old clothes. I'd love for the league officials to go on this train there and back, before telling us just how happy the ordeal made them. Then we'll accept it.

You could be forgiven for thinking that the fixture list was a product of a super-computer that's never been acquainted with a train timetable or a road atlas of Great Britain

Living in Norfolk, I understand the difficulties of getting to and from anywhere from East Anglia's northern reaches. Take one instance, when I was coming back from Villa Park after an evening commentary. An accident and a closure of the M6, and I was stuck for hours, sitting there stationary at midnight. I eventually got home at 3am.

Of course, I'm not alone in my experience. Football fans across the country will each have a bagful of such stories. But they needn't have. There must be ways that the league fixtures can be drawn up where a little more common sense is applied to help the loyal supporter.

For instance, doesn't it make perfect sense to schedule local derbies during intense periods of fixtures over Christmas and Easter, when the frequency of games already places demands on fans' time and money? You'd think it was unquestionably logical, but it doesn't always happen. Take the fixtures scheduled over Easter 2020, for example. Some of these represented an exercise in incredulity. While the likes of Burnley taking on Sheffield United and Watford travelling to Chelsea were perfectly reasonable trips, the fact that Manchester City ventured all the way down to Southampton, while Bournemouth – just 35 miles down the M27 from St Mary's Stadium – were simultaneously doing the journey in reverse to head up to Old Trafford was utterly baffling. In fact, I'm going to deploy capital letters here to highlight the idiocy: it made NO SENSE WHATSOEVER. The obvious scenario should have been the two respective local derbies taking place instead that weekend. And the London sides playing each other too. Surely.

Let's also give much more consideration as to whether certain league games should be scheduled in midweek or at weekends. Imagine you're a Newcastle fan. At least until Sunderland and/or Middlesbrough return to the top flight, you're going to be spending plenty of time on the road or rails en route to and from away games. That's an inevitability. It goes with the territory of being a loyal foot soldier of the Toon Army. You're a victim of geography in this respect. So why not eliminate unnecessary headaches by making it as easy as possible for the travelling Magpie? That would mean saving the away matches closest to Tyneside – those in Burnley, Sheffield, Manchester and on Merseyside – for midweek games, while scheduling the most logistically difficult ones (such as the trio of away games on the south coast, plus the five in the capital) for Saturday afternoons. After all, that's when more time is available to accommodate these marathon journeys there and back again. That's not a crazy suggestion, is it? From where I'm stood, that sounds like the simple application of common sense.

Sometimes, though, common sense seems in short supply. In fact, you could be forgiven for thinking that the fixture list was a product of a super-computer that's never been acquainted with a train timetable or a road atlas of Great Britain – a piece of hardware that thinks Burnley is just down the road from Brighton, or south London is within easy reach of Sheffield. But I'm assured that there is still very much a human hand behind the drawing-up of the fixtures. I appreciate that it's a mind-boggling task if so, but it still leads to infuriating match-ups at inopportune times. And if you're one of those poor souls with no hope of getting home before daybreak after an evening kick-off, you'd probably feel justified in carrying around a voodoo doll of the fixture list supremo into which you stick a pin every time just getting to and from a game required a Herculean effort.

So the best cure for this particular ill of modern football is to force the administrators to recognise and amend some of their seriously ridiculous and illogical scheduling. Before the fixture list is agreed and published, let's insist that they put themselves in the shoes of the typical fan to undertake the same journey at the same hour on the same day of the week, to the same budget and using the same mode of transport.

Then we'll see how they like getting home at some time around 3am, needing to set the alarm clock for just four hours later, while wondering why they have so little change left from buying a service-station chocolate bar…

18
Make the FA Cup Special Again

The FA Cup is certainly in the Sutton blood. My dad played in the competition during his career with Norwich City, Chester and Carlisle United, while my brother John appeared for Millwall in their 2004 quarter-final replay win over Tranmere Rovers. And my son Ollie has played in goal for ninth-tier Wroxham in the FA Cup preliminary round.

My own first-ever FA Cup tie was for Norwich against Neil Warnock's Notts County in the fifth round in 1992. We won 3-0 and I scored twice. That was a huge deal for a young man of 18. One of my most memorable goals for Norwich was in the next round against Southampton, who had my future Blackburn team-mates Tim Flowers and Alan Shearer in their line-up. It was a real bloodbath; Southampton had Matt Le Tissier and Barry Horne sent off. We won it in extra-time when I redirected a miscued shot with my head. It looped over Tim and in. He's always maintained that I didn't mean it, but I clearly did.

We reached the semi-finals but lost to Sunderland at Hillsborough after I missed a really good chance during the game. That scuffed shot is something I still think about now, nearly 30 years on. I never won the

FA Cup, that was pretty much the closest I came. I did play in another FA Cup semi-final when I was at Chelsea, this time against Newcastle in 2000, but came off injured at half-time. Then I was dropped for the final by Gianluca Vialli – and quite rightly so as I was performing pretty awfully at the time.

But it wasn't just from playing in the competition that the magic of the FA Cup was sprinkled on me. The only game my dad ever took me to – other than me being taken to watch him play – was the 1980 final between West Ham and Arsenal, when Trevor Brooking scored the solitary goal with a header that can only be described as 'stooping', and Willie Young cynically chopped the legs of the teenage Paul Allen out from under him when he was through on goal. Obviously it was terrific being at the old Wembley to see the match in the flesh, but whether you were there in person or not, the final was always a big deal – regardless of who the teams were.

Are the memories so long-lasting these days? Will today's FA Cup finals be so wistfully remembered by the current generation?

From watching on television back home in Norfolk, 120-odd miles away from that corner of north-west London, all those classic finals have been burned on to my memory. Alan Sunderland scoring that last-gasp winner for Arsenal against Manchester United in '79. Ricky Villa's dribble and winning goal in the '81 replay against Manchester City. Norman Whiteside's brilliant curling shot in extra-time in the '85 final. Coventry doing over Spurs in '87, partly thanks to Keith Houchen's diving header. Having watched history unfold on our television screens, these memories became indelible. But are the memories so long-lasting these days? Will today's FA Cup finals be so wistfully remembered by the current generation?

Like, I guess, many people of my vintage, when I was young the FA Cup always seemed to be the biggest event of the season. Of course, it was always important to win the league title, but that one particular Saturday afternoon in May felt bigger than anything else in domestic football. There was so much build-up on the television, with special editions of *A Question of Sport* and such like. It was like Christmas Day. The coverage was intense.

The day of the FA Cup final doesn't feel so special anymore. The old European Cup was big (and English clubs won more than their fair share when I was a kid), but the Wembley final was arguably still more important to the English football fan. In the era of the Champions League, however, the FA Cup feels like a secondary cup competition. When traditionalists – and I think I am a traditionalist when it comes to football – look at the way that a lot of the top clubs treat the FA Cup, we have to concede that it's not the big trophy it once was.

And, as we move further away from what's perceived to be the golden age of the FA Cup, current players won't have grown up regarding the competition as special – let alone sacred. As time continues its unstoppable march, they'll be ever more distanced from its history and its heritage. That connection to our premier domestic cup competition will be lost.

When I played in that quarter-final for Norwich against Southampton in 1992, there was a full house at Carrow Road. It was absolutely rammed, with the cracking atmosphere that night showing exactly what the competition meant back then. These days, even the most short-sighted onlooker wouldn't fail to notice the rows and rows of empty seats at cup ties, even in the latter rounds. In the fourth round of the 2019–20 FA Cup, the all-Premier League tie between

Burnley and Norwich drew a measly 8,071 fans. All ways round, that's a depressing statistic. The corresponding league fixture between the two clubs the previous September saw a crowd close to 20,000, almost two and a half times the cup-tie attendance. Meanwhile, as the two Premier League teams sought a place in the fifth round, down in League One, Ipswich Town were entertaining Lincoln City in front of a crowd of 18,795 at Portman Road, almost 11,000 more than had taken their seats at Turf Moor.

Sadly, these attendances tell us that the FA Cup is not the draw that it once was. And you can lay much of the blame for this at the doors of Premier League clubs.

The big clubs don't seem to care about the FA Cup – or, at least, they don't invest it with the appropriate level of importance. They don't disregard it, but they do disrespect it. You can't tell me now that, when clubs play their reserve side in the early rounds, they're treating the tradition of the cup with care. Virtually every Premier League team makes multiple changes to their line-ups, electing to rest their best players and save them for what's deemed to be the superior competition – the cash cow that is the Premier League. Bournemouth once made a full eleven changes to their team for an FA Cup tie against Birmingham City, while Leicester went to Newport County in 2019 having played a much-weakened side.

That particular decision somewhat backfired on their manager, though, with Claude Puel losing his job a few weeks later, partly off the back of that defeat in south Wales. He should have taken more care. Self-preservation is just one reason why managers should value a strong cup run, ideally ending with lifting the trophy at Wembley come May. Winning it can prolong a manager's shelf life. Arsène Wenger hung on to his job for years on the back of FA Cup victories. When you can clearly see the good that taking the cup seriously can do for a manager, for his reputation and for his job, why aren't they trying harder? Why aren't these managers picking the strongest teams?

The FA Cup took a bit of a hit in 1999–2000, the season in which Alex Ferguson withdrew Manchester United in favour of going to Brazil to play in the Club World Championship (a similar dilemma to that faced by Jürgen Klopp in 2019 when Liverpool were double-booked in the Club World Championship and the League Cup). Back in 2000, it was an understandable move and I don't blame Sir Alex. But he should never have been put in a position where he had to choose. In such circumstances, there has to be an alternative that can be worked out. After all, it's a sad day for football when the biggest club in the country doesn't take part. Chelsea

> The FA Cup is not the draw it once was. And you can lay much of the blame for this at the doors of Premier League clubs

won the FA Cup that year, but could their victory ever be regarded as being of a similar worth to victories in other years as Manchester United, the dominant team of that era, were absent?

The particular circumstances for Sir Alex that season were a one-off. Elsewhere, managers have a choice. They can talk until they're blue in the face about squad rotation and giving other players an opportunity, but when they say these things, who are they kidding? They're trying to pull the wool over the eyes of their clubs' fans, all of whom would love a good cup run. I understand about the money, that survival in the Premier League – perhaps even a high-placed finish – is crucial to the club's financial situation. As West Ham's Karren Brady has pointed out, 'you don't have to be an accountant to judge that winning the FA Cup and being rewarded with around £3 million doesn't begin to compare with the riches on offer in the Premier League'. Brady's quite correct. The 2020 FA Cup winners banked £3.6 million for their efforts. The previous season, though, all but one top-flight club received a payout from the Premier League in excess of £100 million. Only relegated Huddersfield failed to be awarded a nine-digit amount. But there's no need to feel sorry for them. They still banked a cool £96.6 million for finishing bottom of the league. Their tears dried quickly.

But whatever happened to glory for glory's sake? The game has become too influenced by finance and that's why the FA Cup is not important, or not *as* important, to many of the big clubs. Do we understand that? Yes. Does it make it right? Absolutely not.

Maybe it's the owners giving managers the instruction that 'We're not bothered by the FA Cup. We need to prioritise the Premier League. That Champions League place is more important.' I'm speculating here. I don't know. But I wouldn't be surprised if, in certain clubs, that's how the conversation goes behind closed doors.

It's not the fault of the Champions League. It's just down to the way the big boys of the Premier League view it. But the Champions League only affects the top four clubs from the previous season. What about the rest of the top-flight clubs? Why do they undervalue the FA Cup?

Solid mid-table clubs like Everton aren't in serious threat of relegation. They're good-enough teams whose continued existence in the top flight isn't really in jeopardy. For them, the FA Cup surely represents the best opportunity to win a meaningful trophy. So why don't they give it a proper shot? The culprits are everywhere. Virtually every Premier League club is guilty of fielding a significantly weakened eleven.

To me, that mindset is baffling. It distances a club from its support as they're not giving the supporters what they should be. And the reputation of the competition suffers as a result. If you asked the average football fan about their memories of their team, a good FA Cup run would outweigh an eighth- or ninth-place finish in the Premier League. And if that run took them all the way to Wembley glory for the first time, it would be the greatest season in their history. And fans want seasons to remember. A campaign that finished with lifting that famous trophy would undoubtedly qualify as one.

Just ask the people in and around Wigan Athletic. They might have got relegated from the Premier League in 2013, but it was also the season they won the FA Cup. You ask the players who played that day, you ask Roberto Martínez the manager, you ask the Wigan fans what their greatest moment was and it would be that afternoon at Wembley when they

> Compared to the modest financial reward of winning the FA Cup, Huddersfield banked a cool £96.6 million for finishing bottom of the Premier League. Their tears dried quickly

shocked Manchester City. They treated the competition with greater respect than others and in the process created an occasion that will be remembered for ever. More of those indelible memories.

It reaches down to Championship clubs, too. Having made nine changes to his team for the third-round tie with Chelsea in January 2020, Nottingham Forest boss Sabri Lamouchi justified the 2-0 defeat with candour. A draw or win meant at least one more match to add to a season dedicated to returning the club to the top flight for the first time in 21 years. 'We can't win the FA Cup,' he said, before suggesting that not putting in the greatest effort to win the tie was supported across the club, including the fans. What a sad state of affairs. Giving up before you've started. I wonder what Cloughie – who famously never won the Cup as player or manager – would think of that.

On 26 January 2020, in the wake of Liverpool's 2-2 fourth-round draw with League One Shrewsbury Town, Jürgen Klopp dropped a bombshell when he explained his plans for the replay, a match that fell within the new, albeit modest, mid-season break for top-flight clubs. 'The Premier League asked us to respect the winter break,' he explained. 'That's what we will do. If the FA doesn't respect that, then we cannot change it. We will not be there.'

Insisting that his first-team players wouldn't be asked to forgo the break – and that it would fall to Liverpool's youth team to fulfil the replay – wasn't so much of a surprise. What was particularly galling was the fact that Klopp himself wouldn't be taking charge of the youngsters for the replay; the reins were being handed to U23 coach Neil Critchley. I've always had a lot of time for Klopp, but absenting himself from FA Cup duties suggested some serious disdain towards the competition. It also showed a lack of respect towards Shrewsbury and their manager Sam Ricketts. Would he have acted in the same way ahead of a dead rubber in the Champions League group stage? Of course not.

And let's not ignore something utterly obvious. A replay – and the whole unsavoury episode – could have been avoided had Klopp, whose side at that point of the season had only failed to win one of their 23 league matches, simply picked a fuller strength starting eleven for the first match. Instead, it wasn't until after Shrewsbury had brought the score level in the 75th minute that the likes of Mo Salah and Roberto Firmino rose from the bench to join the fray.

So what's the answer to weakened sides devaluing the competition? Perhaps a quota system needs to be introduced, whereby a certain number of players who played in the Premier League the previous week have to be picked for the FA Cup tie. That would show that managers actually did respect and value our premier domestic cup competition. And it would reinvest the cup with the kudos it deserves.

There's another remedy to arrest the competition's slide and to get the best players back playing in it – and not just in the latter stages. It appears the pure glory of winning the thing isn't enough these days, so you've got to make the prize at the end worth something that will cause clubs to think twice. You've got to turn their heads, offering something they really want, that they really value. And if the reward for winning the FA Cup was a Champions League place the following season, those heads would be spinning round to pay attention.

> Call an end to semi-finals being played at Wembley. Let's return them to neutral grounds around the country. It's where they belong

Overnight, Premier League sides would treat the competition with greater respect and would undoubtedly react by putting out stronger sides. Managers would pick their best players without a second thought. It's a logical step to take and it would make a real difference. We'd get our FA Cup back.

Yes, there's the argument that the league position has been earned right across the season and so a Champions League berth is just reward for that, but this measure would raise the profile and value of the FA Cup in an instant. It would change the perceptions of managers and owners alike. Being a legitimate route to reaching the Champions League would make it a trophy worth pursuing.

There's another cure to help make the FA Cup special again. It's a simple one – and easy to enact. Call an end to the semi-finals being played at Wembley. These shouldn't be played at the national stadium.

Let's return the semis to neutral grounds around the country. It's where they belong. It's the common-sense approach.

Going back to my childhood, only the final was played at Wembley. It was a big deal to get there. Does it feel like the same level of reward when you've already played the semi-final on that same pitch? It can't do. It cheapens it, it demeans it. Previously, the final was a one-off and, having negotiated a winding route through five rounds of the competition, you'd earned the right to walk on to the hallowed Wembley turf. If you'd reached the final, you'd absolutely deserved it.

The semi-finals had an identity of their own back then, when they were played at the likes of Highbury or Maine Road or Hillsborough, where I played with Norwich in the match we ultimately lost to Sunderland. These semis weren't a dress rehearsal for the final. They were standalone spectacles in their own right. We can all recall that fantastic seven-goal see-saw of a semi at Villa Park in 1990 when Crystal Palace knocked out the seemingly unbeatable Liverpool. And then there was that pulsating match between Middlesbrough and Chesterfield at Old Trafford seven years later, when the third-tier side bravely held their Premier League counterparts to a 3-3 draw and earned a replay.

Holding semi-finals at Wembley dilutes the allure and mystique of the final itself. If the authorities stopped this reaching the final would have a stronger meaning to a player – and to a football fan, too. Many of the dominant teams are from the north, so why should their fans have to pay more money to get to a venue down south for the semi-final? Holding a semi-final at a neutral ground that's roughly equidistant from both teams is fair on everyone. And there can be transportation issues, as Manchester City found in 2019 when they failed to sell their ticket allocation for their semi-final against Brighton, with many supporters concerned they couldn't get home that night via public transport due to a 5.30pm kick-off – and, of course, the possibility of extra-time. A trip to Wembley might be a nice day out and it absolutely is. It's a wonderful stadium with lovely facilities. But a semi-final is not the same as a final. A final means so much more.

I recognise and understand the clamour for tickets and that some fans wouldn't be happy if they didn't get one for a semi-final at a smaller stadium than Wembley, but I always thought that a neutral ground that wasn't Wembley was the more logical option. Although I never experienced it, it was clear that the pride always came from reaching Wembley. That was the final game of the season, the big occasion. And if it was your captain who was proudly lifting the FA Cup, the lap of honour was the crowning moment. It's obvious that only the match which decides it all should be played at the biggest stadium.

It's the final destination.

MY TOP TEN **FA CUP MOMENTS**

Whether as a player, spectator or television viewer, all those FA Cup memories are permanently etched into my brain. Here are my most treasured ones, in no particular order…

WEST HAM UPSET ARSENAL

The first match I ever went to was the 1980 final. I don't know how it all materialised – I was brought up in Norfolk and wasn't a fan of either club – but I suppose somebody must have given my dad the tickets. I remember us driving down to north London and parking the car, then walking to the game in the sunshine along Wembley Way. Seeing the Twin Towers was extremely special. As a sports-mad youngster – who was, I have to admit, a bit of an anorak – it was a big, big deal. West Ham were in the Second Division back then and against the odds they won. Even though I was only seven at the time, I was aware that they'd caused an upset and beaten the holders. I think it instilled in me a lifelong affiliation with underdogs.

RICKY VILLA'S WINNING GOAL

Talk about iconic FA Cup moments. Villa's second goal of the replay of the '81 final was a brilliantly executed individual goal, a twisting run that saw him turn the Manchester City defence inside out. Everyone has their favourite FA Cup goals, but as an eight-year-old allowed to stay up to watch the replay, that was a jump-off-the-settee moment. And I wasn't even a Spurs supporter. If you said the name 'Ricky Villa' to 100 football fans, 99 of them would talk about that goal. It's a little bit harsh to only be remembered for those few seconds of your career, because he achieved much more than that. He was a terrific footballer. But, of course, you could be remembered for far worse things than one of the greatest goals ever scored at Wembley! To decide a final with a goal like that, late on, was amazing. You have to say some finals are pretty bland, but that certainly was an eye-watering moment.

WIMBLEDON DENY LIVERPOOL THE DOUBLE

Everybody loves an underdog but, as a 15-year-old television viewer, I felt there was no way that Bobby Gould's Wimbledon side were going to upset newly crowned league champions Liverpool in the 1988 final. Absolutely no way. The two sides were poles apart in both flair and style – Liverpool had Peter Beardsley, John Barnes and Ray Houghton, while Wimbledon had the likes of Vinnie Jones, Dennis Wise and John Fashanu. Obviously, to reach the final, you've got to be a capable team. It was just that the Londoners were rather rough and ready. Their brand of football wasn't to everybody's taste, but it worked for them – although I suspect that if VAR had existed back then, they might not have made it as far as Wembley. On the day, Lawrie Sanchez's glancing header and Dave Beasant's penalty save were all that were needed. As John Motson said, 'the Crazy Gang have beaten the Culture Club'. The pug-ugly underdogs had become the dog's bollocks.

MY FIRST-EVER GOAL IN THE FA CUP

This was the point at which I felt I'd truly arrived in professional football. It was the fifth found of the 1991–92 FA Cup and I was making my FA Cup debut. We were at home against Neil Warnock's Notts County, another team mired in the lower reaches of the old First Division. I knew the importance of the FA Cup to Norwich, a team who'd never won the competition, and we had a great opportunity to reach the last eight. Just to play in the FA Cup was a proud moment, but then scoring a couple in a comfortable 3-0 win – the second one a diving header – was a fantastic feeling. Having been rejected by Norwich at the age of 12 but then getting in through the back door, that made it all the more special. The magic of the FA Cup seemed to hang around Carrow Road; the following Saturday, we beat Liverpool in the league by the same 3-0 scoreline.

LIVERPOOL'S CREAM SUITS

The whole nation will remember the coordinated cream Armani suits that Liverpool's squad wore as they strolled around the pitch ahead of the 1996 final against arch rivals Manchester United. Can anyone remember any other pre-final attire at all? They were the Spice Boys – the likes of Jamie Redknapp, Robbie Fowler, Jason McAteer and David James. Some of them, such as Redknapp, set the look off with expensive sunglasses too. It was a bad idea, but fair play to them for trying to carry it off. While it made them figures of mild fun, they had plenty of really good players and so their posing beforehand couldn't be blamed for their 1-0 defeat; it wasn't the suits that lost them the game. It wasn't the most riveting match and the fact that it's the suits that dominate the neutral viewer's memories of that particular final – and not Eric Cantona's sumptuous double-sealing strike – says something, doesn't it?

RONNIE RADFORD'S MONSTROUS GIANT-KILLING STRIKE

This particular goal, from the third round in 1972, is everything the FA Cup is about – a non-league team, their top-flight opponents, a pile-driver of a goal and a pitch invasion by a load of kids wearing parkas. I wasn't alive when Ronnie Radford unleashed the 30-yarder that meant Southern League Hereford United equalised against mighty Newcastle

United, but I've see it so many times. I can't think of many better goals in FA Cup history. It is the ultimate piece of footage, a wonder-strike made all the more impressive by the awful state of the pitch, around which a sell-out crowd crammed together. I'm possibly a little ashamed that I don't know more about Ronnie Radford – where he played before he joined Hereford, where he ended up after. But nonetheless he retains a place in the hearts of us FA Cup romantics. When you mention him, you're mentioning the FA Cup.

RYAN GIGGS' WONDER GOAL

Just one of the greatest goals ever scored in the competition, made all the sweeter for it coming in the semi-final replay of 1999 against their great foes, Arsenal. Down to ten men after Roy Keane's dismissal, this was Manchester United from an era when they could dig deep and show great resolve; Peter Schmeichel saved a stoppage-time penalty from Dennis Bergkamp to keep them in the tie. In extra-time, Giggs collected the ball in his own half before singlehandedly destroying the Gunners' defence and flashing a spectacular shot past David Seaman. He was a wing wizard and, of course, he didn't score this preposterous goal against an ordinary team. This was Arsenal with their famously ungenerous 'Thou shalt not pass' backline. To a man they were all brilliant defenders, but Giggs strolled past them as if they weren't there. This was the goal that put United in the final and that kept those treble dreams alive.

WREXHAM KNOCK OUT ARSENAL

The Racecourse Ground was not the best place for the league champions to come to in the cup in 1992 and with good reason. On paper, it was no contest, but this full-strength Arsenal side headed back to London with glum faces on the back of a 2-1 defeat to Fourth

Division Wrexham. They had led at half-time, but two goals in two minutes in the second half did for them. Everybody talks about Mickey Thomas in the context of this game and while his Exocet of a free kick was a terrific strike, it was actually Steve Watkin who put the Welsh team through. I couldn't tell you if Spurs beat Arsenal that season. I couldn't tell you if Liverpool beat Arsenal that season. But I could tell you that Wrexham beat Arsenal that season. That's the power of the FA Cup to create memories that remain crystal clear nearly 30 years on.

GERRARD'S EQUALISER TAKES IT TO PENALTIES

Steven Gerrard's career at Liverpool was phenomenal, the way he dragged the team through over the years. The Cup final of 2006 was an example of this. Having gone two up early on, and then leading 3-2 into stoppage time, West Ham probably thought the cup was theirs. But they didn't legislate for Gerrard's 35-yarder to bring the score to 3-3 and take the match into extra-time, and ultimately a penalty shoot-out. Big players step up in the big moments. He had already done it in Istanbul the previous year, and this strike was another special one. Not many people would back themselves from that far out. 'What the hell are you doing? Why are you shooting from there?' But the technique was exquisite. You sensed the cup was heading to Merseyside right there and then. Watching it on television, I knew that it was the game-changing moment. It was miracle stuff.

WRIGHTY vs MANCHESTER UNITED

We're all aware of Ian Wright's reputation now thanks to his terrific scoring record at Arsenal, but back in 1990 he was an up-and-coming young player at Crystal Palace. He was on the bench in the FA Cup final, having only just come back from a leg break, but with Palace 2-1 down, Steve Coppell threw him into the fray. Within three minutes he'd equalised and then in extra-time he put Palace in front. He turned the game on its head. United were terrified of him, and quite rightly so. Talk about drama. He was hungry and in this performance showed the enthusiasm for the game that he retained throughout his career. It's another great FA Cup story. His career wasn't mapped out at a young age and he's a great example of having to really work at it. And nobody believed that he was going to make the difference when he came on. Other than him, of course. If only Mark Hughes hadn't equalised to make it 3-3 and set up a replay, it might have been the greatest FA Cup final story ever.

19

Improve the Credibility of International Tournaments

I was a little too young – just a couple of months beyond my fifth birthday – to really remember the 1978 World Cup in Argentina. But I've gained a sense of its occasion and identity from the footage I've watched since: Scotland's near miss, the Dutch scoring extraordinary goals from crazy distances, all that ticker-tape cascading down on to the pitches…

The first World Cup I truly recall was four years later in 1982, which fortuitously was England's first appearance in the finals for twelve years. To a football-crazy nine-year-old, it was an extraordinary concept, with live matches on the television seemingly every afternoon when I got home from school and then, as long as I behaved myself, I could watch another one in the evening. It was an exotic experience, with scratchy pictures beamed in from glamorous-sounding Spanish cities like Bilbao and Valencia, Gijón and Valladolid. The players oozed exoticism too, whether it was the fiery and passionate Italians or the laid-back but ridiculously skilful Brazilians. The only downers were unbeaten

England's elimination after the second group stage and my hero Trevor Francis only getting a couple of goals. The player everyone was now pretending to be in the school playground, Paolo Rossi, got six.

Mexico '86 offered more for the England fan, whether cheering Gary Lineker's march to the Golden Boot or jeering Diego Maradona punching the ball past Peter Shilton. And then came Italia '90 in all its operatic glory – arguably the most intense international tournament of the last 30 years. There was high drama around every turn for teenage England supporters like me. It was my generation's 1966. Except without ultimate glory, of course.

> For one month every four years, you were locked into the World Cup, into this thrilling tournament. Nothing else got a look-in. Nothing else mattered

The World Cup. For one month every four years, you were locked into this thrilling tournament. At school, the only talk was of the previous night's matches or the games to come later that day. Nothing else got a look-in. Nothing else mattered.

The World Cups of my childhood and youth were competitions with a strong sense of place and of identity, tournaments which owed much to being held in countries with a wealth of footballing history and heritage. To each of these countries, it probably felt like football was coming home. That hasn't always been the case with international tournaments since – and certainly won't be when the globe's top footballing nations make their way to the sweatbox of Qatar in late November 2022.

That a nation without a strong footballing heritage was awarded the status of host nation shouldn't automatically ring alarm bells. We all want the game to develop and grow, after all. The unprecedented rescheduling of the tournament from high summer to late autumn obviously raised a few eyebrows, but was done very much for reasons of climate and health. What irks the football fan the most is that Qatar of late has used its wealth to pull up a seat at global football's top table, whether luring superstars to appear in its domestic league or buying up some of the cream of European clubs. You don't have to be the most cynical football fan to join up the dots and suspect that this great spectacle might have been sold to the highest bidder.

It isn't Qatar's fault that it was awarded the 2022 World Cup. It's the decision-makers who need to be held to account. Will the tournament itself unite football fans? I've no doubt it will be embraced to some degree. World Cups always are. But was there an option on the table with better facilities and a better climate at the right time of year? Big competitions are never going to suit everybody and there will always be holes that get picked every time. But there's no getting away from it: Qatar was an extremely strange choice. So has the World Cup – *the* biggest football competition, possibly the biggest sporting competition, on the planet – done itself some damage with this decision? Time will tell.

> I love a tournament that's held in a single country. It gives the competition a clear, singular identity, feeding into that nation's history and culture and people

This isn't the only international football tournament to provoke some quizzical looks when its details were announced. In 2012, UEFA head honcho Michel Platini announced that the 2020 European Championships wouldn't be awarded to a single country. Instead, to commemorate the 60th anniversary of the tournament, Platini declared that it would take an unprecedented form: a dozen countries would come together to be joint hosts in a one-off, pan-continental affair. He described this as 'romantic'.

I never envisaged a time when we'd be having the European Championships held right across the continent in so many different countries. Yes, we're used to clubs playing from Porto to Prague in the Champions League – and I'm a huge fan of the competition – but at the international level you expect to be anchored down in one country, two at most.

Personally, I love a tournament that's held in a single country. Again, it gives the competition that clear, singular identity, feeding into that nation's history and culture and people. Take the last World Cup in Russia in 2018. In advance, it was portrayed in a certain way – and an ultimately unfair way. For whatever reason, we were told the people wouldn't be welcoming and that we'd get a rough deal. Some of the more nervous travellers even thought they might be shot. But it wasn't like that at all. The people were terrifically welcoming and friendly, and the tournament itself was brilliantly organised. It was first class. And I was in the privileged position of being able to travel around as part of my broadcasting work with 5 Live, visiting fascinating cities like Kazan, Rostov and St Petersburg and learning their history. It was a wonderful experience.

At the time of writing, in the months preceding the 2020 Euros, for me the competition isn't emitting the same warm feeling as tournaments past. It seems to lack the identity that single-country tournaments are blessed with. The schedule is too unfocused, too diffuse. The effect is like being the ball inside a pinball machine, with teams and fans being pinged all over the map.

At the draw, some teams were put at a distinct advantage for the group matches. The likes of England, Italy, Germany, the Netherlands, Denmark and Spain would all playing their three matches on home turf, respectively Wembley, Rome, Munich, Amsterdam, Copenhagen and Bilbao. Each of the other 18 teams would be based in two different countries during the round-robin stage.

Take Wales, for instance. Drawn in Group A, their group matches would be spread between Rome and Baku, two cities nearly 2,000 miles apart. Were the Welsh to replicate – or even better – their performance in the 2016 competition, their travels would have barely begun. Qualification from the group stage could have meant a trip to Amsterdam, London, Bilbao or Bucharest. If they reached the quarter-finals, it could be back to Rome or Baku, or on to St Petersburg or Munich. If the final four beckoned as it did last time around, only then would they be settled in one location – the familiar turf of Wembley for the semi and the final.

So if Wales were to make the latter stages, their passage could well have been secured by playing in as many as five different countries across thirty days, totting up almost nine thousand air miles in the process. That's pure lunacy, isn't it? A high-reputation international football tournament is supposed to be a test of skill, prowess and tactical sharpness on a football pitch, not a trial of human survival and endurance.

By contrast, in reaching the final of Euro '96, the Czech Republic only had to shuttle between Old Trafford, Anfield, Villa Park and Wembley. Winners Germany had even less travelling to undertake. Having played their first four matches in Manchester, they had just a single 200-mile trip down to north London for the semi-final. Now that's the way to avoid fatigue.

While we might be concerned about the physical condition of players and their levels of tiredness, let's not forget about the struggles of the dedicated fans here. Once again, it looks as if no one's thought about them at all. Unlike the players, they wouldn't be experiencing the smooth comforts of first-class travel and five-star accommodation. For them, planning for the 2020 Euros presented a logistical challenge and, in many cases, a financial struggle that their credit-card balances might be feeling the effects of for a couple of years. After all, you can bet your bottom dollar that the airlines and hoteliers of Europe would be doing their utmost to offer some genuine cut-price deals that month. Not...

> A tournament should be ruthless. There should only be places for those who've truly earned them. It must be a measure of the very best

Speaking of which, let's not forget the impact a multinational tournament has on the planet, thanks to all those short-haul flights buzzing across the continent's skies, carrying cargoes of teams, fans and the media from departure lounge to arrivals hall over and over and over. The carbon footprint of the competition is absolutely horrendous and not at all what a major sport organisation should be encouraging.

As well as the geography, in future there are going to be issues with the maths. In 2016, the number of qualifying teams for the Euro finals was increased by 50 per cent to 24, a figure retained for 2020. In 2026, the World Cup will expand by the same percentage to a distinctly overweight 48 teams. I have issues with this ballooning expansion.

Is the quality of the tournament, the end product, actually *improved* by having this many participants? The finals – whether the World Cup or the Euros – should represent the very best teams who've battled their way to the competition's denouement. This is the purpose of the qualifying stages, after all: to separate the wheat from the chaff, the strong from the weak. Right from the off, a tournament should be ruthless. There should only be places for those who've truly earned them. It must be a measure of the very best. By opening the finals to a broader selection of teams, there has to be an unwelcome dilution of this. It's inevitable.

It's all very well saying you're widening the tournament to be more inclusive, but people don't want boring group games where we know the result before the game starts. It's not a dissimilar state of affairs to that of the 2019 Rugby World Cup. It was a great competition up to a point, but you could have named the quarter-finalists before a single oval ball was thrown.

The smaller footballing nations will say 'We're getting a chance to play in the World Cup. That's great.' A couple of weeks later, they're heading home after getting tonked four times in the pool stage. That's not the greatest experience – and it's a depressingly predictable one. We don't want predictability. We don't want games that fail to offer any competition or shock value. We want to be smashed round the head with a shovel right from the off.

Tournaments need to be credible in every single aspect. Whether there is credibility in the qualifying rounds is a moot point. This time around, the four final qualifying berths for the Euros weren't a play-off between those countries who finished third in the qualifying groups. Instead, they were reserved for those who performed best in the new Nations League.

But once those who had already qualified for the Euros were discounted, the play-offs became a route for teams who had not only failed to qualify outright in the conventional way at the first time of asking, but who had also actually finished bottom of their Nations League group. Cue the likes of the Repulic of Ireland and Iceland getting a *third* bite at the Euros qualification cherry.

Like the 2020 Euros, the 2026 World Cup will also take a multinational shape. But at least the tournament, split between the United States, Canada and Mexico, is being shared by countries with a couple of common borders. Nevertheless, there are some potentially long flights to be made from the depths of Mexico up into Canada. It's a long way from Veracruz to Vancouver. Another hefty carbon footprint.

Again, though, why isn't there a single host? Both Mexico and the United States have hosted it on their own before and shown their infrastructure can cope. Maybe this time Canada should have been given the reins. After all, if Qatar can be the single host, why not Canada? To me, it smacks of trying to keep everybody happy. But in the end, are we getting a better product? Will it add itself to the classic World Cups of decades past? That has to be the bottom line, the overwhelming objective.

To make these tournaments more credible, to make them gripping spectacles, to give them the best chance of being classic competitions, I have three prescriptions.

1. Do not share the love when it comes to awarding host country status. Don't divide the privilege across several countries. Ideally, make it a singular tournament with a clear cultural identity. Two countries could co-host if neither has the stadia and infrastructure to go it alone; Euro 2012, split between Poland and Ukraine, was a success, after all. But definitely no more than two host nations sharing the load.

2. The best international tournaments tend to have been held in countries steeped in the beautiful game. These are the countries that deserve the prize. New host countries are welcome to bid, of course, but they must prove themselves fit for purpose. The right to host can't simply be given to the highest bidder.

3. Reduce the number of qualifying nations. Make the competition as strong as it can be. Be ruthless. Be definitive. Make it count from the very first day.

With these guiding principles, we can get international tournaments back to the classic sporting events they used to be. The next generation need to forge their own memories. It's time to give them their own Italia '90.

20

Stop Moaning About There Being Too Many Games

'The schedule doesn't make sense. It's absurd for all the teams. Of course, there are teams that have three days between matches, but I don't know the particular reason why it's us who have less hours. But it's a concern for all the managers and all the players.'

Nuno Espírito Santo wasn't too happy about how the Premier League fixtures fell over Christmas 2019. And, yes, while his Wolves side had, at 45 hours, the shortest gap between the first two post-Christmas matches of any team, many other clubs only had 48 hours between theirs. Having just three fewer hours to recover really shouldn't make an amazing difference at this level. After all, these are sportsmen at the peak of fitness and conditioning. It was simply how the fixture cookie crumbled.

With Wolves facing both Manchester City and Liverpool during that period, they were always going to be beholden to the timings and demands of television. And what Nuno neglected to mention was that Wolves had had a six-day break before that first post-Christmas game, when a quartet of other clubs only had four days' grace. Swings and roundabouts.

If they were still with us, legendary managers like Bob Paisley and Brian Clough would surely be chuckling at Nuno's comments. In 1976–77 – as they marched to the league title, the FA Cup final and European Cup glory – Paisley's Liverpool side played no fewer than 62 games over 284 days. This works out at an average of one every four-and-a-half days, sustained across a nine-month season. They didn't manage this with a sizeable squad either; the league title, for instance, was secured using just 17 players.

Of those players, Phil Neal missed just one of those sixty-two games. Ray Clemence and Emlyn Hughes went one better, playing every single match. And all three fitted in appearances for England during that season too.

While an extraordinary achievement, it wasn't a one-off. Two years later, as they scooped both the League Cup and the European Cup, Clough's Nottingham Forest went one better, fighting their way through a 63-game season. Two of their number – Peter Shilton and John Robertson, my old coach at Celtic – played in each and every match. Back in the day, a manager would put out a full-strength side without fail, no matter the competition, no matter the quality of the opposition. The concept of squad rotation was some years off.

Although I've never played anything close to 60 matches in a single campaign, I do know what a 42-game league season feels like when you're vying for the title. We won the Premier League at Blackburn in the last season before the number of top-flight clubs was trimmed down to 20. It was tough, both physically and mentally. It felt relentless, with no time to sit and admire the view from the top of the table. The quest required the ultimate focus and application – although we twice did ourselves an inadvertent favour by going out of the UEFA Cup to Trelleborg at the first time of asking, and then repeating the trick against Newcastle in the third round of the FA Cup. That eased the burden. But slogging it through those long, dark months, before securing the title in the sunshine of the season's final day, meant the taste of success was even sweeter. Finishing top of the heap is not meant to be easy, anyway. You have to go the full nine yards. You really have to earn it.

Since then, of course, the Premier League season has consisted of 38 games per team, for which they prepare with the luxury of a 25-man squad and from which the line-ups for domestic cups don't have to be selected. In their domestic treble-winning season of 2018–19, across all competitions, Manchester City used a full 31 players. Paisley and Clough would be chuckling at that too.

One aspect of modern domestic football they would recognise, though, would be the Christmas programme of matches, that intense period that might exercise present-day managers but which continues to separate the men from the boys. If there are too many games over Christmas now, then it means there have always been too many games over Christmas. It's not ideal, but it's never been ideal. And that's why we love it. It's an exciting time to be a player.

Yes, it puts players under a lot of physical stress, but it's a one-off that everyone knows is coming. These clubs have squads of such breadth and depth now that they should be comfortably able to cope with this intense – but, let's face it, short – run of games. Plus, with weakened sides invariably being picked by the top-flight teams in the third round of the FA Cup come the first weekend in January, the big stars know they're going to get some downtime, either on the bench for the cup tie or even a weekend off.

Now I'm a pundit this period is as busy for me as it was when I played. Back then, I probably grumbled about playing on Boxing Day, but at the same time I loved it. You might be a bit tired, but you know what's coming. You go into the period knowing your team's season can change, whether for the better – if you're currently adrift towards the bottom, or for the worse – if you're up near the top of the table. It's a gamble, an exciting gamble. If you win all your games, or if you lose them all, it can be a pivotal moment in the season. It's triumph or disaster. And isn't that what we want from sport?

> The Christmas period is a gamble, an exciting gamble. If you win all your games, or if you lose them all, it can be a pivotal moment in the season. It's triumph or disaster. And isn't that what we want from sport?

I'd hate to see the tradition of matches over Christmas and New Year disappear from the football calendar. And I don't think fans would be in favour of its removal either. They buy into it and really enjoy it. And keeping things exciting for the fans is what the game, fundamentally, is all about. This is a time when most people are off work, so isn't having a quick run of games squeezed together the perfect fan experience?

I'm not sure to what extent fans are wholly sympathetic to players moaning about there being too many games. Isn't that what squads are supposed to be all about? Nowadays, you have players on £100,000 a week sitting on the bench. There's ample opportunity to shuffle the pack, to rest some players without experiencing a dramatic drop-off in quality. They should have enough to cope with any eventuality.

In all this, we shouldn't neglect the fact that the majority of Premier League teams don't have their calendars troubled by participation in European competitions. And if they make early exits in the domestic cups (when, as is likely, most of the eleven players taking to the pitch are largely their second string), their best players are only really called upon for those 38 league games. Not 42. And certainly not 62. They don't know they're born.

Despite my championing of the busy run of games over Christmas and New Year, I'm very much in favour of having a winter break in the league campaign. There's no contradiction here. Have the intensity of that festive-period schedule, but then have a welcome break almost straight after. I experienced this mid-season interval in Scotland and very much enjoyed it. We used to go away to Florida to play some games, and we'd also go away with the family for a week. It gave me the chance to recharge and rejuvenate myself. Mental stress is a large part of being a footballer, especially at the highest level. It might be two or three games every seven days – going again, and again, and again. Just because they're paid tens of thousands of pounds a week doesn't mean they should be run into the ground. We shouldn't be standing over them, lashing them with a big whip.

During the winter break, you go home to your family and you do get some rest and recovery, but your mind is still on the season. You're thinking about the first game back, about the opposition, about the players you'll be up against, about your form at the time, about how you're training…It's a welcome period of rest and reassessment. Teachers get time off over Christmas, so do most professions. So why shouldn't footballers be allowed that right? It would just come a couple of weeks later, that's all.

And, let me assure you, it's not a soft return to the fray when the pause button is released on the season. It's very much a resumption of hostilities. You hit the ground running, full of energy and vigour. You're straight back into it. Refreshed, renewed, recharged. Game on.

But let's not forget – among all this welcoming of a winter break and the period of recuperation that this provides – that players are pampered these days, so much more than a few decades back. I imagine there would be plenty of players from the Seventies and Eighties looking at today's crop of footballers and wondering what all the fuss is about. Back then, the likes of Emlyn Hughes and John Robertson wouldn't have entertained the notion of player burn-out. They just got on with it, plying their trade on lumpy pitches, without the high-end facilities of today. They didn't fly first class to matches. For them, travel home after a game would have meant bumping along the motorway network on a crappy team coach into the wee small hours. But you can't blame the players of today for what they have. It's all relative. And it's a consequence of success. You'd rather be flying first class than not. It's just that players should want to play at any opportunity.

It was unsurprising that double-booked Liverpool made the League Cup the casualty, essentially handing it over to the youth team as an ·experience-gaining exercise

These are the days they should be cherishing, the ones that will live long in the memory. Don't let these moments pass you by.

Playing in the Club World Cup will live long in the memory, so Liverpool's first eleven will have been pleased that Jürgen Klopp chose not to surrender the club's participation in the 2019 tournament in Qatar in favour of the League Cup quarter-final against Aston Villa less than 22 hours earlier. That ridiculous scheduling should have been rectified the moment that Liverpool beat Arsenal on penalties in the previous round after that extraordinary 5-5 draw at Anfield.

Bringing the quarter-final forward even just a day or two would have created enough wiggle room for the club to have done justice to both competitions. It wouldn't have been ideal, but it would have been just about doable. It was unsurprising that double-booked Liverpool made the League Cup the casualty, essentially handing it over to the youth team as an experience-gaining exercise. The 3,300-mile flight to the Khalifa International Stadium in Doha was always going to be more attractive than the 100-mile run down the M6 to Villa Park. Klopp was never likely to turn his nose up at the chance of his boys being crowned the best club in the world, especially as Liverpool had tried and failed at it in the past. Bob Paisley never led them to that particular pinnacle, nor did Fagan, Dalglish or Benítez.

That the club itself had to make the choice as to which competition they prioritised shows that we're not looking after our own. The dilemma should have been taken away from them, with the authorities reassuring them in advance that, should there be a clash of this nature, contingencies would be put in place and flexibility shown. It was pretty embarrassing that Liverpool weren't offered guarantees in this way. They were essentially being penalised for success and that was grossly unfair. It's rather baffling. After all, having officially the best club in the world coming from your domestic league is something of a big deal, isn't it? It would definitely be something to crow about.

Having the best – or, at least, highly competitive – teams in Europe is a point of pride too, so replicating the winter break granted across the European leagues will surely maximise English teams' chances in both the Champions League and the Europa League. The Premier League is the only major league across the continent that doesn't uphold a significant winter break. The 2019–20 season saw a slight relaxing of the Premier League schedule, with one game week in February split across two weekends, thus giving each club a fixture-less weekend. But it's not the same as a winter break as I've known it. And it's far from making us equitable with the other big four leagues. Serie A doesn't close for business over Christmas, but it does give its clubs time off over the New Year, while the Bundesliga, La Liga and Ligue 1 all clock off a few days before Yuletide and don't reconvene until January. The Bundesliga takes the longest break of all – in the region of 26 days.

Why is the Premier League different? Is it to our benefit that it is? Or do we put ourselves at a disadvantage in the latter stages of European club competitions, having declined the opportunity for some meaningful rest? Going by the example of 2019, when the finals of both the Champions League and the Europa League were the exclusive domain of English clubs, the answer may actually be no. But that might just be an anomaly, a blip. Give the guys a break, I say.

There was, though, an issue with the implementation of this first – rather modest – Premier League mid-winter break. The small matter of FA Cup fourth-round replays got in the way for some (namely Liverpool, Newcastle, Spurs and Southampton), cutting into that sun-kissed rest and relaxation. Of course, Jürgen Klopp ensured that this wasn't a problem for his first team, and for himself, by again delegating to the youth team to represent the club in the replay. To guarantee this clash doesn't reoccur in future years, the Premier League and the FA need to sit down together to ensure that their respective competitions dovetail schedule-wise.

Klopp's decision coincided with calls from others for an end to replays right across the FA Cup. But this is short-sighted. Replays are so important to lower-league teams who relish a second match, the gate receipts of which could make a serious contribution to keeping the club solvent.

Klopp wasn't the only leading manager effectively doing down one of the domestic trophies. Pep Guardiola had the League Cup in his sights, claiming too much football was causing injuries and burn-out. 'Eliminate competitions,' was his blunt prescription about the League Cup especially. 'Take out the competition.' Even a squad boasting the depth of Manchester City's was, he believed, showing the strain. 'We push and push. The body says stop. It's enough.'

But while the administrators scratch their heads and try to make all the pieces work, new proposals land on the table for *increasing* the number of matches, such as the mooted expansion of the Champions League group stage. As we've seen, Klopp is no stranger to fixture pile-ups and he swiftly nailed his colours to the mast on this one: 'I am not involved in these plans. That's absolute bollocks.'

In short – and with the extreme case of Liverpool and the Club World Cup aside – top-flight clubs now have ample resources to cope with the demands of what the football calendar throws at them. That said, let's at least put English teams on a level footing with their European counterparts by giving them a couple of weeks off in the middle of the season. But the intensity of that mad period of matches over Christmas is sacred. It should be ring-fenced, never to be touched, never to be tinkered with, never to be changed.

Now that's something to fill Nuno Espírito Santo with seasonal cheer.

PART FIVE
THE SYSTEM

Some of the ideas I've presented so far haven't been a matter of life or death for football as a sport. The world will still keep turning if young players take to the pitch in Day-Glo footwear. As annoying as it is, fans' near-constant use of their phones during matches won't bring the game to its knees. And a fan won't stop supporting their team just because its players aren't as eloquent as a Stephen Fry or a Peter Ustinov in post-match interviews.

Some subjects, though, are more serious. They affect the long-term future of our beautiful game – its quality, its health, its sustainability. A failure to tackle some of these most pressing of issues threatens football as we know it. The system is malfunctioning and is in need of an overhaul. Sometimes it's failing from within; other times it's external cultural forces that are placing it under pressure. The fixes aren't necessarily quick and easy.

For instance, the issue of dementia within the ranks of retired footballers – a subject that's personally very resonant for me – really is a matter of life and death, and yet it's one that's been swept under the carpet by football for decades. For generations, even. The fix for this lies within the sport itself, within the power of those responsible for the game in this country. But, as serious as that subject is, the decline in the number of people actually playing the game in the digital age is arguably the one that eats away at football the most. The repercussions could be grave for the beautiful game unless action is taken to arrest the slide in participation.

I don't claim to have all the answers to these heavy issues, but I can certainly offer some preliminary ideas that could push them higher up the agenda. They can't be ignored any longer. Football's future depends upon them. As fans, we all have a responsibility to make football better. We can't just sit back and watch the game's foundations crumble. We're better than that.

21
Stop Clubs Stockpiling Young Players

I was born at the right time.

I don't think I would have been a professional footballer had I started out in the current era. When I went to Norwich City to play in their youth team at the end of the 1980s, there was a pathway for young players. The route was clear and relatively easy to navigate if you were committed. A long and winding road it wasn't.

When I joined as a YTS at the age of 16, there were 6 or 7 other YTS lads in my year and a similar number in the year above. That was essentially the make-up of the youth team. If you started doing well as a youth player, you were likely to get a run-out in the reserves. Then, thanks to the smaller squads of those times, if a first-team player got an injury, the door may well have swung open even further and you, that callow youth who might still be short of voting age, would be invited in. That was how I got my opportunity. It was as straightforward and as simple as that.

I also don't think that, back then, I would have made it at a big club either – an Arsenal, a Manchester United or a Liverpool. They had squads of greater depth and quality and I would have found it difficult to break through the ranks to earn, and then grab, my big chance. The pathway there would have been far more twisty and labyrinthine, with plenty of other players – both young hopefuls and more experienced pros – getting in the way. It was to my advantage that I was a country boy joining a team in a small city. The numbers were in my favour. Had I grown up in a large metropolitan area – London or Manchester or Birmingham – the world of football may well have not beckoned me in.

Not only was geography favouring me, but a particular time in history was, too. The platform I had all those years ago, from YTS trainee to top-flight regular, was short, direct and pretty darned quick. Nowadays, only the most gifted 16-year-olds get within touching distance of the promised land at such a tender age, such as Ryan Sessegnon and Harvey Elliott. For most young players at Premier League clubs it's all about graduating from the under-18s and moving into the under-23s set-up. Upward progression towards the first team moves at a glacial pace – if it moves at all.

> My route from YTS trainee to top-flight regular was short and quick. Nowadays, upward progression towards the first team moves at a glacial pace – if it moves at all

The Premier League 2, the current under-23s league, was a very distant entity when I was in my late teens. Instead, it was the tough baptism of the reserves that dominated my thoughts, getting bashed around in the Football Combination on a Tuesday or Friday night. It was a short, sharp upbringing, with an extremely large carrot dangling at the end. It was a massive, massive motivation. *This isn't far away*, I would keep telling myself. I'm not the sharpest tool in the shed, but even I realised the close proximity of the old First Division. *There's a real opportunity here...*

If I were that age now, how would I view things? I might be doing well in the 18s but then I've got to prove myself in the 23s. Only then can I start thinking about breaking into the 25-man first-team squad, where my opportunities would still be limited. How would I realistically break through? Because of the numbers involved, that opportunity seems miles away. Unreachable, untouchable.

Clubs cast as wide a net as possible in order to make sure that the big fish of the future don't get away while they're still minnows. They're hedging their bets

In his book *No Hunger In Paradise*, Michael Calvin crunches some numbers and comes up with a chilling calculation: 'Since only 180 of the 1.5 million boys who play organised youth football in England at any one time become a Premier League pro, the success rate is 0.012 per cent.' That's the kind of statistic that would instantly cool the dreams of young hopefuls, and those of their parents. But as long as clubs are opening their academy doors wide and hoovering up the best players at the youngest possible ages, the flames of ambition and destiny are being falsely fanned. After all, who – whether child or parent – is not going to get excited when a top club comes calling? Who's going to get their calculator out there and then to work out the odds of their little 'un ultimately making the big time and thus declining that club's overtures?

Parents ignore the numbers and get sucked in. That's probably human nature. Despite there being 12,500 players in the academy system, the whole environment is seductive, even if a glance around a training session to see just how many other kids are in the same position would provide a reality check. But dreamers are often blind to the truth. There will be scores of kids at that session who've earned their academy place and each parent still thinks it will be their child who's going to be the next superstar. And even if they paid attention to the odds, it would be very difficult to stand in Junior's way and tread on the little one's dreams.

Clubs sign up youngsters on such a scale these days. They're doing so to look after themselves. They cast as wide a net as possible in order to make sure that the big fish of the future don't get away while they're still minnows. They're hedging their bets. Should we blame them for that? I don't know. Would I have recommended to one of my kids that they sign on the dotted line if a top, top club wanted them for their academy? Probably not. Would I have thought that offered the best chance of them becoming a professional footballer? Highly unlikely.

But then try telling them that of the two academy places they've been offered – let's say one's from Manchester United and the other's from Bristol Rovers – a move to the West Country and a League One academy offer the better long-term chance of life as a pro than the glitz and glamour of the Premier League. They won't believe you. Or they won't want to believe you. It's a tricky case to put to someone flattered by Old Trafford's interest in them. It calls for tough parenting and hard talk. Perhaps you can be helped out if you're lucky enough to have a family member or a friend of the family involved in football who could offer the best advice.

It's a tough environment, especially for a young kid. Every year there's a cull. Progress is only on a 12-month rolling basis. And clubs don't mess around; these are not refuges of sentimentality and charity. Eleven-year-old Johnny might have been with the club for half his life, but that won't colour any judgement that is made. If the powers-that-be haven't seen enough of him to be selected for next year's team, they're not bothered about his feelings or those of his parents. It's absolutely brutal. Thanks Johnny. See you around. Have a nice life.

Even if the services of a young player are retained year upon year and they end up being rewarded with a professional contract, they're still a long way from achieving their ultimate goal, from reaching their final destination. All the while that managerial insecurity feeds a short-term culture where signing seasoned, experienced players is deemed a more stable way of achieving success than blooding young talent, the prospect of stagnating in the under-23s, or perpetually going out on loan, remains high. From the manager's perspective, it's perfectly understandable. A young teenager might be showing promise when he stepped up to train with the first team, but if the next match is a must-win game, he's not going to risk putting his livelihood in the hands of an unproven foal of a player.

When players return home at the end of a successful loan spell, there's no guarantee that they're any higher up the pecking order

Chelsea are famously the prime example of this state of affairs, with dozens of their academy graduates denied upward progression by a lengthy series of expensive signings and consequently farmed out on loan. This has certainly been the defining characteristic of the club's youth policy during the Abramovich era. However, since Frank Lampard's ascension to the manager's office – and, more pertinently, since being hit by a transfer embargo that forbade any new signings – youth has finally had its chance at Stamford Bridge.

The likes of Tammy Abraham, Fikayo Tomori, Callum Hudson-Odoi and Mason Mount have prospered as a result. And Abraham and Mount have proved that being serial loanees needn't mean the extinguishing of a future at your parent club. There was a question mark over Mount for me. After doing the business at Derby in the Championship, could he replicate those performances in the more refined Premier League? My doubts about him were shown to be misplaced. He's worked hard and proved himself all over again.

But Mount is an outlier, a rarity, an exception that proves the rule. Lampard had confidence that the midfielder could step up and that faith was shown to be well founded. He got another crack at his parent club. Most loanees don't get that chance. As impressive as they might have been lower down the leagues, when players return home at the end of a successful loan spell there's no guarantee that they're any higher up the pecking order. They're almost certainly not, in fact – especially if a new signing or two has arrived in the meantime. And, to some extent, that's perfectly reasonable. How many Premier League managers will say 'I'm a hundred per cent sure he's ready for the top flight now he's served his time in the Championship'? You could count them on the fingers of one hand and still have some fingers left over.

So it's small wonder when, as it prepares for life in the Premier League, a newly promoted Championship side opens the cheque book and splashes the cash on tried-and-tested players who will guarantee them survival in the top flight. Only there are no guarantees. Fulham provide the salutary lesson here, having spent £100 million on new players ahead of the 2018–19 season, only to slide back to the Championship the following May, with a huge financial burden on its shoulders. If nothing is certain, gambling on transfer fees and wages while stockpiling more players doesn't feel like the most judicious course of action.

There is another way. When promoted Norwich swapped places with relegated Fulham the Canaries weren't in a position to spend, certainly not in a climate where £50 million doesn't even guarantee that you're buying a player who's the finished article. Instead, Norwich put faith in youth, with the likes of Max Aarons, Jamal Lewis and Todd Cantwell asked to make the step up. While certainly no safeguard against relegation, there was at least the reassurance that a return to the Championship wouldn't financially cripple the club. They didn't overextend themselves. No egg was left on the face.

While Norwich have been comfortable blooding their younger players, other clubs stay cautious. The money that's sloshing around the top end of the game is how and why these clubs can embark on stockpiling players in such huge numbers, in the hope that one of these rough diamonds will be able to polish up. It's a waiting game that they can easily afford. The pot of money seems to have no bottom to it.

While the clubs don't feel the pain of stockpiling, the careers of the individual players are put on hold in this purgatory. They're treading water, their time wasting away like a muscle atrophying. They can delude themselves by still believing – as they did when they were ten years younger – that they really are going to make it at their beloved club, or they can choose to make some brave, bold decisions. Ultimately, they've got to find their own natural level to make their dreams a reality.

The problem is that most players go into clubs too high, too early and they stick around for the sake of sticking around. They don't want to damage their pride. But, for the sake of their careers, this pride has to be swallowed. They've got to make their own destiny and find the level of the game – be it Championship, League One or League Two – that matches their ability. This is the route for them out of this purgatory: to be a professional footballer for the next 15 or so years and not an ex-academy player who stagnated and slipped out of the sport in their early twenties. Better to be a medium-sized fish swimming in the right-sized pool for plenty of years rather than a small fish flapping around in a large, overcrowded pool for a comparatively short amount of time.

Playing in League One or League Two is, of course, no barrier to actually rising up through the leagues in time. Take Dele Alli, for example. He learned his trade at MK Dons, becoming the battle-hardened player who, within just five months of playing his last game for them, became an England international. Like me, he saw his pathway clearly too. Make a name for yourself at your hometown club and the big guns will come calling. Had he been scooped up by a Premier League club at an earlier age, he could still be an anonymous under-23 player who no one beyond that club's most devoted fan had ever heard of. Again, it's about making your own destiny. At one point, Liverpool had been very closely linked with Alli, but he instead chose to extend his time in Milton Keynes by signing a new contract. It's a tough life and only the supremely gifted get the rewards handed to them on a platter. For mere mortals, it's about making the right choice at the right time and the right age.

This stockpiling of young talent is unfair on players, both individually and collectively. They're given a glimpse of the promised land, but are highly unlikely to pay it even a fleeting visit. Most at best tread water and almost everyone will face rejection at some point. They are the collateral damage in a system where the clubs put their own self-preservation first.

Clubs get away with treating – or mistreating – young talent this way because they can. There's no mechanism that stops them doing so. Should they be criticised for their actions? Well, they're not bending the rules. The rules are the rules. They're just doing what they see fit for their club to work in the best possible way. It's up to the rule-makers to really change things.

If I were wearing the hat of a rule-maker, I would make reducing the number of players being stockpiled a priority. There should be a limit to the number of players a club can retain and built into this would be a limit on the numbers that are allowed to be sent on loan. This would greatly benefit the wider system. Not so many players would go into the game – or linger – at the highest level, meaning there would be a more natural sharing around of the talent. A player's career wouldn't be put on hold while a club hedged its bets to see whether he was going to be a late developer. And, filtering down to a lower level, a player would be playing meaningful football at an earlier stage, thus improving himself and the quality of the lower-ranked club he's been content to sign for.

> Reducing the quantity of players that a club can retain creates more of a dog-eat-dog environment. While the numbers stay high, there's a lack of competition and an element of complacency

Reducing the quantity of players that a club can retain creates more of a dog-eat-dog environment. All the time that the numbers stay high, there's a lack of competition and an element of complacency. Remove that safety net and it becomes a more perilous high-wire act. It would become the survival of the fittest, which is what it always used to be for players wanting to break through at the highest level. If you're not good enough, you're not going to get the opportunity. Yes or no, black or white. And no more grey areas offered by the loan system. 'We can only pick eight players now, not fourteen or twenty. We've got to be ruthless. I'm sorry, but you'll have to go and try elsewhere.'

Without the luxury of stockpiling, clubs would have to make sure their selections were spot on. The insurance policy of amassing a large pool of players so that none slip through the net (and none get snapped up by your rivals) would disappear. Clubs would have to identify the hungriest talent, those players more likely to prosper at the top. They might be proved wrong in the ones they let go – as Manchester United were when they sold academy graduate Paul Pogba cheap, only to buy him back from Juventus for the princely sum of £89 million. But there would be more peril, more danger and more uncertainty around recruitment and retention. And who doesn't like that?

No more would clubs be allowed to collect players as if they were football stickers.

22
Football Needs to Properly Tackle the Dementia Issue

I ring the buzzer and the doors open. I write and sign my name in the visitors' book, then punch the code I've been given into the lift. I go up a floor and walk out to the left, a few yards through another door and turn right. I wander down a long corridor, with numbered doors on either side. On the wall outside each room are small glass cabinets, mostly filled with old photos, family photos, smiling photos. These are memories of better days and happier times. I walk through another coded door and into a big, bright lounge and spacious dining area. It's full of people, mostly elderly. I look around and spot the man I'm looking for.

He's easy to recognise as he's wearing a blue cap. He loves that cap. He's sat slumped on his own at a table, staring vacantly into space. My stride quickens. 'How are you?' I say. 'It's me, Chris. Remember me? It's great to see you.' The old man just looks on ahead. Nothing. He doesn't budge, he doesn't blink. I grab his hand and tell him I love him. I whisper to him about the things we used to do together, our shared past: the cricket, the football, the stories, the good old days.

I step back and squat down before him and look deep into his eyes. They don't flicker. He looks on through me. I sit down and chat to him for maybe 30 minutes, always holding his hand. He doesn't recognise me and my stomach lurches at this thought. Every. Single. Time. But I persist and carry on chatting away. I want something to register with this man. I think I see a glimmer in his eyes, but it's probably nothing. Maybe I'm just imagining it. I hold his hand tighter. Sometimes the man talks, but he makes no sense. He never makes sense anymore.

When it's time to go, I don't say goodbye. I never say goodbye because if he can somehow understand me, I don't want him to get anxious or angry or upset or disappointed. I leave the man sitting in the chair as before, hunched and staring ahead motionless. There is nothing

> Dementia is a cruel master. It robs you of who you are, of who you once were and of the life that brought you joy, love and fulfilment

there anymore, but I love this man. It's heartbreaking to see any man or woman like this, rotting and wasting away. Imagine a member of your own family dying in such an undignified way.

The man with the blue cap hunched in the chair is my dad Mike. To see him like this breaks my heart. I walk away, leaving him in his own lonely world.

My dad was a colossus. He was a superb athlete and played professionally for Norwich, Chester and Carlisle. After he packed in his playing career at the age of 28 because of a knee injury, he went to Loughborough University, did a biology degree and became a really well-respected teacher for the next 30-odd years. He was a clever guy and a strong character with a great sense of humour. He now has advanced-stage dementia and lives in a home.

Dementia is a cruel master. It robs you of who you are, of who you once were and of the life that brought you joy, love and fulfilment. It wipes out the memories and leaves a blank page. There is life there, but it's no life really. It eats away, minute by minute, hour by hour, until the sad, inevitable end.

> It wasn't until a full 15 years after Jeff Astle's death that the FA and the PFA joined forces to fund what turned out to be truly significant research. What the hell took them so long?

At first, my dad just started getting a little forgetful – not remembering where he'd put his car keys, that kind of thing. We began getting really concerned when, one weekend, he couldn't find his way home after watching my son play football. My dad was born in Norfolk and grew up there, and knew the roads like the back of his hand. That's when the alarm bells started ringing.

Since then, there's been a gradual decline in his condition. If you put a plate of food in front of him, he doesn't know how to eat it. He doesn't know how to clean his teeth, or wash or dress himself, or go to the toilet. He's heavily medicated and needs to be locked in for his own safety. He's had years and years of getting worse. It's an awful way for somebody to die.

My dad is, of course, not the only former footballer suffering from dementia. Far from it. Far, far, far from it.

In 2002, the former West Brom and England striker Jeff Astle passed away from dementia at the age of just 59. At the inquest, the coroner said his death was the result of an 'industrial disease'; that is, his head had suffered repeated minor trauma throughout his career, most probably from the frequent heading of footballs.

You would have thought that following the death of such a high-profile player – who had, of course, lined up for England at the 1970 World Cup in Mexico, as well as scoring the winning goal in the 1968 FA Cup final – the football authorities would have been fired into action, commissioning research project after research project to study the links between heading a ball and degenerative brain disease. But no. It wasn't until a full 15 years after Jeff Astle's death that the FA and the PFA joined forces to fund what turned out to be truly significant research. What the hell took them so long?

After all, it's not as if the PFA didn't have the financial resources to invest in research before then. This is an organisation that reportedly once spent £1.9 million of its funds on a L S Lowry painting and that, for many years, has paid its chief executive a sizeable seven-figure salary, reportedly making him the highest-earning union official in the world. There's no doubt that its money could have been put to more progressive use.

Throughout those 15 years, Jeff's daughter Dawn tirelessly campaigned for some of the money that's been poured into football to be used to investigate this issue. In return, at best she received platitudes. The same drum was being banged again and again, and yet football chose to let the issue slip away. Then, in 2017, my old Blackburn strike partner Alan Shearer made an hour-long, primetime documentary for the BBC about the long-term effects on a player's brain of heading a football. Talking to neuroscientists, administrators, former players and their families, the documentary hit hard, revealing the reluctance of the game to tackle this grave subject.

One interview was particularly telling. Alan sat down with Gordon

Taylor, the long-reigning PFA chief executive, and cut to the chase. 'You've got fifty thousand members,' he said. 'Do you know how many of those have dementia?' Taylor puffed out his cheeks. 'No, I don't.' It had been a full decade and a half since the pronouncement made by Jeff Astle's coroner. That Taylor was not in possession of even a ballpark figure was staggering.

In the same documentary, Dawn Astle observed that 'football doesn't seem to want to know'. She was speaking from bitter experience. She and her family kept getting pushed aside by the sport. An earlier approach she'd made to Taylor about the lack of proactive research on the part of the PFA had been dismissed by its chief executive. His own mother had dementia, he explained, and she'd never headed a ball in her life. It was a crass and insensitive thing to say.

As head of a trade union, it is Gordon Taylor's job to do the best for his members. That has been his responsibility since he took charge of the PFA back in 1981. I can't sit here and say he hasn't done good things for football and footballers, because he has. But on the matter of dementia, for years and years he sat on his hands and didn't say a word about it. I appreciate that the PFA – and the FA – would have been worried about the legal implications if they did admit to a link between dementia and heading a football. But strip that aside. The guy who is in charge, supposedly with his members' best interests at heart, has a duty of care to those players, players who are dying the most horrible deaths in circumstances where their dignity has been lost.

There are high-profile former footballers, with plenty of opinions on politics and other topics, who have stayed silent on Taylor's shambolic handling of the dementia situation. Why is this? I sincerely hope not, but these ex-players – and their families – could regret this in years to come as they may end up suffering from this horrible illness themselves. Players from my dad's generation deserve better support from both my generation and the current generation. I'm sure if the roles were reversed, things would have been different.

In the wake of Alan Shearer's probing, the FA and the PFA joined forces to belatedly commission a study looking into former footballers who later in life suffered from dementia. After 22 months, researchers from the University of Glasgow, led by the eminent neuropathologist Dr Willie Stewart, delivered their findings in October 2019. And these findings were truly significant. The research team compared the causes of death of 7,676 former Scottish professional footballers born between 1900 and 1976 against those of more than 23,000 individuals from the general population. They found that footballers had an approximately 3.5 times higher rate of death due

> In 20 or 30 years' time, there will definitely be footballers currently in the game who will be suffering horribly from this illness. Of that I am absolutely certain

to neurogenerative disease. Within this figure they discovered that footballers were twice as likely to die from Parkinson's, four times more likely to die from motor neurone disease and *five* times more likely to die from Alzheimer's. It confirmed what the families of footballers with dementia had believed for years. Now armed with the hard scientific evidence, they remained perplexed as to why the authorities had taken so long to commission such research. Much anguish had been experienced during the intervening years.

It's now a case of what the authorities do with this research, of how they both improve the lot of those afflicted and safeguard future generations of footballers. And it's an issue of how quickly they act. Within a couple of months of the study being published, three more former players passed away within a few days of each other: Ron Saunders, Jim Smith and another England World Cup hero, Martin Peters. All had suffered from dementia in their later years.

Too much time has been wasted. In 20 or 30 years' time, there will definitely be footballers currently in the game who will be suffering horribly from this illness. Of that I am absolutely certain. And their families will be asking, 'Why didn't we do more? Why did we not push for more funding?' These ex-players are the lifeblood of the game and they need help. And so do their families. People might think it's just about the person who's suffering. And, of course, they are going through hell. But there's also the stress and pressure that their families are under, providing 24-hour care themselves because there's insufficient funding.

> It's been proven that if you head a ball just 20 times in one day, your memory is impaired for the next 24 hours.

I don't worry about myself. I'm retired now. I can't go back in time and retract all the headers I've done in my life. As a kid, I was always practising with my dad – heading, heading, heading. I would have loved to have been told at the age of 14 or 15 about the potential long-term effects on my brain. When I was in my mid-to-late teens, I was heading hundreds of balls every week. I was good in the air. It was one of my strengths. It's why I originally played at centre-half. And how did I get good at it? By practising.

When I joined Norwich, afternoons meant heading practice for attackers and defenders – attacking long goal kicks and heading wet, heavy footballs. The goalkeeper would punt big, high balls out and I'd sprint towards them with great determination and effort, grunting and thinking *I've got to head this back as far as I can.*

If I'd have known the facts, it would then have come down to choice. If I'd have known I was going to damage myself, then I wouldn't have wanted to go out and head a hundred balls on a wet Tuesday afternoon. I'd have been thinking, *Yes, I have to do heading practice, but maybe not on Tuesdays, Wednesdays and Thursdays. Less repetition. And perhaps only one day a week.* Of course I would have thought that. If the coach had pulled out a packet of cigarettes and said 'Here, smoke ten of these', I would have refused. I knew the dangers. But when it came to the damage that heading could potentially cause I – and all my fellow professionals – just weren't in possession of the facts. There was no hard scientific evidence for us to chew over. And the football authorities' inertia on this matter was to blame for us not knowing any better.

It seems obvious now. I'm no scientist, but if you punch someone in the head 30 or 40 times a day for 15 years, I reckon it's probably not going to do them a whole lot of good. But effectively that was what was being asked of us as footballers, being told to repeatedly head footballs with great force every day in training. And it's now been proven that if you head a football just 20 times in one day, your memory is impaired for the next 24 hours. That's a fact.

While it shouldn't have taken a former England captain and a film crew to make dementia such a live issue within football, the Shearer documentary commendably took the issue on to primetime television and opened people's eyes. And it forced a response from the authorities, albeit one of reaction when they should have been proactively leading.

Even so, I found the comment by Marc Bullingham, the FA chief executive, a little complacent: 'Our research shows the number of aerial challenges has already been reduced significantly over the years as we have changed to smaller pitches and possession-based football.' While this situation may well prove to cause fewer cases of dementia in footballers in future decades, it's small comfort to those players and their families who have had to suffer the pain and torment of debilitating disease both in the past and in the here and now. At this minute, though, it's unproven. Suggesting that the nature of modern football may well have lessened, if not removed, the issue for future generations is, to my ears, an irresponsible position to take. Proof is needed of this. Studies and tests must be continually undertaken, otherwise there is the danger that in 20 or 30 years' time we'll be repeating ourselves. And there's been enough complacency.

No one yet knows the effect of repeated heading on a developing brain, but why take the risk of lasting damage?

I'm considering legal action against the PFA or the FA on behalf of my father. I want people to realise that this is a very real, very serious issue that has been neglected and ignored for so long. It's a grave state of affairs. Action needs to be taken now, but football has chosen to do nothing – or very little – about it. It's an outrage, a disgrace. And it should be an issue that outrages people. We're currently in a time when everyone is railing against VAR and the controversies that VAR has caused. But VAR isn't killing anybody. Ex-players aren't dying horrible deaths off the back of an offside call or a penalty decision. If only football fans were getting so apoplectic about dementia.

Banning heading would fundamentally change the game as we know it and, indeed, no one is calling for a wholesale ban in senior football. But we could, and should, outlaw heading in junior football – from under-12 level and younger. No one yet knows the effect of repeated heading on a developing brain, but why take the risk of lasting damage? Why would I want to expose my children and my grandchildren to heading a ball when, at that age, there's no real upside to doing so?

In 2015, the United States Soccer Federation outlawed heading for players aged ten and under, and limited heading practice for eleven- to thirteen-year-olds to half an hour a week. It wasn't a biggie. The world continued to turn on its axis. But hopefully it's a decision that will save a few players from enduring an undignified death when they're older. And that's not all. Two years earlier in the US, the NFL agreed to a $765-million package to provide medical assistance to those of its 18,000 former players suffering from degenerative brain disease. Admittedly the NFL only opened the chequebook after a lawsuit had been filed, but this is the kind of action that football – both in the UK and across the globe – would do well to duplicate. It's overdue. And ideally it will happen without the threat of legal action.

The early months of 2020 saw some promising advances on the issue. In January, it was announced that the Scottish Football Association was finalising proposals to ban heading for kids under the age of 12 both in training and matches, plans that would make it the first European association to take such action.

The same month, the Industrial Injuries Advisory Council revealed that is had been discussing the issue of neurodegenerative disease among older footballers, raising the hopes of campaigners like Dawn Astle that it could officially – and finally – be defined as an industrial disease. Then, in February, the FA – in association with the Irish and Scottish FAs – issued updated guidance on heading for young players. Children at under-11 level and younger will no longer undertake heading practice in training, and a limit has been placed on the amount of heading practice in junior and youth teams.

Certainly more investment in research is urgently needed. While the University of Glasgow study indicated the likelihood of footballers developing dementia later in life, the most likely cause is yet to be pinpointed. At the time of the study's publication, the FA suggested it might be due to heading, but it might also be concussion management or the design of footballs or even what they termed 'personal lifestyle'. They'd better get a move on and find out.

That clock keeps ticking.

23

Don't Disrespect Woman's Football. Love It

The scenes at Wembley were boisterous. All tickets sold. England vs Germany. A fixture that will be for ever a red-letter day on the football calendar.

But this was different. This wasn't the World Cup final of 1966, nor the Euro '96 semi-final. This was just a friendly between the two nations in the closing months of 2019. And it was also a women's international, the first time that England's Lionesses had played at the national stadium since they hosted Germany five years earlier. While the result was another German victory, this time around the attendance was more than 30,000 above the number who turned out in 2014.

If ever there was an indication of the rude health that women's football has found itself in over the last decade or so, that evening at Wembley was it. And this match was no flash in the pan. Four months earlier, a peak audience of 11.7 million people had tuned in to BBC

One at primetime to watch the Lionesses take on the holders, the United States, in the World Cup semi-final. The TV audience was two million more than were watching the *Britain's Got Talent* final over on ITV.

Thanks to BT Sport, Sky and the BBC, women's football is getting the platform it deserves, as well as many more column inches in the newspapers than it did before. It would have been unheard of ten – or even five – years ago that the women's game would have its own section in the papers. Back then, if it were covered at all, it would be a small mention next to the classified ads for lawnmowers and the like.

My daughter's certainly been caught up in the attention that's come the way of England's women and she's developed an interest in football as a result. It wasn't always the way. If you had a daughter 30-odd years ago, playing football wasn't a path that girls were particularly encouraged to venture down. I've got two older sisters and my parents never pushed them to play – and that was despite my dad having been a professional footballer. Instead they were encouraged to take up what were regarded at the time to be 'girls' sports' – netball and hockey and the like.

The platform to play wasn't there back then, but pleasingly it now is for my daughter's generation. Take the classic film *Gregory's Girl*, made in 1980. One of the main plotlines involves a teenage girl who wants to play in the boys' school team because there is no other outlet for her footballing skills. She is seen as an oddity, an anomaly, an alien in the male domain of football. If I showed that film to my daughter she'd think it was a slice of ancient history, but it only reaches back a single generation.

That same year, Japan held its first women's football tournament. But despite the good intentions, there was an underlying belief that women couldn't cut it. It was an eight-a-side tournament played on smaller pitches and with matches lasting 25 minutes each way. And not only were the assembled teams playing with a kids' football, but handballs were allowed if the hands and arms were protecting that particular player's breasts.

Progress was slow. Eleven years later, the first official Women's World Cup took place in China (its actual name was the snappy First FIFA World Championship for Women's Football for the M&M's Cup). Concessions were still being made to the players, with the authorities believing women couldn't last the full 90 minutes of the men's game, so matches were set at 40 minutes each way. As the United States captain April Heinrichs later quipped, 'FIFA was afraid our ovaries were going to fall out'.

Giant strides have since been made. Nowadays, go down to any municipal playing fields on a Saturday or Sunday where there are a few football pitches and you're almost certain to come across a girls' match. Opportunities for players have

I have two older sisters and my parents never pushed them to play – and that was despite my dad having been a professional footballer

evolved and widened. The choice is there. It's more inclusive, exactly as it should be. A lot of young girls are getting really enthusiastic and excited about football and I love that. The forward movement has plenty of momentum. Times have certainly changed for the better.

UEFA's #WePlayStrong campaign is a positive element in this progress, with its objective of making football the number one women's sport across Europe. Mostly aimed at girls between the ages of 13 and 17, the campaign aims to recruit and, crucially, retain female players. Most football-playing girls quit the sport when they hit their teens, which UEFA's research attributes to peer pressure with young women electing to undertake other activities which have more social currency among their friends. Retaining players throughout the teenage years and into adulthood is vital for the continuing growth of the women's game.

At the highest level, the FA Women's Super League helped to usher in the era of the full-time female professional footballer in this country. Before that threshold was breached, football had to fit around work. For instance, Kelly Smith, England's record goalscorer, had to juggle her footballing life with two jobs – working in McDonald's and at a dog kennels – while only training two evenings a week. When, as an international player, she approached Adidas for a boot deal, she was turned down flat.

> Twenty years ago, the average male football fan would have struggled to name more than one or two current female England internationals. Now the full-timers are becoming household names

Now the full-timers are becoming household names. Twenty years ago, the average male football fan would have struggled to name more than one or two current female England internationals. Now – thanks mostly to exposure on the small screen – they can tell their Lucy Bronzes from their Steph Houghtons, their Ellen Whites from their Jodie Taylors. And they can match up players to their clubs. They know Jill Scott is a towering presence in Manchester City's midfield, while Fran Kirby is Chelsea's busy, bustling striker. And among this knowledge comes a genuine appreciation of the high quality and the advanced skills of the professional women's game.

On the other side of the Atlantic, women footballers are even more high-profile, thanks to the sport being further advanced than on our shores. The star of the 2019 World Cup, the United States captain Megan Rapinoe, was named as Sportsperson of the Year by *Sports Illustrated*, beating all the male megastars of the NBA and the NFL to take the prestigious gong. For the game to have evolved that far in the modern era is pretty extraordinary.

For all the good news, though – the full-time professionals, the attendances, the opportunities to participate – women's football is suffering in one respect. Every time a major women's tournament comes around, every time it takes its place in the television schedules, male keyboard warriors emerge from their lairs to stick the boot in. Because the quality on show isn't quite at the level of Salah or De Bruyne or de Gea, they feel perfectly within their right to denigrate an entire sport. Their conclusions are not only wrong, but they also show these moaners as brainless: 'Women's football is crap.' 'Why do you think it's crap?' 'Because it is.'

The sport journalist Martha Kelner has written about this antagonism towards female players: 'Not liking women's football is fine – not every sport is for everyone. But the active antipathy towards it among a section of society is utterly perplexing. Just because more people are watching women's football…doesn't mean men's football is under threat. The two can co-exist without the earth's surface imploding.'

'Active antipathy' is a choice phrase, perfectly summing up the sneering brigade, those sniping anonymously online: 'I don't like it and I don't really watch it, but I'll still give it both barrels.' These uptight half-wits need to get a life. Their anger would be better suited writing letters to the local paper about potholes in the high street than undermining a sport that's increasingly being played and watched by a sizeable portion of the population.

If these moaners are insecure about the women's game encroaching on traditional male territory, they needn't be. It's highly unlikely to reach the same level, or receive the same exposure, in my lifetime. And that's not meant in a derogatory way. Women's football is evolving well at its own pace, forging its own identity away from the men's game.

While the men's game is faster and more physical, comparing it to women's football is the nub of the problem. It shouldn't be the yardstick against which women players are constantly measured. You wouldn't watch Dina Asher-Smith put in an exemplary 100-metre performance and say 'Ah, but she's not as quick as Usain Bolt'. Nor would you watch Ashleigh Barty and say 'Her serve isn't as fast as that of Novak Djokovic'. But the skills and ability of female footballers are continually set against those of male players. The respective games shouldn't be compared. They are separate and distinct, and they can run in parallel. They are each their own thing. It's comparing apples with oranges.

That said, a comparison of prize money is revealing. I've already ranted elsewhere about how the £3.6 million won by the winners of the men's FA Cup was miniscule in comparison to the Premier League payments to clubs. However, compared to the prize for the women's FA Cup it's a fortune. The women's team that lifts the trophy scoops a not-so-cool £25,000 for all their efforts. That's a single day's salary for a Premier League top-earner. Each of the 32 men's teams who progress past the third round receive £135,000 for doing so, more than five times the amount paid to the *overall winners* of the women's competition. I appreciate that the men's and women's games are separate commercial entities, but that extraordinary gap in prize money needs some serious narrowing. The FA needs to dip its hand into those deep pockets. And it needs to be bloody quick about it.

The response of some men to women's football is nothing new. It's been a struggle for the game to get where it currently is, as the history books tell us. On Boxing Day 1920, a crowd of 53,000 watched a match at Goodison Park involving the best women's team of the time – Dick, Kerr Ladies. In the narrow streets around Goodison, around 14,000 disappointed spectators couldn't get in. But this bubble was soon quickly burst when the FA banned women from playing on Football League grounds. The reason they cited was blunt and brutal: 'the game of football is quite unsuitable for females and ought not to be encouraged'. If you think the FA makes some curious and baffling decisions now, those are not a patch on that particular one.

> The men's game and the women's game shouldn't be compared. They are separate and distinct. They are each their own thing. It's comparing apples with oranges

Here's the extraordinary thing, though. The ban on women playing on FA-affiliated grounds – effectively any stadium with spectator facilities – lasted until 1971. It was in place for *fifty* years. Its lifting only came after a rebel England eleven had travelled to Mexico to play at an unofficial World Cup in front of crowds stretching into the tens of thousands. The difference between the two cultures – one cold and forbidding, the other warm and welcoming – couldn't have been more acute.

Sadly, the attitudes of some men towards the women's game continue to be dismissive. This needs to change in order for it to stop being undermined. But how can that be done? While we can't make every critic go to watch a WSL match on a Sunday to have their worldview corrected, we could bring the game to them. Once in a while, simply schedule a women's match ahead of one of their male counterparts' games – the same day, the same stadium, just a couple of hours before the men kick off, with everyone buying a joint ticket. I like this idea. The women get to play in their home stadium in front of a crowd the size of which they'd only otherwise encounter in an international match. At the same time, those stick-in-the-muds in the stands would get to judge the artistry on show from close quarters. Then you'd give this section of middle-aged men, who are totally dismissive of women's football, the chance to reconsider.

And even if they didn't undergo a Damascene conversion, they'd hopefully not be so vitriolic the next time the Women's World Cup came around. As Martha Kelner has prescribed, when writing about England captain Steph Houghton: 'You might not like watching her play, but at least have the good grace to respect her right to do so.'

24
Give Referees the Respect They Deserve

Throughout my time in football, there's always been one particular question at the forefront of my mind. And it's a question that's more pertinent than ever before.

Who would be a referee?

You've got to be a special breed to put yourself out there in the middle, haven't you? You've got to be a little odd. I'm not sure who grows up wanting to be one. It's a bit like picking being a traffic warden as your choice of career. I don't quite understand what goes through your mind to want to take on a role where, let's be honest, no one likes you – or, at least, very few people do. You need to be strong-willed, strong-minded and thick-skinned to be a referee. It definitely takes a certain type. And it's not something you readily advertise about yourself. You don't want to get funny looks when you go down the local pub or the fish-and-chip shop.

I suppose, for some, being a refeeree can be very fulfilling, especially if they never had a chance to play football at a decent level. It's a way of getting out there on the pitch in the thick of the action. But the very nature of it means that at the top of the profession they'll be refereeing in stadiums full of fans, where a decision from them can only favour one team or the other. They'll never please everybody. It's an impossible job.

I used to referee under-12s games and I loved it. I didn't put up with any backchat, but of course it was only a low-level kids' game. That's far removed from taking charge of a Premier League match, which I wouldn't fancy doing at all. Would I enjoy receiving abuse on a regular basis, both on the pitch and after the game? Well, I had that as a player and it's not nice. All referees go into the role to do it to the best of their ability, but they're up there to be shot at. It's a thankless task and more often than not they will have got up the noses of both sets of fans. Certainly referees only get negative feedback from the stands and no one applauds them off the pitch. Well, not without sarcasm.

People might look at the wages of Premier League referees and think that as their income isn't too shabby they can put up with criticism. After all, being paid an annual retainer of around £40,000 and in excess of a grand on top for each match they officiate will be comfortably above the average salary of the fan in the stand. But all the money in the world doesn't give several thousand people the right to abuse them. It's like stepping into the lion's den, while also being called all the names under the sun. I can certainly see how the prospect of that would put referees off making their way up the hierarchy towards professional status. Who else would choose a job where being verbally abused, often very viciously, would happen every time you turned up for work?

The appeal further down the pyramid isn't any stronger. I don't understand why anybody would want to go down a soggy park on a wet Sunday morning and referee a game with the possibility of being sworn at, and maybe attacked There's not even the compensation of a handsome payday. Their fee, varying between £20 and £40, is just pocket money. These referees are doing this not to carve out a career, but because it's their hobby. They're doing it for reasons I can't quite fathom. No one's holding a gun to their head. They're doing it for fun.

Of course, they may well be slipping into a referee's kit out of an admirable sense of altruism. Their motivation might just be to show their love for the game and its long-term future. After all, football can't exist without someone umpiring and marshalling the game. Therefore, as football fans, we all need to show respect to the man or woman in the middle. They're doing a public service, without which a match can't kick off. So we all need to sit back and contemplate how we treat referees. They're not the devil. They are human beings trying to do right by everybody. Whether they succeed, of course, is another thing entirely.

It's a thankless task. Referees only get negative feedback from the stands and no one applauds them off the pitch. Well, not without sarcasm

Take referees in junior and youth football. There have been plenty of initiatives under the 'Respect' banner to encourage parents not to barrack from the sidelines, to not undermine the referee. After all, if full-time professional referees at the highest level are struggling to keep up with all the subtle tweaks continually applied to the laws of the game, what chance does a weekend referee, holding down a nine-to-five job during the week, have to keep abreast of every little rule change? I work in the media now full-time and it's even hard for me to keep up with these supposed improvements. These volunteers are doing the best they can and I think we have to accept it's not going to be perfect.

The abuse that referees are subjected to across the football pyramid means it's small wonder that they're a declining species. Nearly 7,000 hung up their whistles at the end of the 2018–19 season, which was neither a blip nor an anomaly. This kind of exodus is being seen season after season. And if referees are in increasingly short supply, then matches don't get played, teams disband and leagues dissolve. The decline in referee numbers cannot be good for the foundations of the game. And if there's a tremor in the foundations, the rest of the pyramid feels the effects.

The abuse that referees are subjected to across the football pyramid means it's small wonder they're a declining species. Nearly 7,000 hung up their whistles at the end of the 2018–19 season

If you look at the figures, they actually suggest that the churn of referees is equitable – there are as many new referees coming into the game as are leaving. However, many of these new referees are teenagers taking refereeing courses and officiating junior matches as part of their Duke of Edinburgh Award. So they're doing it because it's a requirement, not because it's a passion. It's a duty rather than a dream. And they give it up once their award scheme is complete. So they might only officiate for a couple of years; it's not a long-term activity they want to commit to. This then begs the question: how do you make the role of a ref appealing to someone in their late teens or early twenties?

It's all very well taking charge of junior matches, but once you get to senior football and you're refereeing a bunch of blokes on a Sunday morning who are probably heavily hung over or still half-drunk, why should you be the punchbag, the target for them to shout and swear and hurl abuse at? The most natural thing to do in that situation is surely to ask yourself what the point of being there is. It's just not worth the hassle.

I did chuckle when, after an away defeat to Sheffield United in February 2020, Bournemouth's Dan Gosling publicly complained about the referee, Jon Moss. It wasn't his decisions that had aggravated Gosling. It was the fact that Moss had attempted to engage in banter with the player during the match, making what Gosling described as 'little sarky comments' about Bournemouth's proximity to the relegation zone. 'He should really come out and apologise,' he moaned, 'because I thought he was a disgrace.' Players give referees all manner of verbals during matches, but as soon as a referee makes a comment himself, he needs to make an apology? Don't make me laugh. Thankfully the Premier League declined the invitation to review Gosling's allegations.

To recruit and retain referees, there does need to be a greater respect from players. I do think that there's a lot of clubs around the country who are extremely respectful, but you do always hear about the bad incidents. My son plays for a team at level nine of the football pyramid and when I watch them, I do feel that there's generally a really healthy respect for referees from what I've seen. I may be totally wrong – perhaps Norfolk folk are just generally nicer. Maybe playing in so many Old Firm derbies has skewed my perception of what is normal!

There are still 30,000 masochists heading out on to the pitch come the weekend to suffer the slings and arrows that the players, coaching staff and fans will direct at them. And with each of these 30,000 referees paying a re-registration fee every season, there is clearly some money in the coffers for the FA to launch a recruitment drive and provide more training courses. At present, there are waiting lists for prospective officials wanting to get on a course due to there apparently being only around five hundred or so refereeing coaches in the country. I just went on to the FA's website to find out when there might be space on a course. I was greeted with the words 'Unfortunately there are no available dates'.

So, to increase referee numbers, funds need to be made available to increase the number of courses being offered. At the moment, the FA's referees' budget is around the £1.8 million mark, a figure that needs to not only cover the care of the existing 30,000 officials but also the recruitment of new blood. That £1.8 million is the same as the England manager's reported salary.

But the main factor in recruitment – and possibly persuading those who previously quit to come back into the fold – is to cut out the abuse from players. Refereeing has to become an enjoyable experience for the officials, otherwise it will only be the masochists who are going to sign up. In order for that to happen, the vulnerability of referees has to lessen. They need protection. And, in this respect, I think football could learn from rugby union.

In rugby, only the team captain is allowed to speak to the referee during the game. This would be an easy rule to bring into football, a simple measure that would return respect to the game in very quick fashion.

At the moment, even Sunday-league footballers copy the behaviour of their idols in the Premier League. If the pros act a certain way come Saturday afternoon, that seems to legitimise it. So if a Sunday-league clogger sees a pro offering a potty-mouthed tirade to a linesman, or a bunch of players surrounding the referee insisting that an opponent be booked, these antics will be repeated on park pitches the following morning. If in the Premier League or EFL only the captain could approach the referee to request further clarification on a decision, this too would soon filter down into the lower leagues and beyond. It would become the norm very quickly, especially if a yellow card was brandished each time a player other than one of the two captains spoke out of line. And if that player then spoke to the referee for a second time, his reward would be a red card.

Everyone would know the consequences. If I were playing under that rule, I would abide by it. Even if I were bursting to express my point of view, even if I were desperate to tell the referee he'd made a hash of that last decision, I would know that I couldn't speak to him and so therefore I wouldn't. It's about self-discipline. If I got a yellow for that, I'd have let my manager down and I'd have let my team down. It's about respect and responsibility.

> If a rule came in that only captains were allowed to speak to the referee, it would certainly make their job a hell of a lot easier – not having obnoxious twits chipping away at them

As a player, I must admit that I used to actively try to influence referees and get in their head. If a referee gave a foul against me, I would always question his decision: 'Come on, that was the other way.' If a rule came in that meant I wasn't allowed to speak to the referee, I wouldn't do it. It would certainly make their job a hell of a lot easier if they didn't have obnoxious twits like me chipping away at them.

While this measure wouldn't deal with abuse from the crowd, it would at least relieve the referee's burden on the pitch. They wouldn't be surrounded by a dozen players screaming in their face, telling them how to do their job. The referee would only be dealing with the two captains. It would be less intimidating, and therefore the job would be more enjoyable.

And I think referees would be treated much more respectfully, as they are in rugby, where they even call them 'sir'. There's nothing wrong with that kind of discipline, those old-fashioned values. That's the problem with football. It's just become a bloody frenzy ruled by the voice of the mob.

At the end of a rugby match, the players aren't haranguing the referee all the way back to the dressing rooms. Nor does a rugby referee need to lurk in the centre circle after he's blown the final whistle, waiting for his linesmen and a protective ring of stewards to chaperone him off the pitch. That doesn't happen because there's that mutual respect between player and official. Rugby referees aren't demonised the way they are in football. They're seen as custodians of the game, the crucial cog that's keeping order. We could learn a lot from them.

Let's not get carried away, though. Rugby is still a strange sport. I was having a conversation the other day with a taxi driver who was a rugby man. I said to him, 'You guys smash the living daylights out of each other. You can break someone's jaw and then you all laugh about it afterwards.' While they seem to have a better sense of respect, it's not normal respect. If you walked down the street and some lout came up and broke your nose, you'd press charges against them. In rugby, they think it's funny and then shake hands at the end. I don't care who you are, that's just plain weird.

25

Play the Game – or Lose It For Ever

If you went back in time 40 years or so to the summer holidays of the early 1980s and drove through any village or town or city suburb that had a recreation ground or park, you'd be virtually guaranteed to see local youngsters playing football, with jumpers and jackets for goalposts. Glance down a side street and you'd see the same scene – kids kicking balls, dribbling balls, having fun.

Drive through that same village or town or city suburb four decades later and look across to the same recreation ground or park, or down the same side street. You won't see balls crashing into fences or disappearing into bushes. You won't see kids chasing, tackling, shooting, sweating and laughing. Instead, you'll see them doing exactly what a large proportion of the rest of the population will be doing. They'll be gazing downwards in a trance-like state, oblivious to what's going on around them. Spellbound and solitary. In their own world, on their own planet.

There's no denying that technology has become an integral element of sport in the first two decades of this century. It's everywhere. It's inescapable. But the technological advance that's had the most impact on the sporting world isn't the introduction of Hawk-Eye in tennis, the piece of kit that can show where a ball has bounced. Nor is it the implementation of DRS in international cricket, the system by which teams can refer an umpire's decision to the bods operating the video technology. And, as headline-making as it's been, it's not even VAR in football. As you'll have already read, the jury is still very much out on the benefits of that.

The digital age has seen a sharp decline in active participation in sport. Between 2012 and 2015, an astonishing 2,380 grassroots football teams disbanded

No, the most impactful piece of gadgetry is somewhat smaller and cheaper than any of that hardware. You can fit it in your pocket. You can take it anywhere. Almost everyone has it. It is the smartphone.

The smartphone can be the enemy of the active sportsperson. Anyone who has ever tried to cajole a grumpy, monosyllabic teenager out of bed or off the sofa to encourage them to get out into the great outdoors to take some invigorating lungfuls of fresh air will know exactly where I'm coming from. A whole generation only has eyes for little screens, for this portal into a world unheard of when today's parents were their kids' ages.

Don't get me wrong. There are positive benefits to using a smartphone. Of course there are. It's the way in which these teenagers learn about, and communicate with, the world. It helps them to make social connections and to form interpersonal relationships, while also fine-tuning and honing their aptitude for technology. However…

While I don't want to be seen as an old dinosaur who would prefer to communicate using cups joined together with string, the overreliance on this little piece of technology is dangerous. The average teen who has a smartphone checks it 63 times a day, behaviour that can cause anxiety, stress, depression, attention deficit disorder and sleep deprivation. Their mental health can be seriously undermined.

And then there's the physical aspect. Operating a smartphone obviously takes no effort to do. Being active isn't a requirement. And it's arguably the principal reason why youngsters playing sport has nosedived in recent times.

The digital age has seen a sharp decline in active participation in sport, including football. A few years back, an FA-commissioned study found that in the three seasons between 2012 and 2015, an astonishing 2,380 grassroots football teams disbanded. Clearly, fewer people wanted to sign up for a season-long commitment, content to have their heads turned by the distractions of modern life. And if clubs disband, the natural consequence is that the league system shrinks. At the end of every season, leagues will merge in order to stay alive. An example of one such amalgamation close to where I live was in 2017 when the Norwich and District Saturday League joined forces with the Central and South Norfolk League – both legendary local leagues in their prime.

Other leagues are dissolving altogether, sinking without a trace. And not necessarily at the end of a season. At the start of the 2019–20 campaign, the Herefordshire Sunday League disbanded after just one match after one of its *four* teams moved to Saturday football, leaving the league in an unworkable situation where it had just *three* member teams (two of whom subsequently merged and moved to Saturdays too). Little more than ten years ago, this league was thriving with a healthy forty-one teams. There can be fewer more damning stats than that to demonstrate the parlous, and still-worsening, state of grassroots football. The spiral is inescapably downward.

While participation in organised eleven-a-side football is sharply falling, five-a-side football is in rude health. The number of five-a-siders has commendably increased in recent years. A great deal of this is down to the improvement in facilities which is attracting players. Where previously five-a-side matches at local sports centres would have taken place in the main hall once the badminton nets had been put away, or outside on the unforgiving gravel of an unused tennis court, players can now show off their silky skills on carpet-like 3G or 4G surfaces.

But as heartening as this uptake is, a particular problem seems to persist. This might just be my observation and I don't claim that it's rigorously scientific, but those five-a-side pitches tend to be populated by middle-aged players – perhaps those who had to give up playing eleven-a-side on the weekend when kids came along and domesticity got in the way. Very rarely do I see that teenagers have organised themselves and booked out a five-a-side pitch. They don't know they're born. Me and my pals would have killed to have strutted our stuff on such well-appointed playing surfaces back in the day.

Playing football is no longer the magnet it once was. Life in the 21st century offers too many shiny distractions. People can get their football fix by tuning into never-ending live football from right across the globe that's pumped straight into their living room. Or, if they do have a sense of competition in their veins, they can reach for the PlayStation controller and play *FIFA* for hours on end. After all, why go to the effort of getting changed, getting out and getting muddy as a Sunday-league clogger when you can pretend to be a twinkle-toed Messi or Ronaldo from the comfort and warmth of your living room?

But it's the smartphone and the tablet that have really produced a lost generation, a generation that's forgotten the value of playing sport – if they ever knew it. I've got talented sons. One of them is really talented at sport, but I can't get him off his iPad or phone. And if I do, he goes into a hysterical fit and it all kicks off. If only he'd spent the same amount of time practising football or cricket as he has done texting or being on Instagram, Snapchat, Twitter, FaceTime, WhatsApp and the rest…

> The smartphone and the tablet have produced a lost generation that's forgotten the value of playing sport – if they ever knew it

This isn't a football-specific problem, of course. It impacts right across wider society. And it's a subject which everyone discusses in their own home. The moodiness, the anti-social behaviour, the tantrums – they don't seem to go away. Using technology is addictive. I'd say it was one of the most serious addictions around, due to its negative effect on both lifestyle and face-to-face social interaction.

I guess I'm lucky to be from the generation that I am. We still had the choice whether or not to play sport, but it was an easier decision to make as there were fewer distractions in those simpler times. I do encourage my kids to play sport, but I don't ram it down their throats. That's just counter-productive. But the most important aspect about sport, which I try to emphasise to them, is that it's where you make your friends for life. As members of a sports club you have a great deal in common. It's about shared experiences, shared memories. You win together, you lose together, you socialise together. There's not many better feelings than that sense of camaraderie.

I know what sport has brought me – and I don't mean in monetary terms. It's the happiness, and the stimulation, that comes from being involved in a team. I realised this at a young age. I was out playing football and cricket all the time when I was a kid. I didn't have an unbelievable amount of equipment or the best football or the newest cricket bat, but me and the boys from school would make do, playing down the recreation ground or on the street. It usually involved an old tennis ball.

> As kids, we'd invent our own Olympics, or our own *Superstars* tournament. We used our initiative. We were creative and imaginative. And we were in heaven

That's all we did in the school summer holidays. You'd go out at nine in the morning, play until lunchtime, eat the sandwiches you'd brought with you, play again for a few more hours and head home around four. Sometimes we'd invent our own Olympics, or our own *Superstars* tournament. We'd get some bamboo canes and make them into hurdles, or fashion them into javelins, or create a high jump by using pegs we'd liberated from the washing line. We used our initiative. We were creative and imaginative. And we were in heaven.

Just as technology is a teenage addiction now, sport was my addiction then. I wasn't alone in this. I would say that a strong percentage of the kids throughout my education – at my village school, middle school and high school – would play sport outside the mandatory PE lessons.

Maybe I'm gazing out over the past with rose-tinted spectacles on, but being brought up in that environment in the Eighties was brilliant.

We were helped by having very few options when it came to filling our time. It was either stay in bed or get out and do something. Today, kids stay in bed for hours on end and message each other. 'What are you doing?' 'I'm in bed.' 'I'm in bed too.' 'What are you going to have for breakfast…?' Then they'll take pictures of their breakfast and upload them. Whatever happened to doing some meaningful with your day?

A lethargic, lazy generation obviously impacts on society. The UK currently has the third highest obesity rates in Europe, a situation that's only going to apply, in the fullness of time, additional unwanted pressure to an already overburdened NHS. The knock-on effect will be grave. And playing sport is great for mental health too. I've managed to persuade one of my youngest sons to play football regularly. The difference in him is crystal clear. When he comes home after playing, he's absolutely buzzing. That release of endorphins is addictive in itself, let alone the pleasure of actually playing. He now goes to a gym too. Success!

But persuading your offspring that getting out and getting active isn't easy when they're made aware of the rewards of a more sedentary lifestyle. E-sports are huge now, with tournaments being televised in front of massive crowds. My son told me about this 15-year-old British lad who shared, with his gaming partner, £1.8 million of winnings from the Fortnite World Cup, an e-sports competition that boasts a total prize pot of £18 million. What kind of message does that send out to the nation's youth? Stay in your room during your teenage years and you too could become a wealthy role model to adolescents everywhere. Elsewhere, several football clubs have their own e-sports teams: the likes of Bayern Munich, Manchester United, Barcelona, Arsenal and Monaco are among those who compete in the eFootball League.

And it doesn't stop there. There have even been rumours of e-sports becoming Olympic events at some point in the future. Apparently this has only got to the discussion stage, but the fact that talks have even been held about their inclusion is a disgrace. The Olympics are a test of athletic prowess, one that measures speed and movement and agility. Again, what's the message here? That we can all sit on our backsides, press some buttons, twiddle a joystick and become an Olympic champion? Oh, come on...

How are we going to create top sportspeople if they aren't putting the hours in? If you want to play at the highest possible level you've got to be dedicated, you've got to make the effort. You only have to look at some of the greatest players the world has seen and the sacrifices they made when they were younger. When the likes of Frank Lampard and David Beckham talk about their upbringings, it's all about the endless practice they undertook as kids. That's what I did too. I used to drive my mum nuts, constantly kicking a ball against the outside wall of the kitchen. I also kicked a sponge ball around indoors, pretending I was Trevor Francis while doing my own commentary. It was quite sad, really.

> When the likes of Frank Lampard and David Beckham talk about their upbringings, it's all about the endless practice they undertook as kids

Without putting the time in, no one can expect to play at the top level. But there will be some kids out there who have that desire, that stickability. They'll be the ones to put the tech to one side, to crack on and get everything they deserve. Cristiano Ronaldo now has an incredible 197 million followers on Instagram, but I guarantee that if he'd been glued to social media when he was eight years old instead of forever kicking a ball around, he wouldn't have remotely been the player he is. In fact, we'd have never have heard of him.

The danger is that there's no cure for this decline in playing sport. The population is increasing and yet participation levels are heading in the exact opposite direction. The difficulty is that it's a matter of choice; no one can force their offspring to reach for the boots and shinpads. The parents can try to persuade, but ultimately they're powerless. You can't deny free will.

When I was young, you'd see posters and stickers for the government's 'Sport For All' scheme all over the place. I can still see the era-specific logo in my mind's eye. The campaign made its point well: sport wasn't necessarily about being the greatest, but it was about getting active and healthy. Perhaps some similar initiative could be wheeled out to promote an active lifestyle these days. But would any youngster have their head turned by an official government campaign? It's unlikely.

Technology will no doubt improve how we watch televised sport in 30, 40, 50 years' time. But while the viewing experience will be extraordinary, the quality of the action itself will have suffered across the board from fewer people participating. Instead, we will have become a society of tech-smart but unhealthy oafs in an age when the online gaming world cup may even overtake the actual World Cup in appeal. The future is bleak if action isn't taken now. After all, just imagine how distanced from active sport the teenage kids of our current teenagers will be.

The problem extends beyond levels of participation. All the time that our children's backsides are glued to the sofa, they're not even getting out to *watch* sport in the flesh. Football is definitely suffering. Away from the Premier League and the Championship, the outlook is bleaker than the cheerleading at the very top of the game would suggest. Further down the pyramid, getting bums on seats is proving increasingly difficult. In fact, figures indicate that it's already an acute problem. The Football Supporters' Federation has calculated that the average League Two club needs 5,000 fans through its turnstiles every match in order to keep its head above water. League One clubs need 10,000. Yet, in 2018–19, 31 of the 48 clubs in the lower two divisions of the EFL had average attendances that were less than half their ground's capacity. These are, of course, far from the biggest stadiums in the world.

And all the while that the Premier League and the Champions League ooze glamour from every pore (which, of course, they always will in comparison), the lower levels of football look anachronistic to the younger generation. In the Eastern Counties League Premier Division – the league in which my son Ollie plays – a match attendance can struggle to reach triple figures. And those who are there are far from a representative cross-section of society. They are predominantly men of a certain age – that is, the dark side of 60. It's an ageing support base. The only people under 30 tend to be the mates or girlfriends of those playing.

So what do we do about this?

The message needs to get out that it's not all about the Premier League. People love different leagues, different divisions, different standards of football. Some fans of Championship clubs actually don't want their club to get promoted because they love the cut and thrust of what is arguably Europe's fiercest, most competitive division. People love certain leagues for what they are and for what they give. For them, it's not a competition *between* leagues – which is the fastest, the richest, the most glamorous.

Many supporters of Scottish Professional Football League (SPFL) clubs don't give a monkey's about what's happening south of the border in the Premier League. And why should they? SPFL attendances have increased year-on-year for the last four seasons. Fans like the brand of football being served up and don't need to look elsewhere. As the SPFL chief executive Neil Doncaster rightly identified, these rising crowd numbers are 'testament to the hard work done by the individual clubs to engage supporters in their local communities and the loyalty shown by Scottish football fans to turn out in such extraordinary numbers to support their teams'. Two crucial words there: 'communities' and 'local'.

But elsewhere the problem extends beyond those coming through the turnstiles. Let's not forget the volunteers, those hardy souls who, in all weathers, step up to serve their clubs, whether marking out the pitch, operating the turnstiles or manning the tea bar. Again, they tend to be of a more senior vintage. I go to football dinners where the loyal groundsman gets a ripple of applause for his efforts. But no one really thinks too hard about the hundreds of hours he puts in for love alone. These people are simply taken for granted. And when they and their kind head off to the great groundsman's hut in the sky, who'll be waiting to take their place? No one's stepping forward. The vacancies go unfilled and the club goes under. That particular story ends.

A handful of lower-league and non-league clubs have wisely gazed into their crystal balls and have seen the trouble on the horizon. They can possibly only

> All the while that the Premier League and the Champions League ooze glamour from every pore, the lower levels of football look anachronistic to the younger generation

see decline and extinction for clubs at their level unless action is taken to sign up the supporters of tomorrow. I know it's a cliché, but the children are their future. One such club, Forest Green Rovers, gives out free team shirts to four hundred local Year 3 schoolchildren every year, working on the proven premise that the age of seven is when most football-crazy kids pick the team they're going to support. Get them young enough – when there's less stigma about wearing the colours of the local League One club rather than the ubiquitous kit of a Barcelona or a Juventus – and they'll become fans for life. Hopefully.

Down in the National League South, Dulwich Hamlet are another progressive club who reach out to those around them in the local community. One of their initiatives involves giving free tickets to local kids and their parents, a scheme that can bear rich fruit. A rough calculation suggests around a third occasionally come back to watch them again, 10 per cent return regularly and about 5 per cent become season-ticket holders. While the Premier League becomes this ultra-glamorous product worshipped across the globe, such a commitment to their local team is heartening.

But it's crucial that the other teams in the leagues around them follow suit to avoid catastrophe. As it stands, the prognosis for football lower down the system – whether playing or watching – is far from rosy. The foundations of our mighty football pyramid are crumbling and grassroots football could ultimately become just a footnote in sporting history.

And there's a fair chance that the kids won't even look up from their phones to notice.

Epilogue

So there you have it: my 25-point manifesto for fixing football, for getting it back on the rails, for restoring my faith – and hopefully yours – in the game we all hold so dear.

You may not agree with all of them. For instance, you might be happy to refer to your beloved club's stadium by its latest sponsor's name, easy in the knowledge that the money that the deal is bringing in will be partially reinvested in that 20-goals-a-season striker you've been craving for ages. Similarly, you might not resent spending your hard-earned cash on a high-price replica shirt for the exact same reason. And you might – might! – even think VAR is working brilliantly in its current form. There must be someone, other than the football authorities, who thinks that.

Alternatively, you might agree with each and every fix I've put forward. If so, congratulations. You've got great common sense.

I'm not an idealistic dreamer who believes all of these fixes can be made overnight. But I'd love to think that there was collective agreement on the part of everyone in and around football that the game is currently misfiring in many ways. And I'd also love to think that all of its stakeholders – the fans, the clubs, the media, the governing bodies – share an inclination and a determination to right these wrongs. Utopia is an impossible destination, but we can at least try to get some way towards it. At the moment, it feels like it's disappearing in the rear-view mirror.

We can't just sit on our hands and see football remain un-fixed. We need to help our sport. But it needs to help itself too.

Come on, football…

YOU'RE BETTER THAN THAT!

Acknowledgments

Thanks...

...to my wife Sam for her love and support; my mum Josephine; my lads Frankie, Oliver, George, James and Harry; and to my beautiful daughter Sophia, who makes me laugh every day.

...to Nige Tassell, who helped me put the book together, for his patience and his patience and his patience with me.

...to my literary agent Kevin Pocklington from The North Literary Agency.

...to everyone at Monoray – Jake Lingwood, Alex Stetter, Karen Baker, Juliette Norsworthy, Clare Hubbard, Sarah Kyle and Peter Hunt.

...to my *606* co-presenter Ali Bruce-Ball and our producer Simon Crosse.

...to BBC Radio 5 Live and BT Sport, and to my editors at the *Daily Mail* and the *Daily Record*, for putting up with me. They're better than that...